A Question of Justice

A Question of Justice

New South Governors and Education, 1968–1976

Gordon E. Harvey

THE UNIVERSITY OF ALABAMA PRESS
Tuscaloosa and London

Copyright © 2002
The University of Alabama Press
Tuscaloosa, Alabama 35487-0380
All rights reserved
Manufactured in the United States of America

Typeface: Perpetua

∞

The paper on which this book is printed meets the minimum requirements of
American National Standard for Information Science–Permanence of Paper for
Printed Library Materials, ANSI Z39.48-1984.

Library of Congress Cataloging-in-Publication Data

Harvey, Gordon E. (Gordon Earl), 1967–
A question of justice : New South governors and education, 1968–1976 /
Gordon E. Harvey.
p.   cm.
Includes bibliographical references and index.
ISBN 0-8173-1157-2 (alk. paper)
1. Education and state—Alabama—History—20th century. 2. Education and
state—Florida—History—20th century. 3. Education and state—South Carolina—
History—20th century. 4. School integration—Alabama—History—20th century.
5. School integration—Florida—History—20th century. 6. School integration—
South Carolina—History—20th century. 7. Educational change—Alabama—
History—20th century. 8. Educational change—Florida—History—20th century.
9. Educational change—South Carolina—History—20th century.
I. Title.
LC89 .H28 2002
379.761—dc21
2001007372

British Library Cataloguing-in-Publication Data available

Contents

Acknowledgments

Over the course of preparing this book, I have become indebted to so many people for the countless favors and invaluable aid they have provided me. The staffs of libraries at Auburn University, the University of South Carolina, Florida State University, and the South Caroliniana Library made research in their fine institutions a pleasure. Reference staff at the South Carolina State archives, the Florida State Archives, and especially the Alabama State Archives were worth their weight in gold, and I cannot thank them enough. A few people stood out. Norwood Kerr was a master at locating documents and chasing archival rabbits. John Hardin, Ken Tilley, and Rickie Brunner also deserve heartfelt thanks. David Coles, formerly of the Florida State Archives, provided similar aid. At the Modern Political Collection of the South Caroliniana Library Herb Hartsook was a lifesaver and worth his weight in Pittsburgh Pirate baseball memorabilia. He introduced me to the major figures in John West's world and more than a few essential archival sources.

During my time at Auburn University, many people provided assistance. Jim Hansen and Larry Gerber in their capacity as chairmen of the Auburn History Department allowed me to jumble my teaching schedule to allow for extended research trips. I also want to thank Auburn's History Department for research funds and for providing an intellectual atmosphere conducive to scholarly pursuits. Friends and History Department colleagues such as Jim Ross, Steve Murray, Richard Starnes, Eric Tscheschlok, Gene Barnett, Sheri Shuck, Robert Vejnar, Dan Szechi, Joe Kicklighter, Jeff Frederick, and Scott Billingsley made the grad school experience tolerable and rewarding. My dear friends Robin Fabel and Donna Bohanan provided much-needed moral support and excellent conversation. Steve McFarland always had the same annoying but helpful question while I was writing: "Have you finished yet?" Wayne Flynt in his capacity as advisor and friend taught me more than I can ever thank him for. I treasure his guidance, friendship, and faith in me. I also want to thank the three governors for allowing me to interview them. William Maloy at the University of West Florida, a former Askew aide, also allowed me an interview and has been very helpful in tracking down former Askew staff.

The folks at the University of Alabama Press have been wonderful and patient in answering my numerous pesky questions about the publishing process.

Finally, my love and gratitude go out to my parents, Gordon and Georgia Harvey; my lovely and supportive wife, Marie; and my sons, Preston and Hudson, for their love and affirmation. I hope they know that I could never be more proud of them.

A Question of Justice

Introduction

The South is ready to adjust and become part of the nation.
                                    —Florida governor Reubin Askew, 1971

In southern politics 1970 marked a watershed. That year a group of southern governors entered office and changed the way the nation looked at the South and southern state chief executives. Across the region, southern politicians of a new style were elected governor: from the ranks of Democrats came "a no-liquor-no-tobacco Panhandle Presbyterian elder" named Reubin Askew in Florida; John C. West, a racial moderate who rose through the ranks of the South Carolina Democratic Party; a self-styled "country lawyer" in Arkansas named Dale Bumpers; peanut farmer Jimmy Carter of Georgia; William Winter in Mississippi; and Terry Sanford and James Hunt of North Carolina. Republicans A. Linwood Holton in Virginia and Tennessee's Winfield Dunn also represented this new style of governor. So did Democrat Albert Brewer, who inherited Alabama's governorship in 1968 but was not reelected in 1970. Just as the post–World War II economic boom transformed the southern economy, the combination of the civil rights movement, the Voting Rights Act of 1965, the subsequent political party realignment, and the rise of moderate southern governors changed the South's political landscape in 1970.[1]

These governors benefited from paramount changes in southern politics. V. O. Key had predicted as much when he wrote *Southern Politics in State and Nation* in 1949. Key asserted that for the South to experience a political revival it had to gain its freedom from four major institutions that had constricted the region's political development for decades: disfranchisement; the one-party system; malapportionment of state legislatures; and Jim Crow segregation. Twenty-six years later, Numan Bartley and Hugh Graham examined the three decades following Key's seminal study and found that his analysis had proven correct. *Brown v. Board of Education* (1954), the civil rights movement, and the subsequent legislation expanding voting and civil rights had sounded the death knell for the traditional, one-party, segregated South. In the years after 1950, Bartley and Graham found a neopopulist resurgence whereby loyal New Dealers such as James "Big Jim" Folsom, Earl Long, John Sparkman, and Estes Kefauver gained state and federal offices by appealing to coalitions of white rural voters, working-class urbanite voters, and the growing number of black voters. Thus, over the twenty-six years between Key's study and that of Bartley and Graham, all four institutions of stagnation and disfranchisement in the South had been destroyed.[2]

Of the four developments Key prescribed for a new political South, perhaps the most important to the rise of "New South" governors was the 1965 Voting Rights Act. For most of these governors black votes meant the difference in their victory over segregationist candidates. Before the 1965 legislation black voters were virtually nonexistent in the region. In Mississippi, only 6.7 percent of voting age blacks were registered to vote in March 1965. Next lowest was Alabama with 19.3 percent. In South Carolina 37.3 percent of blacks were registered. Florida seemed progressive with 51.2 percent, well behind Tennessee's substantial 69.5 percent.[3]

By 1967, the situation had changed drastically. Numbers of black voters in the South skyrocketed. The biggest jumps came in Mississippi and Alabama. Black voter registration in Mississippi increased 535.9 percent, Alabama's 167.9 percent. South Carolina black voter registration jumped a relatively modest 37.2 percent. As a whole, the region's black voter registration grew 72.6 percent. This increase contributed to the rise of racially moderate southern politicians as 52.1 percent of eligible blacks were registered to vote by 1967. It also corresponded with, and most likely contributed to, an abatement of racial tension in the region. Essentially, resistant whites realized in varying degrees that blacks and whites would integrate irrevocably. These whites realized, wrote Alexander Lamis, that with integration "the world did not come to an end."[4]

The result of such massive increases in black voters was the creation of new majority coalitions in state legislatures and new faces in state government, especially the governor's office. The change was so dramatic that by 1972, every southern state save Alabama had elected moderate governors who avoided racial rhetoric and advocated progressive policies. But the progressivism of the class of new southern governors in the 1970s was limited largely to their views on race and reform of state governmental structures. On economic issues they could be quite conservative, reflect-

ing the anti-tax mood of their day. These governors were often less progressive than the populist, segregationist governors of the earlier twentieth century. Although contemporary journalists may have labeled these
state chief executives as "populists" or "progressives," such titles are mis-
leading. The reforms of the class of governors of the 1970s more closely
resembled those of "business progressivism" of the 1920s, which emphasized highway improvement, educational expansion, health reform, and
general expansion of public services. Even this comparison is tenuous,
however. The progressivism of the post–civil rights era New South governors rarely extended beyond racial moderation and reform of state governmental structures, prisons, mental health programs, and education. As
noted by political scientist Larry Sabato, the irony of the New South governor is apparent: "The modern southern governors are in some respects
far less progressive on economic policy than many of the populist segregationist governors of earlier times who combined racism with programs
for their poor white constituents (which blacks, of course, shared in)."
Some of their reform measures did not follow the standard model for
reform.[5]

Examined here are three New South governors of the late 1960s and
early 1970s: Albert Brewer of Alabama; Reubin Askew from Florida; and
South Carolina's John West. Most surveys of the modern South address
New South governors in a tangential manner, briefly listing several and
explaining their ascent to power. John Boles's *The South through Time* and
Numan Bartley's *The New South,* as well as Dewey Grantham's *The South in
Modern America,* give passing mention of the election of southern moderate-
to-liberal Democrats and Republicans after 1970, but go no further. Most
discuss Jimmy Carter's rise from New South governor to president and
provide a general definition of the New South governors: supported by
a biracial coalition of moderate-to-liberal black and white voters, outspoken on race, won elections against segregationist opponents, and re-
formed state government and education. Beyond that there exists no in-
depth study of any of the class of 1970 other than Jimmy Carter.

Although John West and Reubin Askew are regularly named, such
survey listings do not include Albert Brewer. I believe this is a mistake,
and it may be the result of chronology more than anything else. It is not
easy to pinpoint the beginning of a historical era or phase. It is much easier
to declare watersheds—in this case 1970—by way of introducing new
political phenomena, namely, the election of moderate governors at a time

when the region was voting solidly Republican with Richard Nixon. But watersheds are artificial constructs, used by historians to provide nice, clean transitions from one era to another. Because Brewer assumed the office when Lurleen Wallace died and served from May 1968 to January of 1971, he does not neatly fit into the commonly held chronology of the New South governors and is often left out of any group listing. Although he lost to George Wallace in the 1970 Democratic primary, Brewer's shortened term resulted in a sweeping education reform package that still stands as the most progressive the state has seen in a generation. Brewer also made the last genuine attempt by an Alabama governor to reform the state's antiquated constitution, while at the same time eliminating to a large degree corruption in the state's executive departments. No Alabama governor has met the standard of reform set by Brewer in 1969. That he does not neatly fit into the arbitrary 1970 watershed model should not preclude Brewer from the group.[6]

The only New South governor never elected by his state, Albert Preston Brewer was born in 1928 in Tennessee and grew up in Decatur, Alabama, where his father worked for the Tennessee Valley Authority. Brewer attended the University of Alabama from 1946 to 1952, where he earned his undergraduate and law degrees. In 1955, when only twenty-five years old, he won election to the state house of representatives and entered the legislature with many of his law school classmates. They represented a core of young, professional, enthusiastic legislators who felt a genuine concern for education and other issues such as reapportionment of the state legislature, modernization of rules for the legal profession, highway construction, and economic development. This reform appetite was whetted even more because they entered office during "Big Jim" Folsom's second term as governor. Brewer's zeal for progressive issues, his solidifying of legislative friendships, and his building of his law practice paid dividends. In 1963, thirty-four-year-old Brewer defeated Hugh Merrill and Rankin Fite to become speaker of the state house, the youngest in Alabama history and in the nation at that time. He became one of the ablest legislators ever to preside over the state house. A large part of Brewer's success in this election was due to his friendships and alliances in the house, to his broad appeal to a variety of interests (especially a growing urban bloc resulting from reapportionment in 1963), and to the Wallace stamp of approval. Although considered a "Wallace-man," Brewer remained relatively independent of Wallace because, as Brewer put it, "the great thing about him

. . . was he didn't interfere. He didn't want to fool with it. He didn't want to be bothered with governing." Although successful as speaker, in 1966 Brewer believed it was time to "move up or move out." In that year he ran for and was elected lieutenant governor.[7]

After Lurleen Wallace's death from cancer in 1968, many in the state welcomed Brewer's assumption of office. The *Montgomery Advertiser* described an "electric excitement" and a "new enthusiasm" surrounding the new governor. He was the only person in Alabama history to hold in succession the offices of speaker, lieutenant governor, and governor. The newspaper also predicted a new approach to state government: "It seems that five years or more of tilting at federal windmills, without knocking a single one of them over, is just about enough." Although Brewer was not a vocal opponent of segregation or an outspoken proponent for integration, capitol watchers did not expect him to follow Wallace's defiant lead. He was generally silent on desegregation. In the legislature, he was a vocal supporter of Wallace measures in the house but bristled at being called a "Wallace man." The *Mobile Register* asserted that Brewer had the qualifications to become one of the best governors the state ever had but that he would have to watch his step. Alabamians could be "highly fickle."[8]

Brewer learned just how fickle in 1970 when he stood for election to a full term as governor. Despite contrary public and private pledges following Lurleen's death, George Wallace ran against Brewer. The ensuing campaign became by some accounts the dirtiest the state had ever witnessed, including bags of cash for the Brewer campaign from President Richard Nixon. The first primary, relatively quiet on the race issue, ended with a slight Brewer victory, 42 to 41 percent, with Brewer leading Wallace by twelve thousand votes. The candidacy of millionaire and perennial office-seeker Charles Woods, however, siphoned almost 180,000 votes that probably would have gone to Brewer, forcing the contest into a runoff. The runoff campaign saw Wallace revert to his old tactics. After suffering technical defeat for the first time since 1958, Wallace used race as a means of scaring Alabamians away from Brewer. When Brewer garnered virtually all the black vote in the first primary, Wallace accused Brewer of making deals with black political leaders to gain the "bloc" vote. Wallace disparaged Brewer and his family and eventually won the election with 52 percent of the vote. Because Alabama Republicans declined to run anyone against Wallace he became governor by default. This race put an end to what many saw as Alabama's best opportunity to contribute to the region-wide political moderation. The victory by the "poor man's segregationist" proved that race was not quite a dead issue in Alabama. For Brewer the irony was thick. Wallace's endorsement helped him become speaker and lieutenant governor, and it was Wallace's candidacy that ended Brewer's gubernatorial aspirations.[9]

Although Brewer's past political ties to Wallace and relative silence on race may seem to preclude him from status of "New South governor," his short time in office clearly reveals a reform impulse. In terms of support from the black community, Brewer enjoyed levels of support comparable to West and Askew. In his loss to Wallace, Brewer received almost all the black vote, polling upward of 98 percent in Birmingham and 89 percent in Montgomery, and this he achieved with an African American candidate also running for governor. Although definitely more conservative than the outspoken Askew, Brewer nonetheless marked a clear departure from Alabama's recent political past and defiant anti-integration posturing under George Wallace.[10]

Reubin O'Donovan Askew was not a native Floridian. Born to impoverished parents in Muskogee, Oklahoma, in 1928, Askew and his five siblings came to Pensacola with their mother in 1937. Abandoned by his father, Askew sold magazines, shined shoes, bagged groceries, and sold his mother's homemade pies to supplement her income as a waitress and Works Progress Administration seamstress. Between stints in both the army and air force, Askew earned his undergraduate and law degrees from Florida State University and the University of Florida. Elected to the state house of representatives in 1958 and the state senate in 1962, Askew quickly rose in legislative respect and prominence. He fast became an expert on government finance. In 1969 he was elected president pro tempore of the senate. Askew's decision to run for governor in 1970 was questioned by many. Political commentators greeted Askew's candidacy by asking, "Reubin who?"[11]

The 1970 Florida Democratic gubernatorial primary was historic in that it was the first time since the *Brown* decision that all the candidates campaigned as nonsegregationists and openly courted more than three hundred thousand registered black voters. After defeating three of the best-known men in the state for the Democratic nomination with 58 percent of the vote, Askew took on bombastic Republican incumbent Claude Kirk. The campaign gave voters a clear choice between Old and New South outlooks. Kirk had seized personal control of the Manatee County

School District in 1969 in order to prevent implementation of an integration court order. Askew supported busing as a means of achieving equal educational opportunity. Askew denounced Kirk as an embarrassment to the state, whereas Kirk called Askew a "momma's boy" and a "permissive liberal." Kirk tried to pull Askew into a racially motivated campaign, but Askew stuck to his main theme—tax justice. Askew argued that Floridians were tired of "government by antics" and ran a populistic campaign proposing his "fair share" program, which called for an income tax on corporations, general tax reform, and increased school funding. Askew defeated Kirk handily, garnering almost 57 percent of the vote. It was the second largest margin of victory in Florida political history. Askew's 821,190 votes also exceeded the total Republican voter registration by 380,474 votes. He soon became an outspoken proponent of racial justice and racial healing. If George Wallace appealed to the alienated voter with the politics of fear, Askew courted the same group, and more, with the "politics of trust."[12]

Like Askew and Brewer, John Carl West rose to power through traditional state Democratic Party connections. Born in 1922 of moderate means, West was raised by his widowed mother on a farm in Camden, South Carolina. After attending the Citadel and earning an undergraduate degree, West served as an army intelligence officer during World War II. Following the war, West earned a law degree from the University of South Carolina under the GI Bill. After a brief stint as highway commissioner, West ran for and won a state senate seat in 1955, serving for eleven years. In 1966, West was elected lieutenant governor, serving under Governor Robert McNair. By that time, West had made his mark on South Carolina politics as a racial moderate. Earlier in his political life, he had publicly denounced the Klan and had even given the keynote address at a testimonial dinner in honor of Roy Wilkins, the national director of the National Association for the Advancement of Colored People (NAACP).[13]

In 1970, with Governor McNair constitutionally unable to succeed himself, West easily won the Democratic nomination and squared off against U.S. senator Strom Thurmond's handpicked candidate, U.S. congressman Albert Watson. A gifted public speaker, Watson was also a fervent segregationist. As in Alabama and Florida, the 1970 South Carolina gubernatorial campaign provided voters with a clear choice, segregation versus moderation. With full backing from Thurmond, President Nixon, and the Republican Party, Watson waged the last overtly segregationist campaign in South Carolina's political history. So conspicuous was this strategy that the *Columbia State,* a staunchly Republican newspaper, endorsed West. Suburban Republicans also repudiated Watson by voting for the moderate West.[14]

South Carolina's 1970 campaign illustrated the great impact of the 1965 Voting Rights Act and the obsolescence of racist campaigns in a region where more than half the eligible black population was registered to vote. In the biggest nonpresidential election year voter turnout in state history (471,000), West won the governor's office with 51.7 percent of the vote over Watson's 45 percent. The black vote clearly pushed West over the top. He received almost 90 percent of the black vote, whereas Watson received only 58 percent of the white vote. Black voters represented 25 percent of the total votes cast. West's victory and ensuing moderate racial course led the *New York Times* to take note: "The stars and bars of the Confederacy still fly above the South Carolina state capitol. But beyond the heroic statue of Pitchfork Ben Tillman and within the walls of the beautiful old building permanently scarred by shells from Gen. Sherman's guns, Governor John C. West has set out upon a new political course."[15] West's victory forced Strom Thurmond to court black voters actively for the first time, winning reelection two years later. To many in South Carolina, West was another in a "long line of moderate governors who have steered [South Carolina] to safety through the swirling waters of Civil Rights changes without major violence."[16]

Although the three governors shared many reform concerns, their efforts to improve education provide the most extensive framework for comparison. Education was usually the most pressing concern for most southern governors in this period. They differed on other issues. Albert Brewer attempted to reform Alabama's constitution; John West did not. Askew's focus on environmental protection was not matched by similar concerns in Alabama or South Carolina. Education, however, consumed all three. They shared a vision for what education could do for the region. It was essential to their plans for the South's economic future, which required a literate workforce possessing the skills to operate modern machinery. All three wanted to advance economic development through better funding of public education. Education was also the largest part of their state budgets and the most visible issue.[17]

An examination of John West's education initiatives reveals that reform did not always include conventional education changes, such as increased teacher pay, accountability and assessment, standardized testing, or revision of school funding formulas. John West provides an alternative definition of reform, or at least an alternative method. West's goal in office was to create an economic condition that would allow the state to pay for reform without raising taxes or entering into massive budget deficits (which, by the way, South Carolina suffered from as West took office). This goal was admirable, but it took West longer than he wished, especially because he was prohibited by the state constitution from succeeding himself. Limited to one term, West had little time left to embark on a reform course, and when he approached the subject, he found that the affluence he helped bring the state had dashed any reform impetus. The economic foundation built in part by West aided future South Carolina governor Richard Riley in passing a massive 1986 education reform program.

The selection of these three governors merits discussion. Alabama is the only state never to elect a New South governor because Brewer assumed the office constitutionally. Nevertheless, he brought to the office reform initiatives and integrity. Reubin Askew is held by many as the archetype New South governor. He has been called "one of the most outstanding of the new breed of southern chief executive" by political scientist Larry Sabato. John West's vision for a new South Carolina directly contributed to the transformation of that state from a symbol of the old Confederacy to Sunbelt stalwart.[18]

Albert Brewer tried to bring to Alabama significant reform in the face of court-ordered school integration. Although disdainful of court-ordered integration, Brewer tried to preserve freedom of school choice and at the same time not to appear as another Wallace-style segregationist. He honestly thought if given a good-faith effort, choice could work. Choice, Brewer thought, would preserve the valuable public support he needed for significant educational reform. Unfortunately, Brewer's call for good faith from the courts was too late, as Alabama under Wallace had dashed any goodwill the courts might spare. Brewer's was an argument used often by segregationists as a means to delay implementation of integration court orders as well as by those who supported honest attempts at school choice as a means to preserve the ideal of the "neighborhood schools." Brewer might have wished for good faith, but the courts had none to give. In addition, at times it was difficult to distinguish his remarks from those of segregationists. Brewer enjoyed his most successful year as governor in 1969, when he passed the most progressive education reform legislation the state had ever seen. Still, indicative of the position Alabama held in the nation, Brewer's reforms remained a generation behind Askew's. Nevertheless, Brewer's education reform success solidifies his status as a New South governor.

In 1972 Florida held a statewide referendum on the merits of a constitutional amendment banning busing. Although it held no legal authority, many thought the vote would serve as a cross-section of national opinion because of Florida's diverse population. Askew risked his political future in campaigning against any such amendment to the constitution. Although Floridians overwhelmingly voted to support a constitutional busing ban, Askew showed the rest of the nation that the leaders of the New South supported racial justice even if it meant taking unpopular positions. Just one year after his sound defeat on the busing referendum, Askew maintained sufficient legislative influence to make his state a national leader in education reform. His successful campaign for school reform also provided further evidence of Askew's vision for the New South, which included equal opportunity to a quality education for all children.

John West perceived that integration meant more than just placing black and white children in the same classroom. He attempted to meet the needs of disadvantaged black children, who had been left behind white students because they had been mired in dual education systems. West also committed himself to allaying fears on the part of both black and white parents that with integration came school disorder and violence. His commitment to order and discipline helped make South Carolina's one of the smoothest transitions to integrated schools. John West was the only governor in this group not to pass substantive conventional education reform legislation. Unwilling to raise taxes on his rather poor state to pay for such reform and inheriting an imposing budget deficit, West was forced to pursue other funding options, including reviving his state's flagging economy and making South Carolina a full member of the rising Sunbelt South. Yet he also had to mollify increasingly militant teachers in search of long-awaited pay increases. Still, he succeeded at both.

These governors may have benefited from paramount changes in southern politics, but they also held a common devotion to and hope in the power and necessity of education. Reflecting the philosophy of southern progressive education reformers of the early twentieth century, New South governors believed that education was a gateway to progress. Like their Progressive predecessors, New South governors viewed education reform and the expansion of educational opportunity as essential steps in the South's post–civil rights growth.[19]

Long dominated by Jim Crow segregation, the South provided for dual economies, societies, and educational systems. Founded upon the principle of separate but equal, such dual systems were anything but equal. Southern white public schools received more money, had longer sessions, paid teachers better, and enjoyed more modern facilities than did black schools. In South Carolina in 1945, the number of black and white students in schools was nearly the same, but the state spent three times as much on white students as it did on black students. It also spent one-hundredth of the money on busing black students that it did on busing white students to school. Mississippi acted similarly. In 1945 the state spent 4.5 times as much on white students. Moreover, this was an improvement: as late as 1929 Mississippi spent nine times more money on white children. It was this condition that the NAACP sought to correct when it took on *Brown v. Board.*[20]

Aside from its racial woes, the South lagged behind the rest of the nation in school funding and led the nation in illiteracy rates. This was true as early as 1890. Still, the region was not without its bright moments. During Reconstruction, the Republican-ruled South experimented with tax-supported school systems. Moreover, the great progressive school movement that began in the 1890s had its roots in the South with business progressivism. The rapid industrial and commercial development of the region, combined with the rise of business progressivism, resulted in scores of education reforms in the South. In North Carolina professionals pushed for a system of industrial education to aid in industrial development. A coalition of Florida businessmen and professionals advocated increased taxes to establish colleges and other schools and to train teachers. In South Carolina a farmers' movement led by "Pitchfork" Ben Tillman demanded the expansion of agricultural and industrial education and succeeded in establishing the Winthrop Normal and Industrial College at Rock Hill, South Carolina. Nonetheless, school reform went only so far. Poor whites and blacks suffered ill funding for rural schools, and reform failed when the public feared that blacks might benefit. By 1954, southern public schools remained underfunded, ill supported, and racially unequal.[21]

The effects of separate schools in the South was apparent. In 1940, 25 percent of southern whites had a high school diploma. Only 5 percent of blacks in the region had reached that level. In many ways, such ill-funded and ill-equipped black schools fit perfectly into the white-defined southern experience. Most southern whites discouraged blacks from doing or learning anything but a basic vocation and the etiquette of race.[22]

Brown v. Board (1954) sounded the death knell for racially separated school systems and for segregation in the South. *Brown* was the vehicle used to create political change and social redemption in the South, and later in the rest of the nation, and it also revealed how ambivalent education reformers had been about race. The great education reform movements of the late 1890s and early 1900s did little to address the racial situation in the South or the rest of the nation. As education historian Lawrence Cremin has written, "*Brown* set in motion a major thrust in the direction of greater social and ethnic equality, in education as well as in many other domains of American society." The fact that blacks sued for an end to separate but equal schools and for better educational opportunities revealed just how central education had become to the American mind in the pursuit of the success ethic and the promise of America.[23]

Following *Brown,* few impediments remained to prevent the dismantling of segregated schools. Nevertheless, massive resistance in the South caused desegregation to move at a snail's pace. Even before *Brown,* southerners had prepared for the day when their dual school systems might end. Leading the opposition were the White Citizens Councils, originally formed in Indianola, Mississippi. The councils planned to rid the South of "liberal" books and teachers and prevent racial mixing. Soon after *Brown,* 101 southern congressmen signed the Southern Manifesto, pledging their determination to fight integration and to overturn *Brown.* Southern governors resurrected John C. Calhoun's principle of interposition, which held that the states could nullify a federal law; they also returned the Confederate battle flag above southern state house domes. Even religious leaders weighed in on the issue. Foreshadowing the white conservative critique of *Brown,* a young minister from Virginia, Jerry Falwell, said that "if Chief Justice Warren and his associates had known God's word, I am confident that the . . . decision would never have been made." Blacks saw hope in *Brown,* but they also perceived a white South more determined than ever to prevent that hope from becoming a reality.[24]

By the late 1960s, southern schools remained largely segregated. It took further action by federal judges and the Supreme Court to force change. Three key Supreme Court decisions finally ended segregation: *Green v. County School Board of New Kent County, Virginia* (1968), *Alexander v. Holmes County Board of Education* (1969), and *U.S. v. Montgomery County Board of Education* (1969). In addition, busing was approved as a means of achieving desegregation in *Swann v. Charlotte-Mecklenburg Board of Education* (1971). Massive resistance folded under the weight of these decisions and their enforcement by federal district judges across the South. The prospect of losing millions of federal education dollars also hastened the end of the dual system. By 1972, 91.3 percent of all southern black pupils attended integrated schools. This figure exceeded the rate for the North and West.[25]

It was in this atmosphere that the governors in this book entered office. Integration was a matter of fact. The courts had ruled, and there was no returning to a segregated system, a fact that in many ways aided the governors in their attempts to reform schools and integrate them peacefully. With the matter settled, it was much easier for New South governors to urge calmness and peaceful integration than it would have been without the benefit of the growing number of federal court cases mandating adherence to *Brown*. Still, each New South governor viewed the matter differently. Although all agreed that court-ordered busing as a means to achieve integration was by no means an ideal solution, they diverged in their acceptance of such a solution. West and Brewer argued similarly that busing was not an effective way to integrate, given hostility to the remedy from both white and black parents. Each argued that school choice was a better solution, but neither did much to stop busing. The most outspoken of the three, Askew posited that short of community desegregation, busing, with all its flaws, was the only answer.

West, Brewer, and Askew shared a belief in the Progressive idea that education could be an agent of liberation and empowerment, that for the South to progress economically and socially, it had to educate all its citizens equally. Education constituted a gateway to southern progress. Dual systems with disparate funding levels damaged the region's chances to grow economically and industrially. With Supreme Court mandates looming in the background, the governors were also able to argue, in varying degrees, that education had to be provided to all children equally in order for the South to prosper. Each had flourished in the public education systems of their respective states. Askew, the poor boy from Pensacola, saw it as his way out of the poverty in which he was raised. Brewer went from a family of moderate means and found himself the youngest speaker of the Alabama House of Representatives in state history. West followed a similar path.

West, Brewer, and Askew also served during a political transformation of the sort the South had not seen in a long time. The southern Democratic Party experienced a veritable revolution in membership and demographic composition that allowed these and other New South governors to follow a moderate path that otherwise would have been a political impossibility.

It would be a mistake to generalize across the region in determining a standard definition of "New South" governor. To do so invites over-simplification of the issue and a dismissal of the divergent histories of the southern states. One cannot argue that Florida's experience with the civil rights movement compares with that of Alabama or Mississippi. In many ways, Florida's relatively moderate and peaceful course through the civil rights movement allowed Askew to be as outspoken as he was. Similarly, Alabama's rocky path to freedom for its black citizens created the atmos-phere in which Albert Brewer had to govern. Political survival in Alabama, even after the 1965 Voting Rights Act, required that candidates not offend the racial sensibilities of white voters. To be identified as anything more than a moderate invited defeat at the polls to candidates not afraid to play the race card. Segregation may have died, but racial politics lived on. The 1970 Alabama Democratic gubernatorial primary serves as a perfect ex-ample of this condition. Wallace avoided race in the first primary and al-most lost. He saddled Brewer with claims of "black bloc voting" and won the runoff.

John West faced a similar opponent in Congressman Albert Watson, an unrepentant segregationist who went so far as to encourage violent oppo-sition to court-ordered integration. So inflammatory was one Watson speech that it fostered the attack on a bus of black students bound for a Lamar County school. Ironically, such violent outbreaks so close to the general election forced many voters to support the moderate West, thereby ending Watson's, and Thurmond's, hopes of controlling the state. Such opposition also shaped the manner in which each governor adminis-tered his state. Thanks to a relatively smooth civil rights period in Florida, Askew faced little of the type of opposition confronted by Brewer and West. Applying the "New South" governor standard of Askew to Brewer or West is to overlook and underappreciate the divergent histories of the states in which they all governed. Their differences notwithstanding, the first generation of New South governors, represented here by Brewer, Askew, and West, helped the region transform itself from Jim Crow South to Sunbelt South.

PART I

Albert Brewer of Alabama

On Audie Murphy Day in Alabama, Albert Brewer welcomes the guest of honor, 1969 or 1970. Courtesy Alabama Department of Archives and History, Montgomery, Alabama.

"Deeper Than a Bus Running Down a Road"

The Integration of Alabama's Public Schools

Albert Preston Brewer did more to improve education in Alabama than most of his predecessors and all but a few of his successors. His education legacy is marked by several successes, including steering a progressive education reform package through the legislature in 1969. The package included creation of the Alabama Commission on Higher Education, permanent establishment of the Alabama Educational Study Commission, and a record appropriation to education. He also had to address the wide-scale court-ordered integration of public schools, a task made extremely difficult by the lingering political presence and legacy of George C. Wallace. Although active in appealing many of the sweeping court orders handed down by Frank M. Johnson and other federal judges, Brewer did not oppose school integration, which he considered inevitable. He did bristle at being viewed by outsiders as another Wallace and resented not being given a chance to integrate schools according to his own schedule. As Brewer related years later, it was hard for outsiders to see him as anything other than the next Wallace minion in the governor's chair. When he attended meetings out of state, Brewer often felt scrutinized by the people he met. It made him feel, he said, that they were looking at him to see whether he "had horns like the last one did."[1]

Brewer spent much of his time and energy resisting the manner and method of court-ordered school integration. He defended school choice as the best option for school integration. Brewer also believed that he could somehow transcend the issue of race and integration by focusing attention on issues that he thought would unite black and white Alabamians, namely, quality education, higher teacher pay, better school facilities, and more equitable funding of state schools. School integration by court order rather than by freedom of choice exacerbated the very racial tensions he wished to avoid. Time worked against Brewer. More than four-teen years had passed since *Brown,* and Alabama schools remained mostly segregated. Federal courts had run out of patience at a time when Brewer needed patience for his reform efforts. Differing from his predecessors, Brewer sincerely viewed freedom of choice and the concept of neighbor-hood schools as sound desegregation methods. This position sent mixed signals to the state and nation, for others had previously touted freedom of choice, only to use it as a means of maintaining segregation.[2]

Brewer became governor in May 1968, following the sudden death of Lurleen Wallace. He confronted many challenges, not the least of which was his effort to change the state's image from that of unreconstructed rebel to a law-abiding state that obeyed court orders despite using legal means to protest those it deemed unfair. Brewer's response to court-ordered integration and the increasing firmness with which the Depart-ment of Justice treated the state were largely determined by his frustra-tion in fighting what he naively thought was a finished battle.

Brewer's problems went back to January of 1963 when Detroit Lee, a black Macon County veterans' affairs employee, filed suit in an effort to obtain entrance for his children in what was then the best high school in the county—Tuskegee High. *Lee v. Macon* forever changed the face of pub-lic education in Alabama. That same month another case was filed in Mo-bile federal court by local civil rights activist and postal worker John L. LeFlore. He had submitted a petition with twenty-seven names of black parents to the Mobile County Board of School Commissioners. The petition requested that the board develop a desegregation plan for the county's schools, the largest system in the state with just over seventy-nine thou-sand students. The board's refusal to consider such a plan resulted in the NAACP and the group of parents filing a suit, *Birdie Mae Davis v. Board of School Commissioners, Mobile.* Although not as wide ranging as the *Lee* case, the Mobile suit absorbed Albert Brewer's attention in the late 1960s.[3]

When the *Lee* case was filed in 1963, not one black student had attended a white school in Alabama since the *Brown* decision nine years earlier. This changed in August 1963 when both courts handed down their decisions. From Montgomery, U.S. district judge Frank M. Johnson ordered that the previously all-white Tuskegee High School must admit blacks. Likewise, U.S. judge Daniel Thomas ordered that the twelfth grade of the Mobile County school system be integrated. White reaction to Johnson's order typified and set the tone for the rest of the state. Although white liberals in Tuskegee urged fellow whites to accept the inevitability of integration, white parents pulled their children out of schools in droves, enrolling them in both established and newly created private schools immune to court orders.[4]

Such opposition to integration was nothing new to Alabama. In the nine years since *Brown,* the state had systematically evaded integration, going so far as to pass specific laws designed to prevent the mixing of the races. The cunning 1955 pupil placement law was perhaps the most segregationist of these acts. Passed in the wake of *Brown,* the law was designed to allow local school boards the power to decide where students would attend school based on ability, availability of transportation, and academic background. Ironically, Judge Johnson allowed the Macon County Board to use this law to assign the first thirteen black students to Tuskegee High.[5]

Two Alabama laws passed in 1956 attempted to give local boards legal means to resist desegregation. One measure allowed school boards to close any school faced with integration and also reasserted local control over education. Another 1956 measure, written by Birmingham native and state senator Albert Boutwell, was a freedom of choice law. Freedom of school choice was widely used in the South as a strategy for preventing integration. Choosing which school one's child would attend became the mantra of integration opponents when massive desegregation orders were issued in the 1970s. Its origins went back to *Brown.* Four separate cases were heard under the rubric of *Brown.* The Supreme Court sent one of these, *Briggs v. Elliott,* back to South Carolina where Judge John S. Parker of the Fourth Circuit Court of Appeals held that the Supreme Court had decided only that "a state may not deny to any person on account of race the right to attend any school that it maintains. . . . But if the schools which it maintains are open to children of all races, no violation of the Constitution is involved even though the children of different races voluntarily attend different schools, as they attend different churches. The U.S. Constitution, in other words, does not require integration. It merely forbids discrimination."[6]

This ruling buoyed supporters of freedom of choice, giving them a tool to fight desegregation. Attractive because it was widely accepted as a constitutionally guaranteed right, freedom of choice, in reality, had never been guaranteed, as such a freedom had never been a reality. The ruling was a thinly veiled defense of separate but equal and was immensely popular. One scholar has written that the South embraced the idea of freedom of choice "as though it were a holy writ."[7]

While Frank Johnson allowed schools in Macon County to use freedom of choice to desegregate, Judge Thomas in Mobile moved faster. Upon plaintiff appeal in 1964, he amended his original order to integrate one grade per year to allow for double that pace. He also ordered the board to abolish dual school zones (separate school zones for blacks and whites) for each grade as that grade was reached in the desegregation process. By the 1965–1966 school year, Thomas had ordered the board to abolish dual school zones entirely while maintaining the neighborhood school concept. This "option plan," based upon freedom of choice, received the blessings of both black and white parents who were fearful of sending their children to school in an "inordinately difficult zone."[8]

If integration opponents in Mobile thought the previous few years had been rough, they were shocked in late summer of 1966 when the Fifth Circuit Court of Appeals in New Orleans reversed the lower court decision of 1965 and ordered that the "option plan" be modified so as to provide for every student "the blanket option of attending the school of his zone, or at his option the nearest black school or the nearest white school." This decision was made in light of recent findings that fewer than two-tenths of one percent of black students were enrolled in nonblack schools. That fall 147 black students enrolled in previously all-white Mobile schools.[9]

Governor George Wallace, reflecting the attitude of most white Alabamians, condemned such rulings. He and other state leaders, including the young speaker of the Alabama House of Representatives, Albert Brewer, adopted and published a resolution condemning such guidelines as "totalitarian methods in the form of threats to deny benefits of educational programs from innocent parties." The resolution urged school systems to ignore such guidelines and requirements from the Department of Health, Education, and Welfare (HEW) and follow only court orders. The few districts that had submitted approved desegregation plans quickly withdrew them after this resolution was made public.[10]

By 1968 Lurleen Wallace had succeeded her husband in the governor's office after he failed to get a constitutional amendment passed allowing him to serve a second consecutive term. Albert Brewer served as her lieutenant governor. It was during the abbreviated Lurleen Wallace administration that Judge Johnson expanded *Lee v. Macon* to apply to ninety-nine other school systems across the state. In his decision, he wrote that he "could conceive of no other effective way" to attain "effective, expeditious, and substantial progress" in the area of desegregation. In a statewide television address, Governor Lurleen Wallace quickly condemned this order as one rendered with "malice and animosity."[11]

It was in this atmosphere of animosity toward the courts and federal government that Albert Brewer assumed office in May 1968 upon the tragic death of Lurleen Wallace after a long battle with cancer. He assumed the helm of a state that had mobilized to stave off, if not altogether prevent, the wholesale integration of the state's public schools.[12] In his first press conference after assuming office, Brewer made clear his views on the Mobile court order ending freedom of choice, stating that he feared that the order would cause "irrevocable harm" and would start a domino effect if it were pursued. Brewer maintained that white parents would refuse to allow their children to attend school with black children and would enroll them in private schools not subject to court orders, as had happened in Macon County in 1963. Because the dispersal of state school funds was based on average daily attendance in school systems, such a mass exodus might erode financial support for public schools and lower the quality of education offered. When asked whether this meant that he supported the continuance of "substantially segregated" schools, Brewer tersely replied, "No sir. I am saying we can maintain a strong public support for education in Alabama." He had a point. Enrollment in Mobile County Schools had steadily declined since 1965, when total enrollment for the system had been seventy-nine thousand. By 1968 it had dropped to 74,875, and it fell to 68,623 in September 1970. Walking a fine rhetorical line, Brewer declared that his administration would depart from the radical resistance of past administrations: "I am a lawyer and a law-abiding citizen and I have respect for the law as have my predecessors in this office. I shall abide by any court order and I won't like so many decide which ones. . . . Our court orders are going to be obeyed by everyone."[13]

By the summer of 1968, freedom of choice in Alabama was on its last legs. Court cases in other areas of the South had set precedents that tore away its foundation. In August, Johnson heard pleas from Alabama officials to continue freedom of choice in the ninety-nine systems recently put under the *Lee v. Macon* umbrella. State attorney Maury Smith said that in his opinion there would always be black schools in certain areas and that only 10 percent of black students had chosen to attend white schools. Fred Gray, the plaintiff's attorney, argued that black acceptance of freedom of choice was a mistake and that full integration should have been ordered from the start. Judge Johnson asked Smith if more whites and blacks would choose to mix if the image of the black school was erased by faculty desegregation. Smith replied that such was the case in systems where Johnson had closed black schools to force mixing. U.S. attorney Stephen Pollack argued that faculty desegregation would not help at all because, under freedom of choice, white students would choose to go to other mostly white schools. Johnson agreed.[14]

It had become clear to Johnson that freedom of choice was not working properly. Although willing to allow it to be used, presumably, as a tool for integration, Johnson had banked on a good-faith effort by the state, which he was not receiving. One glaring example of such failure was the case of Annie Yvonne Harris, a black school child in Crenshaw County whose parents sued the district for the fair operation of school choice and an end to the dual school system. Their contention was that Crenshaw County, which had adopted freedom of choice in 1965, had not used choice equitably for black and white students. During the 1966–1967 school year, 202 black students applied for school choice admission to formerly white schools. All but nine of them were turned down for what the county maintained were overcrowded conditions in the schools they wished to attend. Yet officials accepted all the white students who applied for choice. Under oath, Crenshaw County's superintendent of education confessed that black students who asked to attend black schools were automatically approved, whereas black students who requested to attend white schools had their applications treated not as choice applications but as transfer applications. Furthermore, the county's bus system was designed to perpetuate a dual system. It provided black students transportation only to all-black schools. Johnson's ruling of this case on August 8, 1968, reflected certain southern facts of life and his decreasing patience with freedom of choice. First, he acknowledged that "white students will not elect to attend and will not, if any other choice is available, attend a predominately Negro school." Still, he was not ready to give up on choice and saw it as a "feasible plan" given some modifications and a greater degree of positive action on the part of school systems. To ensure that such affirmative steps would be taken, Johnson closed three substandard black schools, extended the choice period, rerouted the bus system to ensure transportation to all schools, and provided minimum teacher ratios by race for each type of school. He maintained that he was not ordering the admittance of any student but merely guaranteeing the preservation of their freedom to choose.[15]

Albert Brewer was more optimistic about freedom of choice. To him it was the only way to desegregate schools and maintain what he considered to be vital public support for education. Freedom of choice was also the only way that Brewer believed he could move the state forward instead of tearing it apart. To drive this point home he took to the speech circuit in June and July of 1968. Before the Alabama Bar Association, Brewer told the barristers that each of them had a duty to get involved in the "crisis to preserve public education—not a discriminatory education, but a quality education for all our young people of all races." Preserving education, explained Brewer, required defending freedom of choice, "one of the principles of a democratic society." At the commencement exercises at Jacksonville State University, Brewer waxed populistic about education in the state and why he wanted to protect freedom of choice. "We have achieved our education," he said "through the tolerance and differences of our fellow citizens." He urged the graduates to "be as concerned about the fate of the uneducated and poverty-stricken as you are about the fortunes of your football team." Brewer lamented Alabama's educational system, which, he said, did not provide Alabama children the best education in the nation. Brewer warned the Alabama Association of Secondary School Principals that his efforts to make Alabama education superior would come to a halt if freedom of choice fell victim to the courts; the consequence would be "public indignation, chaos, and loss of public support for education." It was clear that the governor was trying to influence Johnson's decision on choice. He was also trying to show that he would stop at nothing to preserve the quality of Alabama's public schools. The two, Brewer thought, went hand in hand.[16]

Johnson was not swayed. He was convinced that freedom of choice was not working the way it should had the administrators of systems given a good-faith effort. As early as the 1966–1967 school year, Johnson had indications that choice was not being administered properly by school authorities. During the 1965–1966 school year less than one half of one percent of black students had enrolled in previously all-white schools. One year later this figure had not risen much: only 2.4 percent of black students attended integrated schools. With this in mind, on August 28, 1968,

Johnson ordered seventy-six systems under the *Lee v. Macon* court order to desegregate faculty at a black-white ratio of 1:6 and closed some previously all-black schools before the first day of school. Each system was allowed to maintain freedom of choice as long as it carried out the two new orders. Johnson's decision drew on precedent from other courts. A New Kent, Virginia, case in the U.S. Supreme Court revealed that freedom of choice had not worked there either.[17]

A shocked Brewer deplored the order and lamented that the court was paying "lip service" to freedom of choice while actually using "devious and roundabout means" of implementing integration. "The effect of this decree," he reasoned, was "to require busing without the formality of busing, because it requires the transfer of students to schools which might not be the choice of these particular parents." In the governor's opinion, the court was not acting alone. It was carrying out the "socialistic claims the Justice Department asked it to." Again Brewer made clear the root of his opposition to the orders. He could not reform schools and provide quality education in an atmosphere of anger and fear caused by court orders. Brewer thus crossed a perilous line and departed from the words and actions of fellow New South governors John West and Reubin Askew. The tenor of his protests against court orders and government interference came dangerously close to the rhetoric of his predecessor, something that did not escape the *Alabama Journal,* one of the more liberal newspapers in the state. The *Journal* called Johnson's decision fair and said that it was not wholly unexpected. Previous court rulings in Alabama and elsewhere had foreshadowed it. The *Journal* chastised Brewer for his reaction, writing that it was "almost indistinguishable from the often inflammatory and ever counterproductive rhetoric of the Wallace administration." The *Montgomery Advertiser* agreed in part, pointing out the irony that Alabama had resisted the idea of freedom of choice when it was first implemented as a desegregation tool. Now the state acted as though choice was something sent down from on high. Johnson had placed the burden of good faith on the systems, and they had not performed to his expectations. "The court has given Alabama schools their last chance," maintained the paper. "They must make the most of it or all children, white and Negro alike, will suffer by the consequences of and disaffection for public education."[18]

The Alabama Education Association (AEA) also protested the severity and timing of the order. AEA president Vernon L. St. John protested that implementing such a massive order so soon before school started was nothing less than a "completely impossible task." Brewer and education superintendent Ernest Stone asked Judge Johnson to hold a modification hearing where the state could present evidence of the hardships involved in carrying out the order. More than 1,200 black teachers were slated to transfer before the start of school, and another 909 would move after school started. The AEA also worried about a mass teacher exodus. More than 1,196 teachers did not return to teaching in the 1968 school year, though this figure was probably more a result of low teacher salaries than integration. Brewer argued that perhaps Johnson did not fully grasp the magnitude of his order. The governor claimed that many teachers would resign to avoid transfer, and teacher tenure laws might be violated when so many teachers were transferred without a hearing. He further contended that closing black schools to force integration would lead to overcrowding and loss of accreditation if too many teachers were forced to teach outside their fields. Above all, Brewer feared the decline in state money that would go to schools based on a decreasing average daily attendance figure, which determined state contributions to school systems. Brewer also cited reports from some black principals who predicted that as many as 60 percent of their pupils would drop out of school rather than accept a transfer. "They simply are not going to be driven by the court to do something against their wishes and against their best interests," argued Brewer.[19]

Brewer redoubled his efforts to point out inconsistencies in Johnson's order and to show that Johnson and the federal government misunderstood the situation in Alabama. Before his weekly press conference, Brewer highlighted what he saw as some of the more ridiculous aspects of Johnson's orders. He observed that in one system white teachers had been assigned by court order to teach at a black school that was closed the previous year by an earlier order. In four separate instances more black teachers were ordered transferred than the system actually employed. Brewer's most fervent arguments came when he talked of closing black schools to force integration. More than 145 black schools would be closed over the next year or so by court orders. This would disrupt school finances, he complained, and "at a time when we are so strapped for money to operate our school systems and when we don't have the luxury of closing down schools, but need many more classrooms it just seems ridiculous to require local school boards to throw away many of the facilities we now have." Brewer cited the closing of a new black school in Lanett, recently built at the cost of $1 million and equipped with a swimming pool. At one of these schools, for newspaper photographers Brewer made his "stand in the schoolhouse window," peering into the windows of a newly built but closed black school. Overcrowding, he argued, would result from the pursuit of "social objectives" on the part of the courts and Justice Department. At Dozier High School, Brewer pointed out that the previous year's enrollment was 220, but the court order increased this figure to 309 (130 blacks, 179 whites). Classrooms were at a premium. The school conducted three courses simultaneously in the school's auditorium and a reading class in the cafeteria. The closed school was only three years old. The withdrawal of forty white students to attend school in nearby Covington County, where desegregation ratios were lower, partially alleviated the crowded conditions. Dozier High School principal George W. Maddox had even complained about the educational quality of the incoming black students, claiming that they did not "measure up" to the standards set by his school in the past. Brewer failed to note that Alabama's own survey of black schools in the early 1960s classified as inadequate 48 percent of black school buildings and 51 percent of black school sites. Only 19 percent of buildings and 17 percent of sites for whites failed to meet standards.[20]

Such "ridiculous" and "arbitrary" court orders left Brewer with what he claimed was no choice other than to take two sweeping actions to stop what he called Johnson's playing "Russian roulette" with Alabama's children. Brewer declined to foster a soothing of tension, fear, and uneasiness, instead choosing to make what the *Montgomery Advertiser* termed his "first schoolhouse stand." Brewer first said he would appeal to the Supreme Court for relief from such "impossible" requirements. Then he would make yet another plea to Johnson for leniency and a modification of the court orders. Brewer maintained that it was not only white students who felt the pinch of reduced educational quality and overcrowded classrooms and schools; black students also suffered from the ramifications. In his hometown of Decatur black children sat on the steps of their former school because there was no bus transportation to their new school three miles away. "It would be tragic," Brewer said, "if these disadvantaged Negro children are denied an education because the neighborhood school they were used to attending had been closed." To Brewer the battle lines were clear: his effort to preserve quality education versus the court's "socialistic" agenda. Moreover, to him the two were in direct conflict. Brewer's was a shrewd but dangerous political argument designed to highlight the almost impossible position in which the state and the governor had been placed, even if it was, ironically, a result of the state's past actions.[21]

Brewer also turned his attention to the Justice Department and HEW. Increasingly, both departments had intervened in the wake of compliance orders requiring desegregation plans and guidelines in order for a state to receive federal funds. Brewer considered the Justice Department his "adversary" in the lawsuits. He asserted to the annual meeting of the Association of Alabama School Boards that they were not "under any obligation to obey any orders which you receive from the Justice Department." The state would follow court orders after they had been appealed, he promised, but arbitrary demands from the Justice Department would not be heeded. The state, said the governor, would "exhaust every legal remedy" to alleviate the detrimental effects of the August court order.[22]

Although some black Alabamians shared Brewer's concern about closing black schools, others clearly did not. Joe Reed, leader of the Alabama Democratic Conference, the organization of black Alabama Democrats, spoke out against the state's efforts to ease the "hardships" of integration. In a damning speech in Mobile, Reed claimed that "every method that human ingenuity can conceive of has been used to circumvent, modify, and flout" court orders. Unfair past and present state policy, he said, had resulted in the "outer-gration" of black principals and teachers from public education. School boards, he added, were asking white teachers to transfer while ordering black teachers to do so. Similarly, Reed asserted, when consolidation of schools occurred, most black principals found themselves demoted to assistant principal or even to teacher when they moved to a new school. Either way, rarely had they maintained their rank upon transfer; most moved down.[23]

Brewer's appeal for some sort of relief hearing on Johnson's August 28, 1968, decision was for naught. On October 15, Johnson denied his request for such a hearing, calling Brewer's claim that the court orders violated Alabama's constitutional rights "simply preposterous." In the interim between the August 28 order and the denial in October, all but nineteen of the seventy-six systems affected had come into compliance with the original order while maintaining freedom of choice. If Brewer seemed to miss the point, Johnson did not. He used it as part of his reasoning for denying a hardship hearing for the other systems. Johnson also took the opportunity to clarify his earlier order. Many school districts had automatically closed black schools, some very newly built, in the wake of the August 28 order. Johnson said that he had not intended for use of such facilities to end. Rather he meant that they could not be used exclusively for black children. Johnson then ordered the nineteen noncompliant systems to show cause why they thought it unnecessary to use means other than freedom of choice to desegregate. Not yet ready to abandon freedom of choice, Johnson was still frustrated with its misuse: "The court cannot make freedom of choice work without good faith and effective efforts on the part of the school authorities." Perhaps what frustrated Johnson was that other states, such as South Carolina, seemed to be able to move past the end of choice and accept integration, whereas Alabama and Brewer maintained a death grip on an increasingly unrealistic option. Johnson also reminded the state that one of its own attorneys had argued in the original hearing on freedom of choice that Johnson should "prod us when you have to." He lectured that all parties knew that to prod meant more aggressive orders.[24]

An incensed Brewer blasted Johnson, arguing that his denial of a hearing was "harsh and aggressive." The governor decried Johnson's "devious attempt" to institute social control and lamented that the judge was unfair not to give him, a new governor without a track record of defiance, a chance to show how hard Johnson was being on Alabama. Brewer looked to a more just future: "Someday, somehow, somewhere, we shall have our day in court and we shall present the evidence we have accumulated on behalf of the school children of Alabama to maintain the integrity of our public school system and to defend it against the callous attacks of those who have no real concern for our children."[25]

In late 1968 and early 1969 Brewer obtained the hearing he wanted, but not in Johnson's court. This opportunity came from the U.S. district judge for the Northern Circuit of Alabama, Seybourn H. Lynne, who decided to grant a hearing to school systems that complained of undue hardships in carrying out desegregation orders. It was a victory of sorts for Brewer because the court addressed the problems of school systems individually, something he had suggested all along. This February 1969 hearing allowed Jefferson County to explain why it had problems closing three county schools and consolidating others. Brewer testified that Alabama could not afford the "luxury" of closing schools because of the state's desperate need for classroom space. He said that freedom of choice had allowed some systems to make "unbelievable progress" in desegregating and cited the detrimental effect of white flight. In Tuscaloosa and Haneyville, Brewer reported, white flight had caused a school, once all white, then integrated, to become all black. Under cross-examination Brewer admitted his belief that it was not necessary for schools to integrate in order to provide quality education and denied that black schools were always inferior to white ones. Later, when state attorneys posited that the state legislature might be more willing to increase education funds if freedom of choice were maintained, they were quickly overruled by Judge Lynne.[26]

Brewer may have lambasted the federal courts in earlier reactions to court orders, but he saved his strongest comments for a March 1969 speech before the Alabama Education Association. After expressing a growing frustration at seeing schools closed, Brewer launched his strongest verbal attack at Johnson. Although he did not mention the judge by name, it was evident whom he had in mind: "I long for the day when a federal judge—sitting in his ivory tower—will go out as I have and view the havoc he has created and the retarding influence he has exercised on the minds of our young children. I have been there—I have seen it first hand. And my heart cries out for the school children of this state who have been uprooted to satisfy social whims. My heart cries out for the future of children who are being tossed about by those who have no interest in quality education."[27]

Such problems, argued Brewer, resulted from the need to "satisfy social whims" and experiment with "social theories and objectives." He lamented the closing of a new brick school in one small southern Alabama town, the overcrowded conditions in another, and the "semi-organized chaos" that the court orders had imposed upon Alabama education. "That federal judge," Brewer belligerently proclaimed, "who has lost all touch with reality, has struck a cruel blow at Alabama's children and her public schools. But he has not conquered the courage of a people accustomed to adversity. He has not diminished our hopes and dreams for the future. And his heartless tactics have not diminished our resolve to provide a place of dignity and worth for our children."[28]

That same day, the governor also addressed the annual meeting of the Alabama State Teachers Association (ASTA), a black teachers' organization that was meeting for the last time before merging with the AEA. His addresses to both groups were basically the same with one major difference. In his speech to ASTA, he did not attack the courts and the effects of massive school consolidation. The changes baffled some black educators who had seen the AEA speech over the state's educational television network. They were more surprised, though, at Brewer's failure to name a date for a special session of the legislature to address education reform. It had been rumored that he would do so in these speeches. The *Alabama Journal* was also puzzled. The paper chastised Brewer for tilting at windmills rather than discussing needed reforms in education. "Efforts to shift the blame for our plight to a convenient whipping boy," wrote the editors, "will get him, and the children of Alabama, nowhere. Only the governor can decide which route he'll take." The *Journal* posited that Brewer probably knew better:

> Whether he doubts it or not anyone with sufficient understanding of Alabama public affairs to be governor of the state also should understand that recent court decisions on education are the natural outgrowth of policies which, over a span of several generations, distributed educational funds on anything but an equal basis to all Alabama youngsters. If those governors, those legislators, and those educators who have managed the state's educational affairs for the past seventy five years had been truly dedicated to the proposition that every child should have an equal chance for equal schooling, federal judges would have been able to go fishing a great deal more frequently in the past several years. And use of their names very likely would have offered little political advantages to today's office holders and office seekers.[29]

Despite such isolated criticism, Brewer received a great deal of support for his stance against the federal courts. White Alabamians of all walks of life wrote him, asking or even commanding him to fight harder for Alabama. One citizen asked Brewer to "stand up for Alabama," obviously borrowing the Wallace campaign theme, and beseeched him to "intervene and just shut all the schools down." Brewer pledged his total effort to "maintain good schools and strongly resist any forces who would seek to destroy" them. One way Brewer silently carried on his fight was by using the governor's contingency fund to help defray legal costs of the nineteen school systems that Johnson ordered to show cause why they could not follow his desegregation orders. Established in 1961 by the state legislature, the fund had a budget of $90,000. Recent appropriations halved that amount but still left more than enough to provide some financial aid to "threatened" school systems. Brewer submitted this idea to MacDonald

Gallion, state attorney general, who ruled that the money was designed for use at the governor's discretion and that payments were not subject to court action or review. Brewer's legal advisor, Hugh Maddox, recommended that the state not agree to pay the total amount of legal bills, which might set a costly precedent. Instead he urged Brewer to set the maximum amount his office was willing to pay at $500. Brewer had not initially intended to help out the systems financially. He had earlier suggested that the state attorney's office would provide services, but when one system asked for help, state officials refused. Other systems had gone directly to a segregationist arm of state government, the Alabama State Sovereignty Commission. Founded by the legislature in 1963, the State Sovereignty Commission was designed to aid "in the conservation of sovereignty of the state and of preventing the usurpation of its sovereign powers by an ever expanding central government." Sometimes called a "Confederate C.I.A.," the commission had a state-funded budget and undertook a variety of covert and not-so-covert operations to stall the march toward civil rights. The specific request for legal aid was a new twist, and it may very well have been the genesis of Brewer's contingency fund idea.[30]

The existence of the Sovereignty Commission in Brewer's administration marks an important transitional phase in Alabama history during this period. Brewer definitely wanted to make a new beginning for Alabama. Not ungrateful for what George Wallace had done for him, Brewer still believed he represented a change in the approach by the state government, though at times it did not appear so. The Sovereignty Commission, which had increasingly come under fire, represented segregationist tradition. Although chair of the commission by statute, Brewer did not walk hand in hand with the organization, which continued to be dominated by Wallace appointees.[31]

Although Judge Johnson had been the recipient of much of Brewer's scorn, because of the wide-ranging implications of *Lee v. Macon,* it was another system and another judge's decision that seemed to occupy the remainder of Brewer's time in office. *Davis v. Board* was filed at the same time as *Lee v. Macon,* but its results were very different. Because the Civil Rights Act of 1964 gave the Justice Department expanded authority to intervene in desegregation cases, the Mobile case attracted the careful attention of both state and federal governments, including President Nixon and HEW secretary Robert Finch. Judge Thomas originally had allowed some latitude in school choice, requiring that the option plan be administered fairly. Additional decisions by him and higher federal courts, however, had finally eliminated choice. These rulings required the establishment of mandatory attendance zones for crosstown busing and mass integration by February 1970, replacing the much-abused "choice plan." They also created great hostility and tension between the federal government and the state. Because choice had failed in Mobile, Judge Thomas made the gradual shift toward requiring massive busing and attendance zones to integrate schools. By late 1971, as the result of orders by Judge Thomas and the U.S. Supreme Court, Mobile had redrawn school zones and begun the widespread busing of students. Much of this change came on the heels of the realization by integration advocates and the Court that choice was either too slow or not working. Indeed, by 1968 only 3,484 black students in Alabama attended formerly white schools.[32]

What raised Brewer's ire was the June 1969 reversal of Thomas's ruling allowing for the implementation of a choice plan with some faculty transfers. The Fifth Circuit Court of Appeals in New Orleans ordered the board of education to engage HEW's assistance in preparing a new desegregation plan for the system. Thomas's August 1, 1969, ruling required both plaintiff and defendant to file desegregation plans with the court before his final ruling. Thomas's decree on the suit was favorable to some portions of the HEW plan, which had suggested the total integration of the system for the 1969–1970 school term. Thomas accepted the part of the HEW plan that called for the immediate desegregation of all rural and metro schools west of interstate I-65 in Mobile; all schools east of that line would remain under freedom of choice for the following year. The board had to file a plan with the judge for further desegregation of eastern side schools no later than December 1969. Thomas required faculty to be balanced racially and for the new zones and the details of the plan to be published in the newspaper. After years of litigation, said Thomas, the school system "must forthwith be operated in accordance with the law of the land. What this school system needs is to educate children legally, and not engage in protracted litigation." Some key state officials privately admitted that they could live with such a decree from Thomas. Brewer's legal advisor, Hugh Maddox, concluded that the "school board and staff can live with it—not unsound from [an] educational standpoint." The school board even urged that the best thing that could happen in Mobile for the coming school year was for school to open without appeal of the ruling.[33]

Brewer was under considerable pressure to do exactly what Thomas urged the state not to do, draw out the fight in court and exacerbate tensions. He received hundreds of letters urging him to "stand up for Alabama." Much of this opposition fed off fears and rumors that had spread about the nature of "barbaric" black children and black schools. One Mobilian wrote Brewer that he would keep his children out of school even if it meant going to jail. "They want to take our children," said the writer, "and put them in a nigger school where dope peddling, prostitution, knifings and shootings takes [sic] place." Another complained to Brewer about the "stinking federal government" and how it had infringed on Alabamians' constitutional rights. A twelve-year-old from Mountain Brook said she favored segregation, and another child sent a letter "sealed with hope" that blacks would never attend her Mountain Brook school. Members of the Citizens Political Action Committee sent their opinion that "virtually no one wants integration. If many did, it would not be hard to get people to integrate. Voices in the dark cry 'forward! Black and White together!' But few move in the blackout. Needed are voices of sanity saying 'stay where you are until the lights come on.'" Concerned citizens' groups of like opinion formed throughout the state during these years, and Mobile was no exception. One Mobile group, Stand Together and Never Divide (STAND), recruited a large membership. At its first meeting in the spring of 1968, more than five hundred attended. Almost one thousand were present at the next rally, and at its third, police reported three thousand in attendance. Not to be outdone, civic groups weighed in on the issue of integration and HEW involvement. Mobile's Canes Club and Exchange Club passed resolutions condemning the involvement of HEW and court orders integrating Mobile's children.[34]

Few voices spoke out for peaceful integration. The League of Women Voters in Mobile supported the court orders, as did one "transplanted Yankee of Scandinavian descent from New Jersey," who suggested that because integration was inevitable why did Alabamians not take the opportunity to "show the rest of the nation and the world that they are able to go ahead and integrate the schools without any outside interference." Brewer did not disagree with the recommendations of this last writer, but he wanted the rest of the nation to come under the same watchful eye as Alabama.[35]

Brewer's responses to such outcries did little to calm fears or strengthen support for the U.S. Constitution. Instead, they were vague and at times inflammatory. Some of the governor's responses straddled the fence, perhaps a reflection of his tenuous political position. Brewer told those who urged the state to obey the court that he was trying to keep people calm and still "preserve our public schools." He responded in like manner to those urging total defiance to all agencies of the federal government. He assured them that he was trying to "resist this effort to destroy our public schools." Calling federal courts "vindictive" and accusing them of intending to destroy public schools did little to show the state that he was determined to obey the courts as a law-abiding citizen. Furthermore, it is clear that Brewer became more outspoken in his opposition to the court in 1969 and early 1970 than he had been before. There are several reasons for this change: his desire to pass other reforms that were predicated on some remainder of public support for public education and the fact that he was serving as governor in the malignant, ominous shadow of George Wallace while Wallace was obviously planning to run against him in 1970. Nor was Wallace quietly waiting in the wings for the campaign season to start. He had never stopped running. Brewer received a letter from Blue Springs, Alabama, in July 1970 saying that citizens knew he could keep open the schools scheduled to close under court order in that town because "George C. Wallace called Blue Springs yesterday and said he had done all he could for our school. That you wouldn't keep it open." The looming specter of Wallace moved Brewer a bit to the political right, somewhat closer to Wallace's point of view. It was a key period for Brewer. He wanted desperately to bring a new attitude to the state in its relations with the federal government, but the political necessities of remaining in office dictated his shift. He began in 1969 to take an active regional and national role in preserving freedom of choice.[36]

Alabama was not alone in its integration woes. The rest of the South faced many of the same issues and problems with court orders and resistance. One of the more zealous southern state chief executives was Governor Lester Maddox, Georgia's own junior George Wallace. In July 1969, Maddox called for a summit of southern governors to address the school situation. Alarmed at the "growing crisis" in public schools, Maddox wrote to each governor expressing his concerns and designs for dealing with common problems. Maddox alleged that with increased participation of the federal government in public education, there had been a corresponding increase in crime, violence, attacks on students and teachers, and "chaos and disorder." Brewer said that a previous commitment prevented him from attending, but he sent in his place education superintendent Ernest Stone. Some three hundred people attended, but only two southern governors, Maddox and Mississippi's John Bell Williams. Stone was the only chief school officer who attended, and he reported that Williams's remarks were "slightly short of belligerent" and designed for the pleasure of the one hundred or so Mississippians present. Stone spoke for Brewer, lamenting the hardships created by court orders and expressing hope that the meeting would be "more profitable than the meeting my Grandfather Stone had in Atlanta 104 years ago when he met General Sherman." Stone reported to Brewer that he believed the meeting was too little too late: "I fear we may be closing the barn gate after the horse has escaped."[37]

For not attending the meeting in Georgia, Brewer suffered the wrath of court-fighting Alabamians. Although it is unclear why he declined Maddox's invitation, it was likely due to his moderate position. One Montgomery citizen sent Brewer a copy of her letter to Maddox, which read in part: "Congratulations! it is very heartening to see our country has one patriotic American Governor." "Mr. Brewer, where were you when the HEW took over our schools?" wrote one citizen. "Now governor," wrote yet another, "if that is the way it is going to be, there will be no need campaigning in these parts for reelection as governor. We don't straddle fences." Still others threatened to withhold their vote from him in 1970 because he chose not to attend. One person thanked Brewer for not attending and stepping on the toes of "other liberals. You will make a great moderate for them, but you are not representing my interests." Brewer tried to reiterate his disagreement with the courts and his sympathy and support for the spirit of Maddox's meeting. He also maintained that he was doing all he could to "resist the federal takeover of our schools," but to no avail. Ironically, during the 1970 campaign, Brewer attended such a meeting to address the school situation.[38]

Wallace's meddling increased. In Mobile and Birmingham press conferences, Wallace called for students and parents to support freedom of choice by marching in school protests and for parents to take their children to the school of their choice regardless of what the courts said. Although capitol observers called this Wallace's first direct challenge to Brewer in the approaching 1970 election, Brewer naively dismissed it as not politically motivated. Still, he did say that if roles were reversed, he would have extended Wallace the courtesy of a call to forewarn him of his actions. He maintained that he supported Wallace, but "I really don't know if the reverse is true." Brewer maintained that any "citizen" can make public statements, but he alone shouldered the "awesome duty" of preserving law and order.[39]

Soon after Brewer's statement about preserving law and order, both houses of the state legislature overwhelmingly passed resolutions reaffirming freedom of choice as the preferred desegregation method in Alabama. The resolution received the governor's full support. Nonetheless, legislative voices of dissent remained. A "staunch" Wallace supporter, Alton Turner of Crenshaw County, voted against the resolutions, as did Stewart O'Bannon of Lauderdale County, who called the resolution "an exercise in futility." The sole house Republican voted against the resolution, asserting that "this is not a matter of freedom of choice, it is a matter of law and order and we in the legislature cannot recommend to the people that they violate the law." Although the resolution was not an outright call for people to violate the law, it did little to ease fear and tension. Brewer's reply to a press conference question about private schools accomplished even less. Asked if he would ever advocate taking children out of school and enrolling them in the parents' school of choice regardless of court orders, Brewer responded frankly that he had privately made the suggestion to a parents' group in the past. Clearly, Brewer had failed to provide consistent positive leadership in the crisis over school integration. He was under tremendous political pressure, however, which increased as the 1970 Alabama Democratic primary approached.[40]

In this atmosphere of fear and dread, instances of disorder escalated. In Aliceville, seventy black students who opposed segregated schools boycotted the mostly black R. J. Kirksey High School for two days. At the request of Mayor Roy Kelly, who feared the presence of "black militants," Brewer sent one hundred Alabama National Guardsmen to quell the protest demonstrations. In Mobile and Choctaw Counties whites picketed schools to protest losing school choice. More than twenty-four hundred black and white students, half the enrollment, spontaneously boycotted Choctaw and Butler County schools for four days in opposition to busing plans, distance of travel, and integration. Tension also spilled onto football fields. At the Ariton High versus Tuskegee High football game on September 11, 1969, the mostly white Ariton parents and supporters were "shocked" to see the mostly black Tuskegee football team give the "black power" sign during the national anthem. Brewer blamed court-ordered integration and the end of school choice for such incidents. He also complained about a desegregation plan for Limestone County that forced black students to travel 113 miles a day to attend an integrated school. Brewer decided to take his cause outside the state and solicit support from other governors. His first step was the 1969 Southern Governors' Conference in Williamsburg, Virginia.[41]

Busing was the hot issue at Williamsburg, and the proposals contained in varying resolutions on the subject revealed how divided southern governors were. At the conference, Brewer attempted to solidify support for freedom of choice and to condemn federal interference in state business. Brewer's proposed resolution accused the president and vice president of hypocrisy in claiming that they opposed "compulsory assignment" of students by race at the same time that their Justice and HEW departments had pressured the South for "racial balances" in the schools. The Southern Governors' Conference, according to Brewer's proposal, should go on record as favoring "quality nondiscriminatory education" for all children, local control and autonomy for school boards, assignments of students and faculty on a nondiscriminatory basis that still took into account the "best interest" of quality education, freedom of choice, and a policy of "desegregation" that did not include massive busing. Above all, Brewer's resolution called for each state, not just those in the South, to be treated fairly and equally under the law, an obvious reference to the seemingly selective enforcement of *Brown* outside the South.[42]

Republican Oklahoma governor Dewey Bartlett, facing reelection in 1970, voiced his opposition to the tone of the resolution. "Partisan embarrassment" of the president and vice president, said Bartlett, was not wise. Nor was penning a resolution that embarrassed the governors. Other resolutions were offered in protest to Brewer's proposal. Marvin Mandel, Democratic governor of Maryland, offered a resolution maintaining that "desegregation is the law of the land. This we must all accept. Attempts to thwart this constitutional directive are foredoomed and inevitably feed tensions and hostilities which we seek to abate." Debate over Brewer's resolution lasted two hours, and it revealed a chasm between governors from the Deep South and Border South. Indeed, Border South governors prevented Brewer's resolution from receiving the three-fourths vote needed to pass. Delaware governor Russell Peterson and Maryland's Mandel voted against it, and West Virginia's Jay Rockefeller abstained. Lester Maddox responded to the defeat of the group that newspapers labeled "Deep South segregationists" by asking, "Who is responsible for bringing these Yankees into the Southern Governors' Conference?" The resolution that became the official position of the conference was a watered-down version of the Brewer resolution, which held, in part, that the group favored "quality nondiscriminatory education" and urged "restraint and good judgment of any 'bussing' [sic] of public school students from one neighborhood to another in order to achieve racial integration." This resolution was not what Brewer wanted to see come out of the meeting, but it did serve to project the issue onto the national stage, although in what light is not clear.[43]

The resolution certainly got the attention of the Nixon administration. At the main banquet, Vice President Spiro T. Agnew, the keynote speaker, departed from his prepared text and addressed the issue. In an effort to diminish criticism of the Nixon administration that had emanated from the meeting, Agnew declared that the administration was against busing "children to other neighborhoods simply to achieve an integrated status of a larger geographic entity. . . . This administration favors integration but not mandatory, artificially contrived social acceptance." He said exactly what antibusing governors wanted to hear: condemnation of the federal courts and social objectives to make the audience think that the Nixon administration was on their side. Agnew had publicly expressed what Brewer as far back as November 1968 had privately hoped about the Nixon administration, namely, that Nixon's election might bring a softer attitude on busing. Increased calls from federal authorities for tighter guidelines and more busing had frustrated Brewer, however, and he saw no relief in sight.[44]

Despite all the press coverage of the Southern Governors' Conference, Brewer still found himself unable to influence Judge Johnson. On October 14, 1969, Johnson rejected without a hearing another petition filed by Brewer for a redress of grievances. Johnson reiterated his previous rulings and addressed the complaint that black schools, some of them brand new, had been closed: "What the court is trying to do is make white students attend formerly all-Negro schools. This same court has taken judicial knowledge that white children will not voluntarily do this." Disgusted, Brewer remarked that "even an accused murderer or Communist gets his day in court. . . . This fundamental American right has been denied to the 900,000 school children of Alabama." What Brewer failed to mention was that Alabama, and the South, had its day in court in 1954. With Johnson's rejection, Brewer's approach to quality education received yet another fatal blow. So desperate was he to achieve this almost mythical goal that he remarked in deep frustration that "if we can't have quality education, we may as well not have it at all." Brewer never seriously considered closing state schools, but his frustration with integration went deep.[45]

In seeking a new venue to hear his complaints, Brewer filed a motion in the Supreme Court against the U.S. government, charging that Secretary of Health, Education, and Welfare Robert Finch discriminated against Alabama in his enforcement of civil rights and integration laws. Brewer argued that even though HEW had judged segregation a national problem, it focused its energies exclusively on the South. Claiming that Chicago had 208 all-black schools, the District of Columbia contained 114, Baltimore 89, and New York City 114, Brewer hoped to show that Alabama was unfairly targeted by the government. He wanted the court to balance the enforcement of school integration and treat all regions fairly. The court refused to hear Brewer's complaint.[46]

Although he agreed with a recent statement by South Carolina governor Bob McNair that desegregation was a fact of life, Brewer nonetheless opposed the means by which schools were desegregated. As for the Supreme Court's refusal to hear him, Brewer said, "It is difficult for me not to be very bitter about this thing. We filed a suit here on behalf of three and a half million law-abiding people in Alabama alleging that we weren't receiving equal treatment under the law." He lamented that the same court would hear a Communist. His latest action received mixed reviews by the state's papers. The *Alabama Journal* described the suit as folly and suggested more realistic options or arguments such as a suit by black and white parents arguing emotional distress over desegregation. The *Journal* also argued that the state could use the original *Brown* argument but with a twist; white children, like their black counterparts, were being "educationally and psychologically damaged" by being forced into certain schools "purely on the basis of race." The *Journal,* like Brewer, accepted the inevitability of integration, thus suggesting that the thrust of any appeal should be an attack on the means of integration, not the end result. "Great care should be taken," advised the *Journal,* realizing the subtlety of Brewer's arguments, "to get across the point that the purpose of the litigation is not just another bold dodge to thwart the Supreme Court's orders for eliminating dual schools." The *Montgomery Independent* was more critical of Brewer's appeal to the Court, saying that it was akin to "Christ going to the Sanhedrin on appeal."[47]

Brewer was too busy to attend Lester Maddox's call to arms in Atlanta in 1969, but he found time in 1970 to attend another such meeting in Mobile called by Mississippi governor John Bell Williams. Williams announced the meeting during a rally in Jackson of the group F.O.C.U.S. (Freedom of Choice in the U.S.). At this meeting, four governors proposed a "last ditch" effort to fight integration. Brewer, John Bell Williams of Mississippi, Lester Maddox of Georgia, and John McKeithen of Louisiana gathered for what Brewer called a meeting "imperative" to preserving freedom of choice. The belligerent Mississippi governor John Bell Williams said he was willing to do anything to curb "judicial dictatorship" even if it meant he would "rot in jail." After the three-hour meeting at the International Trade Club, the four released a statement reaffirming their support of freedom of choice as the only viable desegregation method. Committing themselves to achieving their aims through "orderly, democratic processes and not through violence," they pledged to follow the pattern set by Martin Luther King Jr. of "obtaining justice through dramatic actions which will gain acceptance and support for a just cause." They also lamented the unjust treatment of the South. McKeithen was especially adamant about equal treatment for all regions in integration: "The courts," he said, "are trying to make us do something in Louisiana that they would never even attempt in New York."[48]

Taking his crusade to highlight the inequities of federal enforcement of integration to the state legislature, Brewer called a special session for the week of February 23. He planned to submit the 1970 New York Freedom of Choice Law to the legislature. If it passed, constitutional challenges would have to include both New York and Alabama plans. If the law withstood constitutional challenge, the state could possibly revert to freedom of choice. If struck down as unconstitutional, then the law wherever practiced would be overturned, forcing those states that Brewer believed were getting away with segregation to implement desegregation laws. The session also had a political genesis. George Wallace had announced a press conference for February 26 at which he was expected to announce for governor in 1970. Brewer hoped to steal a little of Wallace's thunder.[49]

In his speech opening the special session, Brewer was interrupted no less than sixteen times by standing ovations. He said he had called the special session because "our children are entitled to fair and equal treatment." "I ask you," said Brewer, "what is fair and equal treatment? Is it fair that the children of New York have freedom of choice and the children of

Alabama can't have it? If freedom of choice is right for New York, it's right for Alabama." Brewer made it clear to the legislature and, he hoped, to opponents of integration that he was not trying to stand in the school-house door with freedom of choice. His purpose was higher than that. "Our problem is not race," said Brewer. "As I have said before, the question is not one of integration or segregation. We crossed that bridge several years ago. The question is about what kind of education we are going to give our children." His goal was simple: equal treatment under law for all states "because our children should have the same rights and privileges as the children of any other state in this nation, not to be above the law, but not to be below it either." His final appeal was more for citizens than for legislators. This problem was one for courts and legislatures and "will not be settled in the streets. Violence is not the answer."[50]

The Alabama Choice Bill unanimously passed the house 92-0 and the senate 33-0. Some legislators attempted to go further. Representative Bryce Graham of Tuscumbia tried to pass a call for a referendum to amend the state's constitution and remove the provision that allowed for dual school systems. This motion was tabled 91-1. Other measures passed the house but had not passed the senate when the session ended. One such measure would have provided a ninety-day exemption for parents and children from compulsory school laws should they "find their position untenable" in integrated schools. Another failed bill prohibited the transfer of teachers and administrators purely on racial grounds and provided that teachers would be retained at their home school on a seniority basis. It was introduced by Senator Eddie Gilmore of Jefferson County, a Brewer floor leader. Yet another would have allowed the state attorney general to represent teachers in court actions where they refused to be transferred. These measures were either introduced or cosponsored by Brewer floor leaders and enjoyed the support of Brewer and Wallace. The entire process was largely a charade. Although the act passed unanimously, the issue had long been settled in the courts.[51]

Albert Brewer's defense of freedom of choice and his appeal of court orders have no simple explanation. It is possible, and perhaps easiest, to make the case that Brewer was merely another Wallace foot soldier in favor of halting in any way possible school integration. To be sure, Brewer enjoyed a great deal of Wallace support while he was a state legislator. He received the "fighting judge's" seal of approval in his run for house speaker, lieutenant governor, and until Wallace formally announced in 1970, even for governor. Nevertheless, this view fails to take into account the complexities of Alabama and southern politics, the difficult position in which Brewer was placed with the death of Lurleen Wallace, and his personal beliefs and motivations for education reform. Brewer's motivation for railing at federal court orders and intervention in Alabama's school integration was rooted in his overall outlook and goal for Alabama's public education system. Motivated by a desire to see the most efficient and effective use of school funds and facilities, he believed that he had no choice but to object vehemently to the manner in which the courts were ordering the integration of public schools. When Brewer was thrust into office with the death of Lurleen Wallace, he honestly thought he offered a change in style of governance, a change in tactics and motivations, and, above all else, a change in perspective. Furthermore, Brewer shared with West and Askew a strong dislike of busing. West even touted freedom of choice as the best way to integrate, whereas Askew preferred other options than busing. Nonetheless, West and Askew quickly recognized that choice was no longer an option.[52]

Brewer's problem was that as much as he wanted to believe that the state had moved beyond simple considerations of race, clearly it had not. His opposition to court rejection of freedom of choice, though different in motivation, sounded indistinguishable from the racist rhetoric of segregationist Alabama citizens and politicians. Brewer supported freedom of choice because he believed it would preserve the integrity of the schools, prevent erosion of the tax base, and maintain a decent level of funding and public support for schools. Others supported freedom of choice because it was a more cunning way to preserve racial separation in the schools, a form of shadow segregation. It was hard to tell the two positions apart. A Bullock County school official summed up the complexity of the issue by explaining what was needed for successful integration. "It will take respect and goodwill among people of both races," he said. "It is just deeper than a bus running down a road."[53]

Even if not clearly apparent, Brewer's motivation and outlook were fed by his desire to reform Alabama public schools. Like John West and Reubin Askew, Brewer saw all education issues as inseparable. Integration was no more an issue in and of itself than was education funding or the quality of instruction offered in the classrooms. If freedom of choice was abolished, Brewer feared that white parents would pull their children out of public schools. This mass exodus would cause the average daily attendance of schools to decrease, thereby reducing the amount of state funds provided for the affected system. More important, Brewer believed this exodus would erode vital public support and enthusiasm for education reform such as better funding, ad valorem equalization, and an increase in instructional quality. In the midst of integration in 1969, Brewer passed one of the most sweeping education reform packages the state had ever seen. Brewer knew that if whites enrolled their children in private schools the last thing they would want to do would be to pay taxes to support what would surely become all-black schools. Nevertheless, unlike West (who promised that order would be maintained in integrated schools, thereby alleviating racial fears) or Askew (who staunchly defended public schools and integration as a means of moving beyond the politics of race), Brewer chose a different path. By defending an idea that had long become a practical impossibility, he did not alleviate tensions and fear among races. If anything, his actions exacerbated the problems of abolishing dual systems.

Albert Brewer acknowledged that integration was inevitable, even if it did not appear entirely so. Brewer supported freedom of choice because he believed that under its provisions integration would come at a pace comfortable to all involved, white and black. This pace was definitely too slow for the time in which he governed, however. Brewer became governor at a time when gradualism and good faith were obsolete. The state had had fourteen years to integrate gradually, and it had chosen not to do so. Brewer knew this. He was elected to the legislature in 1955, a year after *Brown*. His administration marked a change from a state devoted to political shenanigans and the maintenance of power to one devoted to legal means of resolving differences and good-faith efforts at carrying out court orders. Brewer wanted patience and time from the courts and the federal government to carry out a good-faith effort at desegregation through the use of freedom of choice. The courts had run out of patience, however, and the state had run out of time. The political shenanigans of Brewer's predecessor and successor, George Wallace, had frustrated federal officials and exhausted opportunities for toleration.

Albert Brewer clearly moved the state in different directions than his predecessors. Yet he was also closely tied to the past that he sought to change. Whether this connection actually kept him from speaking out more on integration and civil rights is unclear. Never a vocal segregationist nor a visible proponent of integration, Brewer was in a difficult and tenuous position. He had to walk a fine line between divergent political and social interests. In contrast to South Carolina and Florida, Alabama had no state political figure to pave the way for a moderate course on integration. Brewer had no Ernest Hollings, Bob McNair, or Leroy Collins to come before him and carry out the initial assault on the parapets of segregation. The state was still coming to terms with its racial past and not quite ready to abandon race as a determining factor in policy. Brewer lacked the support and the time to do so himself. With Wallace on one side and the courts on another, with racists criticizing his hesitancy and without a silent moderate majority to serve as a counterbalance, Brewer could not help but appear more racially restrained than some of his contemporaries. As a result, his legacy, though cloudy if viewed in comparison with those of Reubin Askew or John West, was probably the best any elected political leader in Alabama could have provided under the circumstances. In short, Brewer's "New South" was as new as Alabama's political climate of the 1960s would allow.

2

"Why Not the Teachers?"

Education Reform in Alabama, 1968–1970

Court-ordered school integration troubled Albert Brewer for several reasons. He believed that Alabamians would accept integration more willingly if they could do it themselves, on their own schedule. He also thought that public uproar over what many people in Alabama considered federal intrusion into public schools diminished support for much-needed education reform. Federal courts disagreed and ordered wholesale integration, much to Brewer's chagrin. Still, amid such disapproval and angst, Brewer succeeded in steering through the legislature one of the most important and wide-ranging education reform packages the state had ever witnessed.

Reconciling urban and rural legislative rivalries and ignoring the detrimental effect integration had on public support, Brewer enjoyed what was perhaps his brightest moment as governor in 1969 when he called a special session of the Alabama legislature to enact a sweeping education reform package. He displayed a masterful skill at cajoling and coaxing. Although not able to right Alabama's educational list fully, Brewer brought the state a measure of respectability. Most important, he brought much-needed changes that improved the chances of Alabama's children to succeed in life.

Ironically, Brewer's reforms were only a small step forward for the state. Compared with Florida, Alabama remained years behind the trend in southern education reform. Nor would the state undergo a Sunbelt economic transformation as did South Carolina. No matter how much Brewer changed the state's education system, Alabama lagged behind many of its southern neighbors.

No one disputed the fact that in terms of educational quality, Alabama ranked among the worst states. In 1968, the state spent less on its children's education than any state save Mississippi. By 1969, Mississippi surpassed Alabama in this category, leaving Alabama last nationally. South Carolina ranked forty-seventh, whereas Florida rated twenty-sixth. Alabama teachers received almost $600 a year less than some neighboring states and $571 below the national average. Even after several hundred dollar raises in the mid-1960s, teacher salaries still languished, ranking forty-eighth in the nation in 1968 at $6,159 per teacher. Alabama spent more than $200 less per child than other states in the nation. The state ranked near the bottom in several key educational indicators: fiftieth in per pupil expenditures; forty-fifth in literacy; forty-fifth in the number of military draftees failing army intelligence tests; and forty-seventh in per capita income. A year later, Alabama dropped to forty-eighth in teacher salaries, ranking only ahead of South Carolina and Mississippi. Florida paid its teachers $8,511, ranking it fifteenth nationally. Alabama's education system was clearly in dire straits.[1]

Albert Brewer's concern for education extended to his earliest days in the legislature. Elected in 1954 with a group of young lawmakers, Brewer took particular interest in education. By the time he became governor in 1968, he had been instrumental in creating the Alabama Educational Study Commission. Originally designed to take political heat off Governor Lurleen Wallace, the commission eventually provided the foundation of Brewer's 1969 education reform package. The group consisted of twenty-one members, including the lieutenant governor, the speaker of the house, three house members, three senators, the state superintendent of education, and thirteen gubernatorially appointed members. This was not the first such group to study education in Alabama. In 1919, 1934, 1945, 1951, and 1957 other study groups had highlighted many of the same problems plaguing the state. In large part, Alabama's legislature paid little heed to their collective recommendations. The 1919 study revealed that illiteracy in Alabama was greater in that year than in 1840, that the state ranked near the bottom in virtually all categories by which people judged educational success, and that the state's 1901 constitution was "entirely inadequate" to solve any of those problems, much less provide a suitable education for the state's children. Each subsequent study echoed conclusions and recommendations from this earliest study with equally scant results.[2]

The 1919 study also revealed that since the end of "carpetbag rule" in Alabama, state provision for education had actually dwindled. The 1868 "carpetbag" constitution had treated education better than the constitutions of 1875 and 1901. It created a strong state board of education and made no restrictions on the legislature in taxing localities for education. In order not to give legitimacy to pre-Bourbon rule, the 1919 commission's report asserted that the funds raised for education under "carpetbag" rule had often been embezzled by crooked legislators. The 1875 constitution abolished the state board and denied the authority of local taxation, requiring the legislature to increase education appropriations only "from time to time." The 1919 report judged this constitution as the "most illiberal and inadequate method of support to be found in any State." The 1901 constitution improved little. Allowing for only three mills of state taxes for education, it remained "entirely inadequate." Although in 1915 the legislature allowed local government to increase millage, "limitations on taxation [were] still the most dramatic of any State in the Union." The commission recommended a nine-month school term for all children. At the time some black schools met only for two and one-half months, and certain white schools met for four months. The 1919 commission also recommended reestablishment of the state board of education, increases in teacher pay, and better training for teachers. More than one-third of the state's teachers had only an elementary school education. A majority of the rest had only a high school degree.[3]

After a series of widely ignored studies, in 1957 the legislature appointed a study commission to make a two-year survey of the state's educational system. The group made several recommendations, including election of the state board of education. It urged the state to allow local governments to vote increases in ad valorem taxes up to a limit of twelve mills. The report also recommended a one-cent sales tax increase, the bulk of which would go to salaries. A dissenting minority insisted on complete state relinquishment of ad valorem tax collections to allow localities to increase education funds. Alabama Supreme Court chief justice and future U.S. senator Howell Heflin argued that a one-cent sales tax was too much of a burden for lower-income families. Instead, he recommended that industrial and corporate income taxes be increased: "I am for the industrial growth of this state. . . . However, there are other southern states which, industrially, are growing faster than the State of Alabama, and yet, industry and corporations are bearing their equal load of increased taxation."[4] He also called for property tax equalization, less burdensome taxes on lower-income groups, and removal of sales tax exemptions from all commodities save agricultural goods.[5]

By 1957, education in Alabama still had not improved much. Only 81.5 percent of school-aged children were enrolled in school, a minuscule 3.4 percent of Alabama's population had spent four years in college, and the average educational level attained by Alabamians over the age of twenty-five was 7.9 years.[6]

The 1968 version of the Alabama Education Study Commission sought finally to address and correct these deficiencies. Members of the 1968 group included established and rising political figures. Auburn University president Harry Philpott chaired the committee, which contained such powerful members of the legislature as John Cook, a member of the Jefferson County legislative delegation; the former and future speaker of the house, Rankin Fite; state senator Hugh Merrill from Anniston; and state senator Joe Goodwyn of Montgomery. Alabama Education Association president Vernon St. John also held membership. One of the criticisms of the 1957 study was that those in positions of power had not paid heed to its recommendations. With such a lineup, the 1968 group claimed greater authority and legitimacy. Albert Brewer and his commitment to education ensured that reforms would have a much greater chance than eleven years earlier.[7]

With a firm belief that industrial growth went "hand in hand with growth in education," the 1968 commission judged education in Alabama to be at crisis stage. By most educational indicators, education in Alabama continued to rank near the bottom of states. In many other categories as well, the state had fallen in rank since 1965. That Alabama ranked forty-seventh in per capita income and that only 28.4 percent of voters cast ballots in 1956 only compounded educational deficiencies. Those state leaders who cared about reform saw a citizenry who lacked money, education, and the will to vote. Albert Brewer's assumption of the governor's office after Lurleen Wallace's death brought renewed interest in education. Many in the state believed Brewer marked a positive departure from the turbulent Wallace years.[8]

As lieutenant governor, Brewer had spoken strongly for ad valorem equalization and other reforms. Equalization and increased local support were but a few of the methods Brewer wanted to use to help Alabama education and state government "keep its house in order." Accountability was the key. Brewer admitted that the state needed to increase its share of funding. Nevertheless, he also demanded that local communities do their share and use their existing funds more wisely. Before the Alabama Association of Secondary School Principals in July 1968, Brewer stated his "deep and abiding interest" in education and his plans for the future. "Quality education," said Brewer, "is the answer to many of the pressing problems that face us in Alabama—social and economic." He conceded that money was not the total answer. "Frankly, I have often wished for an educator to tell me something he was doing to operate his school more economically." Never, he reported, had a superintendent told him that he had reduced his administrative staff to free up money to hire more teachers. He wondered aloud whether too much education money was going to places other than the classroom. Administrators were too busy building a "cumbersome bureaucracy," which had grown at an "alarming degree." To do his part and "go to bat" for Alabama's children, Brewer announced several possible solutions. To give taxpayers their true dollar's worth, he suggested repeal of the "repugnant" tenure law. If teachers wanted to be considered professionals, like doctors and attorneys, Brewer contended, tenure had to go. Job retention based on merit, he explained, would not only rid the profession of incompetents but also lend legitimacy to the field. As part of tenure abolition, Brewer recommended basing higher salaries on merit and competence as well as professional degree attainment.[9]

Brewer also called for an expansion of Alabama's trade schools. Like South Carolina's John West, Brewer believed that a literate workforce, trained to succeed in specific industries, was vital to the state's economic future. He rightly believed that an illiterate workforce unable to operate new equipment stood no chance of luring industrial development. Before commencement exercises at Northeast Alabama State Technical School, Brewer called for expanding the state's trade and technical schools, a productive means of supplying industry with well-trained workers. The state's trade schools had to reach their potential, he explained, and it was up to the state to carry the system "forward to even greater achievements . . . to provide an even wider opportunity for Alabama's youth to gain vital skills for useful and productive employment."[10]

The *Geneva Reaper* called Brewer's proposal to end tenure a "giant and courageous step" to remove what had become "job protection for the poor or lazy teacher." "No competent teacher," wrote the *Reaper,* "should have any fear of the loss of a job with the removal of the law." Perhaps, responded Joe Reed, no white teacher should worry. For black teachers it was another story. As executive secretary of ASTA, which represented the state's black teachers, Reed appealed to Brewer to end his tenure abolition campaign. Although ASTA agreed with the governor's desire to eliminate educational waste and inefficiency, the group believed that losing tenure would prove most damaging to black teachers. "The odds were stacked against the Negro teachers," explained Reed, especially with the surrounding tension from integration. If black teachers lost their job protection, their jobs would follow, Reed contended. Even with tenure, he asserted, black principals had suffered demotions.[11]

The *Auburn Bulletin* agreed, predicting "calamitous" results and a return to the days "when selection of teachers was subject to political and petty personal considerations which resulted in widespread injustices and employment insecurity." The *Montgomery Advertiser* wondered whether Brewer's tenure ideas might be motivated by desegregation orders, something Brewer tersely denied. Nevertheless, education "bigwigs" were riled. Reed was "shocked and appalled." AEA president Vernon St. John ambivalently stated that he had no choice but to defend tenure, given his position. The AEA delegate council was more firm. Delegates vehemently defended tenure. The AEA argued that the current tenure law allowed for dismissal in cases of insubordination, incompetency, neglect of duty, immorality, and justifiable decreases in teacher positions. To dismiss a teacher for anything else, argued the council, "[smacked] of partisan politics or arbitrariness and capriciousness on the part of a board dealing with its employees." AEA officials reminded Brewer why tenure was established in 1939. It was not uncommon, they asserted, to see wholesale teacher dismissals in a local system after they supported the wrong candidate for board of education or superintendent. Brewer stood his ground, however. Administrators had to be able to dismiss incompetent teachers without lengthy hearings or potential lawsuits. "We do not expect this of a private businessman," Brewer argued, "and there is no reason to expect it of a principal." Brewer opined that he saw no reason why "any good capable teacher [needed] any protection." He reiterated that the need for teaching to be seen as a true profession dictated tenure abolition: "As we strive to raise salaries to a state level commensurate with professional status, we will seek professional attributes for the high calling of teaching in our state." Critics noted that the state's teachers were overwhelmingly female, whereas attorneys and physicians in Alabama, and most other places, were mostly male.[12]

Brewer continued campaigning for his reform efforts before commencement exercises at Troy State University in early summer 1968. He questioned people's fear of change and the unknown. There was nothing to fear about change, he argued.[13] Brewer lamented that Alabama had urgent needs in so many areas: increased teacher salaries, better-equipped classrooms, adequate school buses, free textbooks, better lunchrooms, and lower teacher-pupil ratios. Yet most important to Brewer was ending waste in administration, stunting bureaucratic growth, and unifying fragmented and wasteful educational programs. All of these deficiencies diverted educators' attention from the classroom and schoolchildren. Brewer hammered the state education department for what he considered widespread waste. "I sometimes wonder if anybody knows what's going on," Brewer said. "I just don't know how you cope with the sheer magnitude of that department." The governor admitted that he was unsure that every facet of Alabama education was underfinanced, that perhaps education's priorities needed adjusting.[14]

In September 1968, Brewer released $7.2 million in conditional appropriations for education passed the year before. Tax revenues had increased enough to allow the governor to release the money, which provided a 4 percent raise for teachers. Depending on teacher rankings and seniority, educators received increases of between $140 and $240 per year. Also, thanks to a $4 million increase in revenues, Brewer announced that Alabama's Special Education Trust Fund (SETF), which funded public schools in the state, then held a surplus of about $22 million. Much of this money was expected to fund Brewer's ambitious education reform package.[15]

The 4 percent raise did little to stop a hemorrhage of teachers out of Alabama. Young teachers, frustrated at the prospect of low pay, left the state in droves. Of 3,230 teacher graduates in 1968, only 50 percent remained in state. The vast majority of those who left relocated in Florida and Georgia, which employed almost two-thirds of the emigrants, usually at much higher salaries. A 1969 study reported that Alabama spent more than $3.7 million educating teachers for other states. Only three out of four trained in Alabama planned to teach, and of those eligible to do so, only 28 percent planned to teach in Alabama in the near future. Of those already employed in Alabama in 1968, more than eight hundred left the state or the profession altogether. The out-migration of young teachers left Alabama with an aging faculty. One-third of Alabama teachers in 1966 were older than fifty years of age. One teacher from Prattville thanked Brewer for the raise that, after adjustment for inflation, resulted in his making $1.79 less than her previous year's salary in "take home pay." Others in Alabama seemed to get their fair share of state revenues, she wrote, so "why not the teachers?" The *Montgomery Advertiser* agreed, announcing that the raise allowed Alabama's teachers to retain their "traditional position at the bottom of the nation's teacher pay scale." Teachers in Mississippi, Florida, and Georgia had received raises of $1,000, $1,800, and $558 respectively. Alabama teachers, however, "languished in the cellar," with raises that averaged less than $200, or $6 a week.[16]

Brewer agreed that salaries were inadequate and planned to end the deficiencies but reiterated that there were no easy answers. One possible solution involved reform of ad valorem taxation, annual assessments on property value. Brewer maintained that reform in this area did not require further legislation. Counties could act without the legislature to equalize their assessments, but they had chosen not to do so. Because the state revenue board selected representatives to county assessment boards from nominees chosen by local education boards, Brewer posited that the simple solution was to choose individuals "qualified and dedicated toward a fair and just tax equalization program." Although property tax adjustment would show no immediate results, support for reform grew. Even the Associated Industries of Alabama supported this reform. Before a public meeting of the Education Study Commission in November 1968, representatives of this group called for more local support of education. They advocated an increase in the state sales tax and argued that sales tax exemptions should be fairer and proportional to the amount of business exemptions fostered. They also reiterated their support for ad valorem equalization, which they had advocated since 1967. For years certain regions in the state had paid different assessments on similar properties.[17]

One member of the Alabama Education Study Commission hinted at proposing 30 percent ad valorem equalization. The state average assessment in 1968 was 16.1 percent of fair market value based on property values determined in 1939. There was room for reform. State senator Joe Goodwyn, author of the bill creating the Education Study Commission, pleaded with legislators not to let urban-rural rivalries distract them from the more important task of education reform. Goodwyn's appeal fell on deaf ears as long as tax assessors valued and assessed property at varying rates. Many urban legislators had complained that although their constituents paid a higher share of property taxes, they did not receive a corresponding share of tax revenues. In 1967, rural and urban delegations fought bitterly in a newly reapportioned legislature over larger shares of gasoline tax revenues. With newfound strength from reapportionment, the urban group won a surprising victory in that battle. That same year a similar fight over property taxes ended in a change in property tax law limiting ad valorem assessment to "no more than" 30 percent of fair market value.[18]

Organizations such as the Alabama Real Estate Association were partly to blame for ad valorem abuse. Realtors urged a ceiling on ad valorem assessment of 1 percent of full market value, twenty-nine points below the mandated rate. Their recommendations were not surprising given that most counties taxed between 5 and 30 percent of full market value. In 1969, assessment ranged from a low of 6.7 percent in Hale County to a high of 26.8 percent in Jefferson County. Just a year earlier, in 1968, the SETF received $9,673,144 from ad valorem assessments. Had assessments been equalized at the highest rate statewide, the SETF would have received an additional $6 million. Legislators from Jefferson County's urban areas conducted a state ad valorem taxation study. They reported that more than half the state's ninety-nine school systems levied below the authorized millage for school purposes. As a result, funds distributed from the SETF came mainly from high tax urban counties. Some smaller rural systems received almost 259 percent of their local effort. Other systems, more often large metropolitan areas, received only 38 percent of their contributions to the SETF. For every $100 paid to the SETF, Montgomery County received $38, Jefferson $41, Mobile $58, and Madison County $51. On the other hand, Lowndes County received $259 and Wilcox County $252 per $100 paid. Urban legislators recommended changing state education finance laws to provide incentives for maximizing local effort. Local systems, they concluded, should not lose state funds but should be required to make a minimum effort. They also recommended lengthening the school year, which, at 175.5 days, was tenth shortest in the nation.[19]

By October 1968, Brewer had talked a lot about reforming education, but his plans remained unclear. He invested a great deal of hope in the recommendations of the Education Study Commission, preferring to remain vague until the commission released its final report. Despite Brewer's coy political behavior, many saw him as earnest and sincere in his desire to reform education. He also hinted at calling a special session to focus exclusively on education matters so that meaningful reform proposals would not get lost in the shuffle of a regular legislative session as they had in the past.[20]

Rumors of a special session caused urban legislators to hold a hastily called strategy session in Birmingham. Summoned by the chairman of the Jefferson County senate delegation, Hugh Morrow III, representatives came from Birmingham, Mobile, Alexander City, Tuscaloosa, Florence, Decatur, Montgomery, and Opelika. Labeled the "rat pack" after it formed to fight the victorious 1967 gasoline tax revenue battle, the group agreed to push for all counties to assess property at twelve mills. Their small-county rivals had the aid of Alabama's most powerful lobby, the Alabama Farm Bureau Federation. The Farm Bureau Federation flatly opposed equalization and had urged property declassification and reduction in ad valorem assessment for timber land. Stung by their 1967 defeat, the bureau was better prepared the following year for the urban bloc. Many small-county legislators had also vowed revenge. One promised that "never again will I permit raising taxes in my district and at the same time lowering the revenue—not for Albert Brewer or anyone else." Whatever education reform plan Brewer proposed to the legislature, he was certain to face, as one newspaper predicted, "tough sledding." Steering a safe path between urban and rural interests posed Brewer's greatest challenge. "It is a distinct possibility," opined the *Phenix City Citizen-Herald,* "that this rural-urban split could wreck an ambitious education program."[21]

In December, though not yet formally releasing their recommendations, the Education Study Commission provided a glimpse of its intended proposals. The committee planned to recommend $100 million for education over the following two years, including a 25 percent teacher raise, retention of tenure, a total revamping of school funding formulas, an appointed state superintendent of education, and new taxation to support schools. New taxation would come from proposed increases in state sales and income taxes, removal of certain sales tax exemptions for state industries, and property tax equalization. Regardless of urban-rural rivalries, wrote the *Birmingham News,* legislators ran away from tax increases "like rabbits." One legislator notified Brewer that he would do well to get $25 million for education, much less $100 million. Equally important, and a key cause of opposition, was the fact that voters would see the effects of any new tax increase when they filled out their 1969 tax returns, which were due only two weeks before the 1970 state primary. Reminding voters of tax increases so close to an election was political suicide. Legislators did not wish to have higher taxes as their running mate. Even Brewer acknowledged he had an "uphill fight."[22]

Attempting to distance himself a bit from the shock of the recommendations, Brewer explained that he wished to use the report as a jumping off point for discussions over legislation. He reiterated his aspiration to fund his proposals without a "direct statewide tax." One way of accomplishing this task without offending large numbers of voters was to remove existing exemptions in the state sales tax. As it stood, current exemptions in the state's 4 percent sales tax were valued at almost $100 million. Instead of passing a score of new taxes, Brewer explained, "we might revamp and realign what we have and cut off escapes." Nevertheless, Brewer admitted that his program would "involve a lot of money." Still, there was a trade off, he argued: "I am convinced the people of Alabama are willing to pay for a quality education, but they want more for their money than they are now getting."[23]

By January 1969, support for substantive education reform peaked. Brewer received scores of letters and petitions from parents, teachers, administrators, and entire faculties urging him to act. One teacher notified the governor that he had accepted a teaching job in Florida making $690 more per year. He had no other choice but to leave because "I simply cannot afford to live and work in the State of Alabama!" Most letters did not recommend specific reforms, preferring instead merely to urge Brewer to "take a stand" for education. "Now is the time to come to the aid of our state!" wrote one teacher. Education superintendent Ernest Stone encouraged Brewer to continue his program of austerity and economy. Nearly all the letters called for a special session in order that education might have top legislative priority. Others lent Brewer the authority to do whatever he deemed necessary to improve education.[24]

Brewer made it clear that there were certain things he would not do in his attempt to reform education. He told the Alabama Cattleman's Association that he was "unalterably opposed" to eliminating tax exemptions on farm supplies such as seed, feed, fertilizer, and pesticides. He also refused to sign any legislation raising state sales or income taxes. Many thought this was a sure way to win votes but an equally easy way to doom serious reform. A suggested general income tax increase would have netted between $9 and $31 million. A half-cent sales tax hike was projected to draw $20 million. Because these were apparently out of the question, the only remaining revenue options were the elimination of certain sales tax exemptions and ad valorem reform. Combined, the two would bring in only $56 million, far less than the estimated $100 million needed to change the state's educational fortunes.[25]

Although many capitol watchers concluded that a special session was guaranteed to be explosive, few, if any, realized how close Brewer came to not calling a special session at all. The governor feared that legislators were ready to splinter between urban and rural factions in the legislature, thereby dooming any reform legislation. Brewer maintained that he would "not be a party to playing political games with the future of our children." Legislative agreement over reform, Brewer concluded, was tantamount to the success of a special session. Moreover, it had to be gained before the session convened. "To call the legislature into session without any hope of success would be the most demoralizing thing that could happen to education," asserted the governor. "If we get an educational program through at all it will depend on legislators not drawing lines."[26]

Looking back to the bitter 1967 fight over gasoline tax revenues, many state newspapers and politicians predicted turbulent days ahead. The *Brewton Standard* in Escambia County lamented urban legislators' gain of power. The "urbans," complained the editors, had designs on how any new money should be distributed, much to the harm of rural counties. To ease the tension, Brewer met with most legislators over several weeks in early 1969. Meeting in his office with twelve legislators at a time, Brewer used his amiable personality and easygoing manner to make personal pleas for his reforms. He balanced these groups between rural and urban legislators in an attempt to break down some of the barriers between the two groups. This balanced approach also prevented any one group from dominating the discussions or ganging up on the governor. After meeting with more than two-thirds of the legislature, Brewer announced that he was "optimistic" about his chances for success.[27]

Brewer's optimism suffered a damaging blow when Representative Quinton Bowers, chairman of Jefferson County's legislative delegation, announced that his group planned to block all legislation unless Jefferson County received a share of education money proportional to what it had paid. Bowers claimed support from forty-seven other urban-area house members, giving him control of sixty-seven votes in the house. With that many votes, he could hold the legislature hostage. At a joint meeting of Jefferson County representatives and senators, Bowers pounded the table and declared, "We're going down there to get that money. If we can't get some legislation for a fairer split in school money, then we'll block all legislation." Although Brewer had earlier downplayed Bowers's obstreperousness, this clear and uncompromising statement created more than a little concern on the governor's part. Jefferson County senators also pledged to stall legislation. Nonetheless, they took a moderate position and only threatened to prevent tax measures from coming to a vote, allowing nonrevenue legislation to flow through the senate unimpeded. These senators wanted Alabama's twenty-two largest counties to get their fair share of education money, even if it came at the expense of smaller counties. Historically, rural political interests had dominated the statehouse, thereby providing rural counties with a disproportionate share of education funds. Although he had promised not to call a special session that might turn into a "prize fight," Brewer realized that he had no guarantee of success. "I thought we were in great shape until yesterday," he lamented.[28]

The *Montgomery Advertiser* agreed with the "urbans." Stronger than ever, urban legislators saw an excellent opportunity to match, if not exceed, their 1967 coup. The 1967 fight had left a bitter legacy in Alabama politics, however, and many looked to the coming special session for a rematch between state interests. If the battle ensued, education reform was doomed. The *Advertiser* suspected that "urbans" had more bark than bite. They stood to suffer lasting political damage if education reform died at their hands.[29]

Brewer's plan was not anathema to urban lawmakers, though rural legislators had grave reservations. To the *Advertiser,* it was "revolutionary" in two respects. First, the plan distributed funds on 28:1 ratio. That is, for every twenty-eight children in average daily attendance (ADA), the district received money for one teacher. This kept state per pupil expenditures equal for every district. Second, the plan required a minimum local financial effort for schools. Urban legislators had long complained that rural counties continuously underfunded education, yet received the lion's share of school funds. Brewer's plan rated counties on their ability to pay, not what they actually paid. If the state per capita income was $2,100, and in "County A" that same figure was $1,050, that county would receive a 50 percent rating. Then, if the state spent $66 per child, the county had to spend at least $33. If not, then "County A" would not receive state education funds until it rectified the deficiency. Rural lawmakers were sure to oppose this plan. This sort of penalty withholding was ruled unconstitutional in Florida in 1973 by that state's supreme court. In 1971 it was ruled unconstitutional in Alabama.[30]

The potential for a rowdy session did not escape the *Advertiser,* which compared it to a cowboy drama. Each side wanted to be seen as the men with the "white hats." The newspaper saw Brewer as the sheriff trying to avoid a shootout. "If a special session does come," wrote the editors, "there may not be gunplay, but there will be considerable pushing and shoving." The session, concluded the *Huntsville News,* promised to be a real "pier sixer." The *Anniston Star* opined that if nothing else, the session might finally settle the question of who was in charge on Goat Hill, "the still unjelled urban bloc or the crafty, more experienced rurals." In the recent past, wrote the *Star,* "the latter by their wits managed largely to outmaneuver the city boys."[31]

Despite the clear possibility that "considerable dissent, if not actual discord" might develop, Brewer made the call for a special session to convene on April 1. The legislature had just five weeks to get the job done before the opening day of the regular legislative session. A shrewd move on Brewer's part, setting the date at that time gave lawmakers a heightened sense of urgency and a clear deadline for results. No one disagreed that education needed more money. Where it would come from was the question on everyone's mind.[32]

Brewer opened the special session on April 1 with a speech broadcast over statewide television and radio. He reminded legislators that they were not there on behalf of teachers, administrators, or parents. They were in extraordinary session to help one group only: Alabama schoolchildren. The state's future was in their hands. "Money alone is not the answer," he admitted, though additional revenues were "vitally needed." Improvements in education would make the state more competitive in business and industrial development and would surely attract top-flight teachers. Nonetheless, Brewer made it clear that he would not sign into law new taxes unless he was given a corresponding guarantee of education quality. It was time, said the governor, to give "not only more money to education, but more education for our money." He then set out explaining his proposal to a legislature he had wooed for the past month. Brewer wanted the Education Study Commission to gain permanent status in order to chart the state's progress in education. He wanted the establishment of a Commission on Higher Education to "coordinate the efforts of institutions of higher learning in Alabama, to avoid the duplication of programs, to assure the utilization of every tax dollar which goes to a college or university in this state." Brewer also wanted the state education superintendent appointed by an elected state board of education, so the state may have a strong administrative organization.[33]

As for fund allocation, Brewer wanted state school funds provided equally per child throughout the state notwithstanding where they lived. He also suggested a minimum financing effort required of local school districts to ensure that they were properly funding their children's future. To raise instructional quality, Brewer suggested the establishment of a system of merit pay for teachers. Brewer did not call for an end to tenure. Opposition to that proposal had convinced Brewer that it had no chance of passage. Still, the fractional legislature had been given quite a task. "Here tonight," declared the governor, "we have reached the hour of decision in Alabama."[34]

The next day, Brewer's floor leaders in the legislature introduced nineteen bills that totaled almost $100 million (only half the $200 million the study commission recommended to correct fully state educational deficiencies) in new education spending and reform over the next two years. The session was relatively smooth for Brewer and his allies. Urban senators gave the governor a brief scare in late April when they staged a filibuster, threatening to delay all bills until rural legislators and the governor agreed to equalize property taxes. Senator George Bailes of Birmingham symbolized his group's plans by wearing a lapel pin that read "NEVER." Bailes explained that the one word was an abbreviation of a paraphrase of a famous Revolutionary War phrase, now applied to Alabama: "Never taxation without equalization." Brewer was not opposed to equalization. On the contrary, he had advocated that reform for years. Nevertheless, he knew that to bring up equalization in what had become a tense session would have doomed any chances at reform. Still, the governor was not above compromise for the good of his package. To mollify urban legislators and ensure passage of his education package, Brewer did not remove exemptions on urban-related taxes, such as sewer, garbage, taxicabs, cable television, and industrial water. Brewer exempted all utilities save electricity, natural gas, water, phone, and telegraph. Although the filibuster lasted only one week, it placed reform in serious doubt for several days. By the time the filibuster ended, with only one week left in the special session, opposition to the reform plan had all but died. Realizing that rural legislators would not give in on equalization, urban senators were not prepared to take responsibility for killing an education reform package that many in Alabama deemed crucial. The *Birmingham News* agreed in principle with the filibuster but admitted that the timing was bad. The education package took precedence, wrote the editors, so "get it done!"[35]

By all accounts, the 1969 special legislative session was a tremendous success.[36] All of Brewer's twenty-nine bills passed. Brewer praised the legislature for following his reform lead. "You accepted the challenge and today we are on the road to a new approach in education," declared a happy Brewer. "We are beginning a new day when we can completely discard the concept of dealing with our educational problems on a crisis to crisis basis and begin to deal with them in a businesslike and orderly manner." Brewer had much to be pleased about: a $100 million increase in education spending over two years; the creation of the Alabama Commission on Higher Education; permanent status for the Education Study Commission; a minimum requirement for local school support; $1 million to expand the free textbook program; and a 12.9 percent pay increase for teachers with a conditional increase of 8.2 percent more. Legislation also passed that allowed local school districts to devise their own systems of merit pay. Brewer gleefully reported that for the first time in many years the state enjoyed a surplus of teaching applications. This success was a "remarkable accomplishment" and the highlight of Brewer's first year in office, if not his entire administration. Brewer's first real dealing with the legislature as governor was quite an achievement and a testament to his ability to create legislative consensus.[37]

The budding controversy over property taxes spilled over into the regular legislative session. It had been a long time coming. As early as October 1968, Brewer had called for reform. So had others. The *Birmingham Post-Herald* noted that there had been little effort at equalization in the twentieth century except for a failed attempt to equalize at 30 percent by former governor John Patterson in the 1950s. "We're waiting," wrote the editors. Besides the urban filibusters during the special session, other organizations and municipalities had called on Brewer to act. Mobile County's PTA, school board, and legislative delegation passed resolutions demanding equalization. They also called for an end to the "illegal taxing of residential property higher than industrial property, and city property higher than rural property." Still others had argued that property tax equalization was a better way to "spread the burden" and raise revenues than was increasing consumption and income taxes. The Education Study

Commission's subcommittee on finance reported that uniform assessment at 30 percent would produce an increase of $17,588,936 a year. There was no doubt that gross inequities in ad valorem assessment existed. The ad valorem system was a tangle of confusion, including divergent assessments on similar property in the same county and outrageous assessment differences between counties. Property tax collection fell far below taxes on consumption. In 1966, Alabama property taxes averaged $33 per capita, ranking the state last in the nation. Per capita sales taxes were $15 higher than that amount.[38]

The problem with the property tax issue was the wording in a 1967 change in property tax laws. The original law calling for assessment at 60 percent of fair market value was replaced by a new law lowering that assessment to "not more than" 30 percent of fair market value. This gaping loophole left county assessors with an easy way to reduce assessment rates to almost nil and make a mockery of ad valorem collections. To be sure, local assessments had never approached 60 percent, but now assessors had legal authority to underassess further. The state Department of Revenue was little help. In a 1967 tax assessment court case in Montgomery, the court could not find where the department had ever endeavored to equalize assessment even at 20 percent. Brewer reiterated that the problem could be solved if only county assessors would choose to assess property properly. It was a good thought, but it proved impossible to convince voters to elect assessors with the political courage to do so. Because county assessors and tax boards were elected at the local level, they feared local voters more than state officials. Property tax reform had to originate in the legislature, a virtual impossibility given the split between rural and urban blocs. There was another option if equalization failed, posited Brewer. He advocated that the state consider getting out of the property tax business altogether. "In the event that statewide equalization cannot be accomplished," Brewer stated, "then I will join with those of you who favor the removing of the state from the property tax field in order that all revenues from this source may remain in the counties where collected for local service." A simple solution, but with disastrous potential for utter confusion and abuse, Brewer's suggestion might solve the problems of urban areas, which had complained about not getting a corresponding return on their investment. It would also compel assessors in underpaying counties to raise their assessments in order to make up for the money they stood to lose.[39]

Although many agreed with the governor that passing equalization laws through the legislature faced "almost impossible odds," they disagreed on doing away with statewide collection of property taxes. The *Mobile Register* accused Brewer of not pushing equalization hard enough. Brewer, accused the editors, seemed ready to "raise taxes on everybody and everything in Alabama, yet [treated] tax equalization in a manner remindful of lip service." The editors expressed frustration that "Brewer hems and haws and passes the buck on property tax equalization." The *Birmingham News* agreed, opining that Brewer's statement was "cracking the escape door gratuitously." It was also dangerous. Allowing counties to proceed in sixty-seven directions with property taxation made no sense, wrote the *News:* "It could, and very likely would do grievous harm to thousands of school children, even now denied a quality of instruction." The hope that urban legislators placed in Brewer for a strong effort on property tax equalization now that his education package had passed soon disappeared. They had come not to expect reform from the Wallaces and now doubted the impetus would come from Brewer.[40]

As much as Brewer was criticized for vacillating on the issue, there was little he could do. Brewer realized he had a greater chance to see some form of equalization under existing laws than to push something through the legislature. It did not help that he rejected a group of bills authored by the Department of Revenue because there was little support for them in the legislature. One bill proposed a $10 million bond issue to finance statewide reassessment. Instead, the governor supported a bill authored by Jefferson County senator George Bailes to provide a feeble $1 million in each of the following two years for equalization. Brewer asserted that this legislation was a "vehicle to travel on" in enforcing existing ad valorem law. Yet this vehicle had no wheels and no engine. The money was too little and the urge to reform even smaller. Brewer later dropped his suggestion to abandon statewide property tax collection. He admitted that to go through with that plan, even if it had some semblance of a chance to pass the legislature, would change nothing; counties would continue to under-assess with no accountability. No solution to ad valorem tax problems came during Brewer's term, nor for that matter in the administrations of any of his successors. Although no previous governor had succeeded in implementing significant property tax reform, Brewer probably had the best chance to bring about some type of improvement. His public appeal and popularity in both chambers and with both legislative blocs gave him perhaps the best opportunity of any modern Alabama governor of pushing the issue to a positive conclusion. He simply ran out of time.[41]

Regardless of his failure to enact property tax reform, Brewer still enjoyed his most successful year as governor in 1969. He also began to reap dividends from trips outside the state to recruit business and industry. He made visits to New York and Los Angeles to show these states the face of a new Alabama. In many respects, he was highly successful. The year 1969 was the state's "most prosperous year ever," with the creation of twenty-eight thousand new jobs and new industrial development totaling $500 million. In the first ten months after the 1969 special session, tax increases on sales, income, and utilities brought in a total of more than $237 million. The Special Education Trust Fund ballooned because of increased investment and tax increases passed in the 1969 special session. By October of that year, the SETF had a surplus of almost $24 million and was growing. Brewer then released $27 million in conditional appropriations passed the previous year. By July 31, 1971, the SETF contained almost $306.8 million.[42]

In June 1970, Brewer lost to George Wallace in a bitterly fought state Democratic gubernatorial primary. After the loss, he released all conditional appropriations passed in 1969 and 1970, thereby depleting the SETF of its surplus and preventing Wallace from using it for pursuits other than education. One Brewer department head commented on the rash of spending: "We will put the money where it will do the most public good." By the time he left office, Brewer had spent almost all of the $24 million surplus, leaving a scant $2 million for Wallace. The funds went to teacher salary increases and capital improvement of schools. This distribution brought an end to Brewer's greatest success as governor.[43]

When compared with the two other New South governors, Brewer ranks in the middle of the group. He clearly did more than South Carolina's John West to remedy basic education ills. His reforms compare with those of Florida's Reubin Askew in scope and impact, but Alabama's reforms were closer to the system that Askew replaced in Florida in 1973. Although innovative in Alabama, Brewer's revisions only kept his state one pace behind the South's education leader. West enjoyed an economic boom in his state that dashed any education reform impetus until the mid-1980s. Although Alabama enjoyed a prosperous 1969, the economic benefit was not enough to cover the multitude of Alabama's educational inadequacies. Nevertheless, Brewer's reforms were a sound first step in bringing his state a measure of respectability in the region.

Albert Brewer spent only thirty-two months as governor of Alabama. In that abbreviated tenure, he did more for Alabama education than most of his predecessors or successors. He brought to the office a businessman's zeal for efficiency, quality, and accountability. Implementing these standards on all facets of state government, especially education, Brewer not only justified increasing education appropriations but also, with his education reform package, improved quality of instruction and increased accountability in school administration. He also tried to educate citizens in the value of a solid educational system to economic growth. This was not a new concept, but many Alabamians had seen too many state leaders give lip service to these concepts only to see no action taken on attaining them. Brewer's efforts to reform Alabama education stood out in stark contrast to the politically motivated actions of the Wallace years. Many Alabamians saw Brewer as possessing "good faith, obvious intent, honest intentions, and [an] above board manner." Even if Alabama did not jump to the head of the list in educational performance, which it most certainly did not, Brewer's reforms certainly improved the state. Alabama was much better off than in 1967 but lagged behind other southern states in the absence of a concentrated, long-term effort to reform education, ad valorem assessment, and a regressive tax structure. The ill-fated 1970 campaign only cut short what would have been a prosperous time in Alabama's educational and economic growth under a full-term of a Governor Brewer. Nevertheless, Brewer left a legacy of reform that would not be matched in the remaining years of the twentieth century.[44]

Ironically, Brewer's standard of reform in Alabama failed to match that of Reubin Askew in Florida. To be sure, Brewer's reforms brought Alabama education into the twentieth century, but compared with Florida's condition the state remained a generation behind. Askew's state also enjoyed a less tense racial situation than existed in Alabama, which allowed the governor to speak more openly about racial matters than Brewer. That Brewer accomplished as much in such a short period of time makes his term all the more remarkable.

PART II

Reubin Askew of Florida

Askew, with Education Commissioner Floyd Christian (*left*), meets with black leaders of a march from Marianna, Florida, protesting racial strife at a local high school, January 25, 1972. Courtesy Florida State Archives.

3

A Question of Justice

The 1972 Florida Busing Straw Vote

To Reubin Askew, what made the New South new was actually something quite old. To the optimistic Florida governor, the humanitarian South had always been a reality, though concealed beneath a thin veneer of racism and ignorance. To Askew, this positive expression of the region asserted itself when southerners realized that their problems could best be solved by working together and rising above the divisive politics of race. This moral, humane, and just South merely waited for "a chance to assert itself . . . a chance to lead." Askew believed that by the 1970s race was no longer a detriment to reform. The South's problems were being solved by a union of whites and blacks, he said, who reached an understanding that they shared common concerns, "that the man at the lunch counter is worried about many of the same problems which have been pressing down on us." Askew's goal as governor, his chance to lead, consisted of showing Floridians that it was entirely within the realm of possibility for blacks and whites to fight together to reach common goals and to solve common problems. To be sure, Askew acknowledged that racism remained "still the greatest obstacle to southern maturity." Racial discord still cast a dark shadow over the South. Askew knew that there were those who still saw the South as the "errant stepchild of the American dream, a tainted land of recalcitrance and reaction. They suspect the South. They have suspicions about southerners. And these suspicions have not been easily dispelled." Askew strove to confront these negative sentiments about and within the region during his eight years as governor. Public school integration rekindled age-old racial fears and animosities, if indeed they had ever been extinguished. Askew chose to embrace integration, including busing, as an opportunity for the South to lead the nation by example in overcoming America's racial dilemma.[1]

Askew's opportunity to exhibit this leadership came in 1972 when the Florida legislature passed a measure placing a nonbinding straw vote on busing on the March 14 Florida presidential primary ballot. Political commentators predicted that the results of such a ballot would reflect national opinion because Florida's population was largely non-native. Askew had previously pledged that Florida's government would henceforth guarantee equal rights for all Floridians, black or white, urban or rural, rich or poor.

Askew's action and leadership on civil rights was not exclusive to education. Upon entering office he found that a vast majority of blacks in state government held menial jobs, and more than 89 percent received pay below the poverty level. Askew quickly rectified this condition, and by 1972 the number of blacks in state government had doubled, including the first blacks to hold statewide positions such as the governor's education coordinator, members of the Florida Board of Regents, and the state's first black supreme court justice.[2]

The 1972 straw vote and the national publicity it attracted provided attention for an issue that Askew used to show the rest of the nation just how far the South had moved from its segregationist days. The vote also demonstrated how complex the busing issue really was. He also hoped to show that white southerners were not natural racists but were like most other Americans. Askew's vigorous moral leadership and plain, honest talk benefited him greatly. This kind of leadership helped lead Florida to a smoother transition from a dual to a unified school system.

Askew's election as governor marked a drastic departure from the administrations of his two most recent predecessors, Haydon Burns and Claude Kirk. The Republican Kirk had created a great deal of the racial tension that still existed when Askew took office. Kirk's greatest shenanigan, and probably the one that did most to raise tensions, was his personal takeover of the Manatee School Board in 1970 to prevent implementation of a desegregation court order. On April 7, 1970, facing personal fines of $10,000 a day from U.S. District Judge Ben Krentzman, Kirk relinquished control after only one day and allowed the school board to begin busing to achieve a ratio of 80 percent white to 20 percent black. Kirk also sought delays in the opening of the school year to avoid integration and filed an amicus curiae brief before the U.S. Supreme Court in the appeal of *Swann v. Charlotte-Mecklenburg.* He further investigated the legality of withholding state school funds from school districts that used busing as a means of integration. These and other capers created an atmosphere of racial tension, black distrust of white political motives, and white fear of a black invasion of formerly white schools. This tense climate resulted in the formation of several parents' groups, including Parents Against Forced Busing (PAFB), led by former governor Kirk, and United Citizens, Inc. In 1970, these groups scheduled funeral services for neighborhood schools, called "Operation Last Rites," complete with mourners dressed in black following a makeshift casket symbolic of dead neighborhood schools.[3]

Seven months into his first term, Askew was forced to make some public pronouncement on school integration and busing. He had spoken frankly on race during the campaign and during his first few months in office, but he had yet to speak out on busing, perhaps the most emotional issue of the day. Askew's education coordinator, Claude Anderson, the first black to hold that post in Florida and a self-described "education provocateur," illustrated the issue's complexity by quoting from *Alice in Wonderland:* "Oh, what a great puzzle I am." In August 1971 Askew received a petition bearing forty thousand signatures calling for him to request that Congress amend the Constitution to ban busing. In response, he spoke out with an eloquence and a candor that left a lasting impression on his state and the nation.[4]

Askew perceived the court's decisions on integration and busing as final, to be carried out forthwith. The states had a duty to comply with court orders in good faith and to do so with the least possible school disruption. Askew did not resort to court baiting or court appeals, instead striving to provide the positive moral leadership that he believed the South was ready to provide the nation.[5]

Askew served in a state that "did not react emotionally" to *Brown* in 1954. Newspaper editors had urged restraint and acceptance at the same time they deplored the ruling. Florida's small black population helps explain this mild reaction. In 1950, 21.8 percent of the state's population was black; the percentage fell to 15.3 percent by 1970. Florida followed V. O. Key's prediction that the lower a state's black population, the less racial animosity it experienced. Nonetheless, gubernatorial leadership also played a large part in this "acceptance" of *Brown.* Thanks to Leroy Collins, who served as governor from 1955 to 1961, the state pursued a course of racial moderation. Collins had publicly supported segregation but also maintained that Supreme Court decisions were the law of the land and would be followed. He also told the state that it had to realize that blacks had equal rights and that "hate is not the answer." Collins and Askew were Florida's only gubernatorial voices of the era supporting easing racial tension.[6]

In late August 1971, Askew chose the unsuspecting audience at commencement exercises at the University of Florida to make his most complete statement on busing since his election. Askew chose this event for several reasons. Most important, Askew was keenly aware of the rapidly approaching opening of public schools and wanted to make a statement that might calm anxious parents in the crowd. Askew also chose to speak at this event, however, because his audience was comprised of many of the same people he hoped to calm, a cross section of Florida citizens from nearly every county, some wealthy, some poor, but the vast majority from that middle class that bore the brunt of funding and supporting public schools. In addressing graduates, he was also speaking to the next generation of Florida leadership.[7]

Askew told the audience that the coming September would be the "most crucial September in the long and remarkable history of our public schools. . . . How sad it will be if the emotions of the hour become the legacy of a generation." The responsibility for ensuring calm in the coming days lay squarely upon their shoulders, he said, for they came from nearly every county, and virtually all of them were products of public education and knew full well how beneficial it was when effectively operated without disruption. They also had the opportunity and choice, said the governor, to make busing unnecessary by seeking "broad community desegregation and cooperation." No one liked busing, admitted Askew, "not you, not me, not the people, not the school boards—not even the courts." Inadequate and artificial as busing was, it still presented the best solution for desegregating schools. "Yet the law demands," declared Askew, "and rightly so, that we put an end to segregation. . . . We must demonstrate good faith in doing just that." Tolerance was the key that Askew prescribed: "I hope that we will use it in the days ahead. It is easy for us to sit in our own homes, churches, or classrooms and put labels on others. It is more difficult and far more productive to meet the other person, to hear what he has to say, to discover that he is basically decent and sincere, and to seek ways in which we can live and work together in peace and understanding. I'm convinced that the maturing of America depends upon this kind of effort."[8]

What surprised the audience was not so much Askew's candor on the issue but that he came out so strongly for busing. This admission was a far cry from the earlier court baiting of Claude Kirk or the current cajoling of Alabama governor George Wallace. Ironically, at the same moment, Wallace was a mere seventy miles away in Jacksonville giving a speech of his own. Whereas Askew called for tolerance and understanding and a greater sacrifice to achieve racial justice, Wallace threatened that failure by President Nixon to halt busing would "force" him into running for president. When Wallace employed demagoguery, Askew appealed to the idealistic nature of the recent Florida graduates and their parents by quoting Carl Schurtz: "Ideals are like stars; you will not succeed in touching them with your hands. But like the seafaring man on the deepest of waters, you choose them as your guides, and following them, you will reach your destiny." This bold contrast of two major southern political figures, speaking in such proximity, symbolized the conflicts and disunity afflicting not only the Democratic party but also the South.[9]

Reaction to the speech was what might be expected with such a provocative issue. Florida's Republican Party chairman, L. E. "Tommy" Thomas, accused Askew of playing politics with Florida's children and gleefully reported that Askew's stand on busing put Florida Democrats "four square in favor of hauling our school children all over their counties in school buses." Many letters to Askew disapproved of his views. To these and the many others who inveighed against him, Askew stressed the importance of enforcing the law, arguing that "in my opinion, most of us in the South recognize that this is a new day and that we cannot continue to operate in the mood of yesterday." Askew also reminded them that there was a better way to prevent busing—community desegregation.[10]

Community desegregation was an idea more fully developed by Askew's education coordinator, Claude Anderson. A Detroit native, Anderson had served as professor of educational foundations at Florida A & M University in Tallahassee before his appointment. Anderson believed that education would play a critical role in breaking down segregation's lasting effects. Like Askew, Anderson believed in the necessity of busing and for exactly the same reasons. Housing patterns, said Anderson, long segregated and not easily changed, made busing an absolute necessity in order to end segregated schools. Busing was more than just moving students around in order to make the numbers look good. Education was the key to breaking the cycle of black poverty and exclusion, he argued, because "housing patterns are based on the economics of income and income is

based on education." Anderson related his experience as a marine to support his argument. He believed that his hopes of becoming a pilot had been
dashed when lack of education excluded him from flight school, even
though aptitude tests proved he had the ability. Such exclusion led him to
maintain that America was not a true melting pot of cultures. "Blacks have
never melted," he concluded, "because they've never been in the pot—
they've always been outside the pot."[11]

Askew needed all the support he could get in late 1971. The rapid implementation of integration had heightened tensions all over the state.
These tensions manifested themselves in the staunch defense of Confederate symbols by white majorities at many integrated schools. One of several major incidents took place at Dixie-Hollins High School in St. Petersburg. The student council had voted to replace the Confederate flag and
rebel mascot with new, less divisive symbols. The students, who had been
elected by their peers, chose three options for school flag and symbol, of
which none was the rebel flag, though all three retained some elements of
the old Confederacy, such as the St. Andrew's cross or the silhouette of a
rebel soldier. Principal Nick Mangin implored students to put the issue to
rest by voting in large numbers for one of the options. "This is your
chance," he said, "to rise above all the hassle of recent weeks, your chance
to show the community and the administration that you can handle the
situation." Mangin also wanted the issue to remain solely among students
and not involve the public. The day of the vote was tense. Rumors of a
mass walkout by white students and the threat of rebel-flag write-in votes,
even though write-ins were not allowed, swept through the school. Although the walkout never happened, students en masse wrote in votes for
the battle flag. Of 2,250 students voting, only 197 voted for the flag eventually adopted, a white cross on blue background with a shield in the center depicting a rebel soldier on horseback. The second choice—the St.
Andrew's cross with a "heavy jowled" C.S.A. soldier in the middle—
received 139 votes; and the third, a blue flag with "Dixie" written across
it, garnered only 98. The other 1,816 students voted write-in for the rebel
flag.[12]

Although an overwhelming number of students voted for the rebel flag,
the principal and board of education disallowed the vote and proclaimed
that the leading vote getter of the three alternatives would be the official
symbol of the high school. Although the ballots had contained explicit
instructions that no write-ins would be recognized, the response to the

decision was immediate. A group of parents formed Parents and Students for Dixie, determined to see the rebel flag fly over the school. After threatening a lawsuit, the group found an unlikely ally in Lieutenant Governor Tom Adams, who said that because the flag was only a school symbol, he could see no reason why it should not be allowed on campus. Another, more ominous group re-formed. The Pinellas County Citizens Council, inactive since the early 1960s, gained new strength. Field Director Roger Cole spoke for the group, arguing that "to allow a vote and then to disregard the wishes of the majority is against the principles on which our government was founded."[13]

As if the flag vote had not created more than enough anxiety, an upcoming football game threatened potential violence. Just a few weeks after the flag vote, on November 19, Dixie-Hollins was scheduled to play mostly black Gibbs High. A biracial advisory committee of the Pinellas School Board predicted that the game would be a "powderkeg of potential violence" and urged cancellation in order "to prevent a daydream from becoming a nightmare." The leader of Parents and Students for Dixie, James A. Jones, was hopeful of another outcome. "If we do take the flag to the game there will be trouble," said Jones, "and that will be bad for the cause. And if we don't take it to the game, there'll be trouble anyhow, and this is good for the cause." Jones expected some action on the part of blacks at the football game. His group stood to gain politically if they did not provoke blacks who attended the game. One member of the biracial council, a local member of the NAACP, expressed great fear: "The game scares me to death. If the Dixie-Hollins band decides to play 'Dixie,' we'll have a racial revolt on our hands." These and other concerns did not force cancellation, but kickoff was moved to late afternoon instead of night, and all rebel flags were seized at the gate. A sparse crowd saw a closely fought game with no outbreaks of violence. Gibbs won the game with a late score, which ironically caused the jubilant Gibbs band to rub a little salt in the wound by playing "Dixie."[14]

Integration foes, left without a sympathetic ear in the governor's office, gravitated to George Wallace, then making his third run at the presidency. Askew received much correspondence demanding that he "stand up for America" and fight busing. More than a few of these letters contained copies of Wallace literature and even a donation thank-you letter from the Wallace campaign. Capitol watchers anticipated an exciting campaign season in which busing would be the focus of all the candidates, especially

Wallace, and in which there would likely be a symbolic showdown between Askew and Wallace. It would also be the campaign in which Askew
made his mark by demonstrating a moral courage that set him apart from
other southern governors and made him a national political figure.[15]

With much work to do in changing racial attitudes in the state, Askew
began a whirlwind campaign in January 1972 with a speech in Tampa at
the Symposium on the Contemporary South. Here he proclaimed a new
day in the region and criticized those southern leaders "who cater to fears
and prejudices." He hoped that those "who would exploit racial discord
and empty rhetoric will be influencing very few southerners from this
time forward." Ironically, his presence at the University of South Florida
attracted protests by black students who followed him around campus
holding signs that read "Southern Whites have not changed—the same
thing with southern politics." Askew disagreed with the message: "I believe the people of the South aren't going to merely join the Union.
They're going to be faced with the opportunity, perhaps even the responsibility, to lead it." One way the South could exhibit such leadership, said
the governor, would be to reverse the "tragedy of urban decay and poor
housing as well as the blight of uncontrolled development." At the end of
Askew's remarks at the symposium, the protesting black students entered
the auditorium and shook his hand, symbolizing the reunification for
which Askew strove. It was a positive start to a trying political year for
Askew. As in 1971, when he gave his busing speech at the University of
Florida, Wallace was again in the state, this time campaigning in Tallahassee. The differing messages of these simultaneous appearances summed up
the question of 1972: to bus or not to bus.[16]

In late January more school disturbances put Askew in the role of mediator. Four black students had been permanently expelled from Marianna
High School in Jackson County for fighting with several white students.
The white students were not punished. State NAACP director Reverend
R. N. Gooden threatened a one-thousand-person march on the capitol if
the governor took no action. On January 21, Gooden led a thirty-car cara-
van with two hundred blacks from Marianna to Tallahassee. He added fifty
more followers along the way to the capitol. Askew acted swiftly, meeting
with Gooden and promising to work out a settlement, believing that
"when people stop talking, they start fighting." From Gooden he solicited
the names of twelve blacks to serve with twelve whites on a biracial committee in Jackson County to address this discord. At this "comforting

news," Gooden canceled a planned camp-out on the lawn of the governor's mansion. Askew's quick action and decisiveness showed blacks that
he was sincere in his wish to restore black trust in government.[17]

A recent rule change in Florida senate procedures, made just before
the session began, allowed senators opposed to busing to place the straw
vote on the presidential primary ballot. The rule let senators place two
bills per session before the senate for priority consideration. These "gold
star" priorities were designed to help senators place their pet projects on
the senate calendar. The first senator to take advantage of this new rule
was Republican contractor and St. Petersburg realtor Richard Deeb, who
used it to propose a straw vote on busing. Voted unanimously out of committee, the bill was passed by the senate 36-7 over the objections of senate
president Jerry Thomas, who urged the senate to shoulder responsibility
instead of "tossing it to the public." In the house, which had no gold star
rule, house speaker and Askew ally Richard Pettigrew, a Democrat from
Miami, quickly assigned the bill to committee where he and Askew hoped
it would bog down and die. The bill had too much support, however, and
was voted out of committee by a vote of 79-32. The vote for passage
followed similar lines. The bill received a great deal of support inside
and outside the legislature. Antibusing groups around the state staged a
concentrated effort to ensure passage. Many of these correspondents relied on form letters, preprinted postcards, onionskin reproductions, and
newspaper clippings of form letters, all of which contained identical language. One of the few handwritten letters summarized the sentiment of
many busing opponents: "Down with busing. Down with idiocy. Down
with liberalism. Up with sense. Up with education. Up with Senate Bill
421."[18]

Local political commentators immediately recognized the potential of
the straw vote for the political atmosphere of the state. The straw vote,
said one commentator, was "just the thing to breathe life and meaning into
our March 14 election." Others praised those who fought against the bill
in the legislature, especially Jerry Thomas and Richard Pettigrew. Although a conservative, Thomas fought against such a "pointless . . . action." Political pundits also recognized Askew's dilemma. The passage of
the bill by the legislature put its fate in Askew's hands and put the governor
under a spotlight. Askew could have exercised several options. Because
the legislature was still in session, he had only seven days to sign or veto
the bill; otherwise it automatically became law. If he vetoed the bill, Askew

surely would incur the wrath of voters for not allowing such a controversial issue to become a matter of public debate. If Askew chose to wait the required seven days for passage without his signature, it would have been in effect a pocket veto, for the state would not have had enough time to print ballots before election day.[19]

As much as Askew wanted to veto the bill, enough legislators supported the measure to override his veto. Reconciled to the depressing fact that he would have to sign the bill, Askew worked hard to soften its language. To make the desired changes, Askew fought on several fronts. He contacted his ally in the house, Speaker Pettigrew, whom he told that as a general rule he opposed these types of ballots. "I feel," he wrote, "that they usually represent an abdication of responsibility by elected officials, and they mislead the people into thinking that something has been accomplished when, in fact, it has not." What troubled him about the straw vote, he admitted to Pettigrew, was how a strong antibusing vote might damage Florida's image. "Florida is not a racist state," maintained Askew. "I believe, and certainly hope, that a minority of the people who oppose busing are motivated solely by race." Faced with a certain veto override, Askew asked Pettigrew to help him change the language of the bill to more neutral phrasing of the question. He also wished to add a new question that tested voters' opinions on ensuring equal opportunity to education for all children. Where the original question had read, "Do you favor an amendment to the U.S. Constitution that prohibits forced busing and guarantees the right of each student to attend the appropriate public school nearest to his home?" Askew wanted the word "forced" removed. He also wanted to add after the word "busing" the phrase "solely to achieve a racial balance." Because he knew a strong majority of voters would vote against busing, Askew wanted to soften the conclusion that Florida was a "segregationist state." Askew designed his proposed question—"Do you favor providing an equal opportunity for all children regardless of race, creed, color, or place of residence and oppose a return to a dual system of public schools?"—to counter the expected overwhelming antibusing vote and prove that Floridians disapproved only the means of school integration, not the ends.[20]

Askew reiterated these and other concerns in a February 15 press conference. He expressed fear that the vote would dominate an emotional debate among presidential candidates. Although such a debate might be profitable, the campaign most likely would get nasty, especially because

Wallace had raised busing to an emotional crescendo. It was especially important, said Askew, that Florida voters express themselves on both issues and have both questions before them so that those who opposed busing might show the nation that they did not oppose equal opportunity to education for all children. Askew announced that he had no choice but to sign the bill but would do so only if the legislature amended the questions as he requested. Asked if his campaign against a busing ban put him into open opposition to Wallace, Askew replied, "I think that's been apparent from the beginning." Askew admitted that he and Wallace agreed on one point: neither of them liked busing:

> I don't like it, the people don't like it, the courts don't like it. The question is, however, how do you address yourselves to achieving an end, and the end is to ensure an equal opportunity. . . . I say that somewhere along the line we've got to break the cycle, the cycle by many people, particularly black people in this country of not having a chance at an adequate education so that it could help them as they pursue their desires in life to improve themselves economically and in turn improve the whole economy of our entire country. And I think that I felt from the beginning that it's not a question of transportation, I say that it's a question of justice.[21]

Askew made it clear that he intended to speak loud and hard against the antibusing resolution, if not to defeat it, then at least to reduce its expected margin of victory. He wanted to turn the question around on those who opposed busing, whether they were Floridians or presidential hopefuls campaigning in the state. The crux of the question, as Askew restated it, was not whether busing was unpopular. Rather, the question was, if not busing, then how would the state ensure equality of educational opportunity? How else would these opponents of busing solve the larger problem of desegregation? Askew hoped to stress this question, not busing's popularity, during the campaign.[22]

With little pomp, Askew signed Senate Bill 421 into law on February 17, 1972, and began his determined effort to convince voters that questions larger than busing were at stake. With all the attention on whose children were going to what school, state leaders, especially Askew, fell under scrutiny for where they sent their children. The governor's children attended desegregated Kate Sullivan Elementary School in Tallahassee, where 42 percent of the students were black. His children were not bused because they lived less than two miles from the school. A firm believer in public schools, Askew as governor refused the opportunity to send his children to University School, an advanced and somewhat elite school run in conjunction with Florida State University. This choice increased his credibility and provided his supporters one more example of how he led by example.[23]

Askew's first public speech after the bill became law came only three weeks before election day in Orlando, which was enemy territory for him. Almost 90 percent of Orlando voters had voted against busing in their own recent straw poll. Despite this expression of local sentiment, Askew admonished his audience: "It's time we told the rest of the nation that we aren't caught up in the mania to stop busing at any cost." Busing was only a temporary means to a greater and just end, he argued. Furthermore, no one was committed to busing as an end unto itself; it was merely an "artificial and inadequate" solution that should be abandoned as soon as possible after all remnants of segregated schools had disappeared. Askew maintained that Florida had made "real progress" in dismantling the dual system through busing. Still, racial disturbances had kept southerners from addressing more important matters, leaving them little time to "demand a fair shake on taxes, on utility bills, on consumer protection, on government services, on environmental protection and other problems." Race always got in the way of real progress, he said. "It seems so often when someone has attempted to actually do something about the problems of the people, the race issue has been resurrected, in one form or another." It was time for the South to show the nation that "we know the real issues when we see them, and that we no longer will be fooled, frightened, and divided against ourselves."[24]

Besides help from Pettigrew and Thomas, Askew received some vocal support from the otherwise hostile legislature. Florida's only black legislator, Representative Gwen Cherry, a Miami Democrat, echoed Askew's words. Not only was busing a necessary step in alleviating the inequality of years of segregation, said Cherry, but also busing had long been used during Jim Crow to transport thousands of black children past segregated white schools. How ironic, she stated, for the same people who condemned busing in 1972 to have had no objection to its past use. Fred Karl, Democratic state senator from Miami, agreed with Cherry, but with more pointed words. He called the straw vote "pure and simple" politics. "However you try to mask it, and however you try to cover it, the issue again is race." Like Askew, Karl maintained that there were only two directions the state could go with a vote such as this: a "no" vote meant moving toward the future and a more just South; a "yes" vote was a vote for segregation and the past. Quoting from an ancient Hebrew prayer, Karl summarized the bill's opponents' hopes for the election: "From the cowardice that shrinks from the new truth, from the laziness that is content with half truths, from the arrogance that thinks it knows all truth, O, God of truth, deliver it."[25]

Askew also received valuable support and encouragement from religious leaders across the state. Eleven different church leaders representing Jews, Episcopalians, Greek Orthodox, Presbyterian, Catholics, and Baptists lent their support. One Miami rabbi promised to call five hundred friends and urge a no vote.[26]

Most people agreed that Askew entered "rather warm political waters" with his antibusing amendment crusade. The *Tallahassee Democrat* believed Askew's words fell on deaf ears because no amount of logic about why busing was necessary could overcome its emotional baggage. In an effort to show that there actually were Floridians who supported Askew on this issue, the governor's office kept a tally of the hundreds of letters Askew received. In the last several weeks before the vote, Askew's office received more than seventeen hundred handwritten letters (not including form letters, onionskin reproductions, or newspaper clippings), which ran almost six to one for Askew. A Gulfport woman said she felt like "shouting from the housetop" that she had finally found a "man who is governor of all his people and appeals to their best." A black mother of two from Tampa told Askew that busing was not her choice, but it was "preferable to the school system that educated me." Not all letters were positive. One teacher from the Panhandle wrote and spoke for many in Askew's home region: "You are not doing what the people of Northwest Florida elected you for." Another writer told the governor that he might make a better car salesman because "you're trying to sell us something that's no good." In response to the announcement of the positive letters, busing opponents swung into action, and several parents' groups formed. Representatives from a group named Dade County Citizens in Favor of Neighborhood Schools delivered to Askew's office two suitcases full of 39,935 "straw votes" clipped from the newspaper, 33,322 of which opposed busing. They also brought more than one thousand signed form letters from North Dade County parents of schoolchildren and forty thousand signatures on a petition calling for a busing ban in the U.S. Constitution. One member of the group, Lynn Freeland, said Askew was "misinformed, misguided, or uninformed" as to the public's sentiments. If Askew would just talk to "everyday people," she said, he would realize that they did not want their kids taken out of the "security of the neighborhood schools." Freeland maintained that they did not oppose integration, only busing to achieve it. Askew also wanted "neighborhood schools," only he wanted them in desegregated neighborhoods.[27]

Firm in his determination to get his message across to the state, Askew organized a political action group called Citizens for Equal Education. Funded by donations from supporters, this organization eventually received more than $32,000 that Askew used to combat the antibusing message sent out by his opponents. The money bought newspaper, radio, and television advertising. He announced the formation of this group on the same day that he attacked ban supporters with another argument. An emotional Askew condemned efforts to "tamper" with the Constitution. There were better ways of stopping busing, more progressive ways than changing the law of the land on an emotional whim. Good-faith legislation for desegregation, selective placement of new schools, and widespread community desegregation were but a few of the alternative methods that Askew suggested to stop busing. If the Constitution were to be amended, how exactly would it be done? Askew inquired. "Would it be done like we say in most of our statutes—'notwithstanding any other provision of the Constitution, the right to attend your neighborhood school will supersede any other right guaranteed hereunder'?" To amend the Constitution in order to ban busing would risk a repeal of *Brown,* would nullify the Fourteenth Amendment, and would restrict the very liberty that busing opponents cherished in neighborhood schools. Askew "recognized the reality" that his side might lose the vote. What he wanted to accomplish with his crusade was to "cause a sober reflection by the people who obviously have intended to vote that way."[28]

Just over a week before the March 14 election the *St. Petersburg Times,* one of Florida's most liberal newspapers, polled two hundred Floridians on their straw vote choice. More than half were "flatly opposed" to busing. Less than 20 percent accepted busing no matter the distance, and about 25 percent approved of busing under certain circumstances. The most revealing part of the survey, however, was an interview with a forty-year-old black woodworker from Key West, Eddie DeLong, who put the busing question into a grim but all too real perspective: "Oh man. I know all about busing. I got bused eighty miles a day so I could go to a one-room school for blacks that had about seventy kids and one teacher who wasn't even a high school graduate. And while I was riding that bus, I rode right past five nice white schools, two of them within walking distance of the shanty where I was raised. Don't no whites come to me crying about busing."[29] Askew made the same point earlier, maintaining that busing had been used as a tool of segregation. "Black children," he said, "were bused from kingdom come to preserve segregation." It was the great contradiction of busing foes. Jim Crow had bused black children extensively to preserve all-white schools. Before desegregation in Mississippi, one system had bused black children 93 miles a day past a white school. Some Florida systems bused black students into other counties; in one case the one-way trip from Collier County to Lee County was seventy-four miles. After desegregation, busing distances declined, although the number of students bused grew slightly. In the twenty years prior to 1971, an average of thirty-two Florida children out of one hundred were bused. In 1971 Florida achieved 90 percent integration while busing only thirty-five out of one hundred. No longer were children bused into adjacent counties. In Dade County, the longest bus ride for desegregation was twenty minutes. Tampa's longest bus ride for desegregation was nine miles, compared with its longest ride for nondesegregation purposes, twenty-five miles.[30]

The *St. Petersburg Times,* a vocal Askew supporter, summarized the issue in its endorsement of a "no" vote in the straw poll. Florida's reputation was at stake, the editors argued. To vote for Wallace and against busing would tarnish Florida's progressive reputation. The state had grown in moderation and tolerance in the 1950s and 1960s. When Wallace had pledged that he would never be "out-segged" again, wrote the *Times,* Governor Leroy Collins had called for toleration and understanding. In 1962, when Wallace promised that segregation would last forever, Governor Farris Bryant asked Floridians to treat each other with "fairness and equity." Even Republican governor Claude Kirk, the *Times* recalled, had maintained that Wallace did not speak for the New South. Now, in 1972, the paper editorialized, the issue came down to Wallace against Askew. "The question Floridians must ask themselves," wrote the *Times,* "is whether they are going to let outsider George Wallace—his own record tarnished by extremism, turmoil, and division—blacken Florida's prestige?"[31]

Antibusing voices were by no means silent. On March 6, Wallace spoke to a joint session of the legislature, praised the body for passing the straw vote legislation, and predicted that it would give national leaders a "rude awakening." Wallace proclaimed that America was tired of welfare, waste in foreign aid, and the breakdown of law and order. Busing, however, was the "straw that broke the camel's back," Wallace explained. To solve these problems, Wallace recommended a "yes" vote for a busing ban and a "strong vote" for him. At a Wallace rally later that night, the Association of Florida Citizens' Councils passed out leaflets urging a "no" vote on equal educational opportunity for all students. The PAFB also urged voters to ignore the second question.[32]

In a speech before the PAFB, one of the bill's cosponsors, state senator Richard Deeb, lashed out at Askew. He accused the governor of trying to make himself attractive to the Democratic National Committee by supporting busing and claimed that Askew had joined those people "who want to use our children as pawns in their grand dreams of controlling our social order." Deeb later charged that Askew cried race for political gain. The governor, said Deeb, "should stop shouting 'racism' . . . and 'segregation,' trying to infer that those who oppose forced busing are prejudiced." Echoing Deeb, former governor Kirk condemned Askew's "holier than thou" attitude and charged that Askew acted like a demagogue. Ignoring his own seizure of the Manatee school system in 1970, Kirk asserted that Askew used Florida's children as "political pawns." Askew was a hypocrite, Kirk charged, because he had voted against busing in 1970 but had changed his tune when confronted with an opportunity to be vice president. Askew had voted for an amendment to an educational bill that sought to deny public funds for busing. The governor offered a spirited defense of his earlier vote. He had voted for the bill in order to prevent a worse antibusing bill from replacing it. Most important, the language of the amendment— that public funds would be denied for any busing used "solely" for racial balance—guaranteed that the amendment was worthless. Busing had never been used "solely" for racial balance, at least not prior to 1970 in Florida. Students had to get to school somehow, and busing was the dominant mode of transportation. The straw vote question also contained the word "solely," however, and even one of Askew's former allies in the senate, Jerry Thomas, backtracked. Aiming at a future run against Askew in 1974, Thomas joined many other legislators and busing foes in attacking Askew's position.[33]

At a large rally in Clearwater two days before the election, Askew addressed the importance of a "no" vote on the amendment question. Askew admitted that busing was an unattractive alternative. Nevertheless, the South had to ensure that it did not return to "segregation, fear, and misunderstanding which produced the very problem that led to busing in the first place." The task ahead was bigger than busing, he argued; the South had to find a cure for racial misunderstanding and prejudice. Askew argued that fear and ignorance had prevented the races from actually becoming close, that "ignorance is the father of cruelty." Addressing accusations that he was merely playing politics, Askew insisted that his purpose in opposing the antibusing scheme reflected a higher calling. He acted as a matter of personal conscience. "When I leave the governor's office," said Askew, "I want to be able to walk down any street in Florida and say in good conscience that I kept the faith, that I kept the faith with my principles and with myself."[34]

The culmination of the campaign came on Sunday, March 13, with television appeals by both sides. Statewide broadcasts allowed each side fifteen minutes to make last appeals. Speaking first from his Washington office for the busing opponents was Florida's U.S. senator, Ed Gurney, who told Floridians that America was watching and that their vote would have a powerful impact on the rest of the nation. A strong antibusing vote, said Gurney, would prevent the Supreme Court from ruling on the issue and would end the controversy once and for all. It would stop busing proponents from using the state's children "like cattle." Askew responded that proponents of the measure were deluding themselves into thinking that a busing prohibition would end racial imbalance in schools. Busing was the bad-tasting medicine needed to cure a serious ailment. Until housing patterns changed, allowing for a more natural and less disruptive pattern of integration, busing was necessary. Askew then sounded a grave warning: "My friends, you be sure, you be very sure, before we start amending the United States Constitution. . . . When we start putting into cement something in the Constitution, we should think long and hard."[35]

Although the turnout was less than the predicted 70 percent, over 50 percent of Florida voters cast ballots and overwhelmingly approved the busing amendment proposition, 74 percent to 26 percent. Every county in Florida voted for the proposition. George Wallace also won an easy victory over his opponents, more than doubling the vote of his closest opponent, Hubert Humphrey. Wallace won 42 percent of the vote to

Humphrey's 18 percent and Edmund Muskie's 9 percent. George McGovern scored only 6 percent. The results of the busing referendum surprised no one, but the victory was smaller than expected. A January 1972 poll measured the vote against busing at 86 percent. Senator Deeb claimed that the vote was a congressional mandate.[36]

More telling were the results on the second question of whether voters supported equal educational opportunity. With almost the same number of voters, this question garnered a larger percentage of the vote than the busing query. Almost 79 percent voted in the affirmative: 1,066,1123 to 290,003. Whereas every county had voted against busing, all but Orange County voted for equal educational opportunity. These results provided Askew a "partial victory," which gained him and the state positive media coverage. The divergent votes also represented the nation's dilemma, Askew argued in a postelection analysis. Most people did not oppose providing children with equal opportunity to education. They merely disliked busing as the means for providing it. Askew then placed the results in perspective. "How many of us back in 1954 or even 1964," asked the governor, "would have expected the people of a southern state to voluntarily vote . . . against segregation as an acceptable condition of life?"[37]

The demographic breakdown of the vote revealed that perhaps Askew was a little too optimistic about the outcome. Every county in Florida supported a busing ban, many by majorities of two, three, and four to one. In Duval County, where Jacksonville is located, even a slight majority of blacks voted against busing while giving a strong "yes" to equal opportunity. The white vote in Duval was five to one against busing and three to one for equal opportunity. In Gadsden County, blacks voted 4,639 to 1,727 against busing. Most urban areas voted by large majorities against busing. Still, some signs encouraged Askew. Counties that had suffered recent racial flare-ups voted at or below the state average on both questions, showing that perhaps they sought solutions, not confrontation. As positive as question two turned out to be for the governor, he still suffered a "stinging defeat" on busing.[38]

Askew's political foes looked forward to 1974 with renewed hope for his defeat. Surely he was doomed by his crazy stance on busing, they thought. One of the bill's cosponsors, Senator Charles Weber, a Republican from Ft. Lauderdale, predicted an ominous future for Askew, giving him not a "ghost of a chance" of reelection. Instead, opined Weber, the state needed "far more conservative leadership." Senate president Jerry

Thomas, an old Askew ally, now rode the political waves toward a run for the governorship. Where sixty days earlier Thomas urged his senate colleagues not to bow to "government by straw vote," he now claimed that the referendum matched his philosophy on busing. He even hosted a celebration party on the night after the vote, where many of the white party-goers expressed surprise that blacks attended. Even former governor Kirk hinted at a comeback.[39]

Reports of Askew's political death were greatly exaggerated, however. Although opponents saw his busing position as his death knell, Askew exhibited a resiliency that surprised even his most ardent supporters. A public opinion poll conducted four months later in July 1972 revealed that Askew actually made slight gains in popularity. In the fall of 1971, 61.8 percent of voters rated Askew favorably, compared with only 26.7 percent who rated him unfavorably. By the summer of 1972 his favorable rating had grown to 64.5 percent, with a corresponding gain in his unfavorable rating to 29.3 percent. These results correspond to an earlier poll conducted during the primary campaign that revealed that whereas Askew's positions were at times unpopular, his personal appeal and reputation for honesty and plain talk made a favorable impression on voters.[40]

For all of the governor's optimistic talk about how far the South and Florida had come since segregation, he realized that old feelings die hard. Integration made many whites feel uncomfortable. They believed that their way of life was being taken away. In such a crisis, they fell back to Confederate symbols to ease their pain and reestablish their identity as southerners. Many of these symbols made their way into schools. For example, at Escambia High School in Askew's hometown of Pensacola a conflict over Confederate symbols became one of the most heated school disturbances during Askew's tenure. At issue was the board of education's decision to remove divisive symbols from the school in the wake of student disturbances. Built in 1958 to serve a growing suburban area near Pensacola's navy base, Escambia High had thirty-four hundred students, with a ratio of almost ten whites to one black, who comprised a non-threatening minority.[41]

The board had appointed a biracial committee of students, parents, and educators, which was 60 percent white, that proposed the symbols' elimination. Vehement white opposition to the proposed removal shocked the board. At the board's January 11, 1973, meeting, whites threatened a student walkout if the issue was not resolved to their satisfaction. The uproar and tension were exacerbated by a local television station and two area legislators. Earlier in the day on January 11, thirty white students protested the committee's recommendation. The night of the board's meeting, state legislators W. D. Childers and R. W. "Smokey" Peaden met with three thousand whites, ostensibly to form a new organization called Concerned Parents and Students Association. After hearing the board's decision they changed their plans. The following Monday, January 15, the board reversed the recommendation of the biracial committee and announced plans to allow the student body to vote on which symbols they preferred.[42]

The decision eased the tremendous white pressure on the board, but it infuriated a vocal black minority. Reverend R. N. Gooden, who had been active in the situation for weeks, blasted the decision, leveling charges of hypocrisy at the board's reversal. More astonishing to Gooden was that board members had earlier appealed to students to follow their lead in charting a path of "moderation or elimination" of "racial irritants." Gooden also rebuffed offers from Childers and Peaden to explain to the NAACP the "seriousness of the white backlash." He also lashed out at the governor, who chose not to interfere in a local matter. Askew's "namby-pamby" approach to the situation was only an effort by the governor to save his image, charged Gooden. "One word from the governor would have helped to settle the problem." Instead, said Gooden, Askew "just sits up in his ivory tower doing nothing." He also threatened that further inaction by the governor would cause him to camp out on the lawn of the governor's mansion. To this threat Askew replied, "Reverend Gooden has camped on my lawn quite a bit." Gooden then condemned racist parents for pressing the school board to abandon its earlier moderation and appealed to the silent white majority to control the "small white racist minority" that had caused the problems.[43]

The school's 340 black students boycotted the vote scheduled for Tuesday, January 16. For the next few days black systemwide attendance remained low because of fears of racial disturbances and in protest of the vote. As expected, both the Rebel flag and "Dixie" as the school's fight song were overwhelmingly chosen over options provided by the board's biracial committee. Gooden and the NAACP quickly filed suit in federal court arguing that such symbols represented "symbolic resistance . . . to the concept of a unitary school system and the philosophy of equality inherent in the Fourteenth Amendment." Education commissioner Floyd Christian had forewarned the board of the possibility of a lawsuit and its good chance for success when he notified it of a 1970 Louisiana district court ruling, later upheld in the Fifth U.S. Circuit Court in New Orleans, which ruled that the retention of such symbols hindered the elimination of racial discrimination and that school boards were "charged with the affirmative duty to take whatever steps necessary to convert to a unitary system."[44]

U.S. district judge Winston Arnow ruled that the symbols had to go, arguing that "these are symbols of white racism in general and offensive to a substantial number of black students at this school." Arnow's order came in three parts, the first two of which dealt with the flag. No students could display or wear the flag on their person, and the flag could be displayed by the school only in the trophy case. The third held that "rebels" could not be used to identify the school or its athletic teams or cheer squads. The judge did allow certain exemptions. Class rings, yearbooks, athletic and cheer uniforms, a plaque with the alma mater and Confederate symbols, a memorial to Escambia High students killed in Vietnam bearing a rebel flag, and the word "rebels" at center court of the gymnasium could all remain. Other objects, however, had to be removed or concealed. A large rebel battle flag on the football field press box and the wall of the gymnasium that read "Home of the Rebels" were ordered concealed. On the day the order took effect, black students returned to school.[45]

Childers and Peaden worked to raise money to fight the order that, according to them, "crushed the spirits and destroyed the pride" of white Pensacolans. Peaden did urge parents to allow their children to attend school and confine their fight to the courts. An emergency meeting of the Escambia County Citizens Council proved an ominous sign, however. Peaden also failed to follow his own advice. A Tampa television station quoted him as saying that "those niggers make me so mad. . . . If I had anything to do with it, I would get a shotgun—no, a submachine gun—and mow them down." Peaden quickly retracted this statement, apologized, and explained that the remark was made "in jest." Escambia sheriff Royal Untreiner supported Peaden's right to free speech: "These men are the duly elected representatives of this county and have a right to say what they feel." Gooden, the state NAACP director, threatened to file impeachment proceedings against Peaden.[46]

The effects of the Escambia and Dixie-Hollins troubles did not remain local. Just after Peaden's remarks, more than two hundred Escambia students clashed, causing classes to end early. Askew finally intervened and sent twenty state troopers to the school. Although Escambia High quickly calmed down, blacks stopped attending, and with the large number of local and state police on the scene, the school seemed "quiet as a tomb." Students remarked that the school felt like a prison, and one teacher confessed that racial feelings were more polarized than ever. "The atmosphere for compromise is almost non-existent," said one teacher, "and that's the only thing that's going to ease the tension." Although Escambia remained calm, schools across the state experienced similar clashes, all over the flag issue. In Boca Raton, Chipley, St. Petersburg, and Palm Beach, tension increased and fights ensued, many of them started over the sudden appearance of "white power" graffiti on walls and students wearing Confederate symbols. Askew legal counsel Edgar Dunn wearily commented that unrest "just ripples across the state."[47]

Askew could not stop emotions from getting out of hand, white students from fleeing to private schools, or legislators from working to pass nonbinding busing referenda, nor could he singlehandedly change the attitudes of white or black Floridians. What he did was to remain firm in his determination to become Florida's moral conscience. Askew entered office free of political debt, with no real national aspirations, and with an honest desire to make state government serve all citizens. Such freedom from ambition, combined with his strong religious faith that all were equal under the law and in God's eyes, allowed him to speak frankly and honestly to Floridians to implore them to search for and release the southern humanitarian impulse that he believed rested just below the surface of racial prejudice and fear. Such consistency helps explain Askew's later successes after supporting an almost universally unpopular position in the busing straw vote. Although many expected his busing stance to doom him politically, his favorable rating actually rose. Whereas many saw him as a lame duck governor sure to suffer defeat in 1974, he won a landslide victory, garnering more than one million votes. Askew's consistency left a mark on the voters. In an atmosphere where state political figures and southern demagogues changed positions and utilized emotional issues and race to gain political advantage, Askew offered instead meaningful solutions to real problems. His more popular positions on corporate income taxes, tax relief, environmental protection, and education reform outweighed his relative unpopularity on busing.[48]

Askew was the first Florida governor to proclaim Martin Luther King

Jr.'s birthday a state holiday and to sing "We Shall Overcome" with students at historically black Florida A & M University, and his commitment to minorities was unequaled among contemporary southern governors. More outspoken on racial reconciliation than many of his contemporaries in the South, Askew did not hesitate to tell Floridians what was on his mind and conscience. Voters respected and rewarded him for his honesty and moral leadership. His actions on behalf of blacks puzzled many in his home region, the traditionally conservative Florida Panhandle. An elderly, toothless man from Pensacola confessed that he liked Askew but wondered about "Rube's funny notions 'bout the colored." In Askew's first campaign for the state legislature, one man called Askew a "nigger lover." Askew pleaded guilty, adding, "but I don't love them enough." The difference between him and his critic, Askew explained, was that "I'm trying to overcome my prejudices and you're not." The one place that Askew believed he could do more for blacks was in education. Although he later downplayed his role in reforming education in Florida, Askew was a key figure, a catalyst of change, during his tenure. Reforming education, however, also meant supporting school integration, busing, and ensuring that children had equal opportunities to education. To help change the black educational experience in America (which Askew advisor Claude Anderson described as something akin to the Old Testament: "chapter one—hell, chapter two—hell continued") Askew spoke firmly and eloquently for busing as a means, however inadequate and temporary, to provide black students with the same educational experiences that white children had enjoyed for many years.[49]

Reubin Askew's hope for the South was that the region would finally reveal its humane side and assume leadership of the nation in racial reconciliation. He wished for southerners to realize that they had bigger, more important problems to solve that could be addressed only when they finally put aside the petty and divisive politics of race. Because he could not mandate changes of heart, Askew became Florida's moral conscience, appealing to Floridians not to let their emotions rule the day, to look deep into their souls and do what they knew was right and realize that all were equal under the law. He believed this so deeply that he put his political future on the line in the busing straw vote.

Like John West in South Carolina, Askew benefited from the initial assaults on racial injustice made by past governors. Florida's Leroy Collins, like South Carolina's Ernest Hollings and Robert McNair, made verbal assaults on segregation and proclaimed that the law of the land would be followed. As a partial result of this effort, both states reacted relatively mildly to *Brown* and the downfall of segregation. Alabama had no one to pave the way for Albert Brewer. He was left alone to make the initial assaults on racial discrimination while at the same time desegregating schools. It was a task too big for any one person. Askew's successes came in a state with a small black population, 15.3 percent in 1970. Almost 27 percent of Alabama's population was black, along with 30.5 percent of South Carolina's. Nevertheless, Askew's political courage was second to no other New South governor.[50]

By 1975 Askew proudly proclaimed that a new day had begun in Florida. "We have abandoned the old premises in Florida," reported Askew. "We have tried to correct old mistakes. We have renounced the old politics in which the needs of the people, black and white, were seldom ever considered." Askew was responsible for moving the state in this new direction, favorably altering the negative image of Florida's racial policies created by the confrontational style of Governor Claude Kirk. Conditions would not change overnight. Askew knew that "discrimination will not vanish simply because we wish it away." Although he was not an unrealistic optimist, Askew chose to accentuate the positive and not dwell on how far the South still had to go. In one of his most impassioned speeches, Askew quoted Thomas Wolfe: "To every man his chance, to every man, regardless of his birth, his shining, golden opportunity. To every man the right to live, to work, to be himself. . . . This is the promise of America." Askew added that "this too must be the promise of Florida."[51] Despite many policy initiatives, perhaps Askew's greatest contribution as a New South governor was to use his office as a "bully pulpit," from which he convinced many white Floridians to examine their own consciences and realize that the New South ought to be about justice for all Americans.

4

Building a Better Florida

The 1973 Florida Education Reforms

In July 1973, Florida education commissioner Floyd Christian reported to state teachers that "better days are here." Christian had good reason for his claim. In June, Reubin Askew had signed into law one of the most sweeping and progressive education reform packages in Florida history. Not since 1947, when the state established the Minimum Foundation Program (MFP) for education, had the state experienced such drastic change. Most education experts agreed that the 1973 education legislation made Florida a national "model" for education reform. The moving force in this watershed in Florida history was Governor Reubin Askew. Shortly after assuming office in 1971, he created the Florida Governor's Citizens' Committee on Education (CCE) to study Florida education and make recommendations for its reform. Askew's appointment of the CCE, its concrete and specific recommendations, and the governor's moral suasion constituted, as Christian pointed out, a "major turning point in education."[1]

Compared with its neighbors, Florida's education system did not appear to need reform. In almost every index, the state ranked ahead of every southern state except Virginia. In 1968, Florida spent more per pupil than the rest of the South, $554 per child compared with Georgia's $498, South Carolina's $418, Alabama's $403, and Mississippi's $346. The nation spent on average $619. In 1970, the average salary of a Florida teacher was $8,300, ranking it first in the South and twenty-second in the nation. Alabama ranked forty-fifth, paying its teachers $6,817, and South Carolina ranked forty-seventh, paying an average of $6,750. Mississippi ranked last in the nation with $5,870. A substantial number of Florida teachers, more than 28 percent, also made more than $8,500 a year in 1970. Virginia was highest in the South with 30.4 percent, though still well below the U.S. average of 45 percent. By contrast, only 5 percent of South

Carolina's teachers earned more than $8,500. Alabama paid only 7.3 percent of its teachers that much.[2]

Reubin Askew knew the state could do better. Not content with continually outpacing most of the South, Askew believed Florida should lead the nation. His vision for the state included serving not only as a national example for racial reconciliation but also as a model of how to finance and run schools effectively. Two months after taking office, Askew elaborated on his vision of what education should be. "Education is the hallmark of our democracy," he said, "a democracy which cannot exist without an enlightened citizenry." Later he added that "ignorance is the midwife of demagoguery and oppression." He suggested that one of the first things the state needed was tax reform. Education could not operate effectively without increased funds and accountability: "We have overburdened those least able to afford additional taxes while continuing to allow the politically influential to escape paying their fair share. As a result, Florida today has one of the most regressive tax structures in the United States." Askew demanded that the state institute a corporate profits tax. As it stood, Florida did not tax incomes earned by corporations operating within the state. This had made Florida an attractive place for industry to relocate or expand. Askew declared that the free ride had to end. His campaign to amend the state's constitution and install a corporate income tax was the first step in his 1973 success.[3]

In the fall of 1971, Askew began a campaign to amend the state constitution and institute a corporate income tax. The battle to get a referendum scheduled by the legislature was only a portent of things to come. In a compromise, Askew and tax opponents in the legislature agreed on holding the referendum in an extraordinary election in the fall of 1971. With the date set, the state witnessed one of the "bitterest 'nonpolitical' campaigns" in state history. Askew campaigned on a populist platform, asking voters, "Who runs this state?" Opponents charged that corporations would pass the tax down to the consumer, in effect making it another sales tax. They also misled voters into thinking the governor wanted a general income tax increase, not a tax on corporations. If approved, the corporate income tax meant almost $100 million for the state in the following year alone. Askew pledged to use the money to relieve sales and lease taxes and to aid education. Askew won a "miracle" victory, gaining more than 70 percent of the vote for the tax. The *St. Petersburg Times* called it a "landslide" and announced that the vote gave "final notice of a new direction in Florida politics." The victory was a testament to Askew's integrity and personal appeal with the voters. An aide described it this way: "He's a very easy guy to believe in." The trust expressed by the voters in this campaign carried over through the rest of his administration and lent legitimacy to his education reform efforts.[4]

Still, Askew knew that more money was not the whole answer to education reform in Florida. The state had to change the way it distributed that money. Those who knew best how the money should be spent, local school districts and their schools, had the least influence over spending. Askew also wanted communities to become more involved in the everyday life of schools and even to help formulate policy, and he used the CCE to assist him in this effort. Askew charged the committee with several duties. He asked it to determine how best to preserve and restore public confidence in education, "without which our system of education would surely collapse." He also wanted it to suggest improvements that would make Florida's educational system worthy of its children. Given a two-year period in which to conduct the study, the CCE planned to use the first year examining school governance and administration. The second year of the study would focus on education finance. With $50,000 from the legislature, and hoping to gain another $50,000 from private and public donations, the CCE embarked on one of the most important studies of Florida education in state history. Later, the CCE received a $93,000 Ford Foundation grant for its education finance study. By the time the committee disbanded at the end of the 1973 legislative session, it had provided the state with the most far-reaching reform program since 1947.[5]

If the CCE was to have any legitimacy with the public, it had to represent accurately the state's population. Askew enjoyed tremendous flexibility in pursuing this goal. Twenty-two members, including three each from both houses of the legislature, comprised the commission. After legislative selections, Askew had sixteen appointments with which to seek diversity. He chose Jacksonville businessman and former house speaker Fred Schultz to chair the committee. Legislative appointments included current speaker Terrell Sessums, house minority leader Donald Reed, and Kenneth MacKay, member of the house education committee. From the senate, Askew selected Robert Haverfield and Raleigh Greene, along with the chairman of the senate education committee, John Broxton. The other sixteen appointments came from a variety of backgrounds and organizations, among them state NAACP director Marvin Davies; Theodore Gibson, rector of Miami's Christ Episcopal Church; former state school board member Sara Harllee; Ed Price Jr., chair of the Florida Citrus Commission and vice president of Tropicana Orange Juice, Inc.; and Betty Staton, president of the Florida League of Women Voters. In all, the CCE represented a variety of backgrounds and groups, from attorneys to doctors, clergy to homemakers, media to minorities.[6] Askew's admonition to the committee was brief but encouraging. The "climate" was right for the committee to do a "great service" for Florida: "My charge is brief. Avoid preconceived ideas. . . . Keep an open mind. . . . Look at all options, all alternatives. Then don't be afraid to build a bold plan, a plan whereby education will serve us even better than it has in the past. Go to every group you can for information and ideas. You need them all to accomplish your task."[7]

Askew wanted this committee not only to devise workable solutions to the state's educational problems but also to earn statewide respect for its hard work and sincerity of purpose. He was not above terminating committee membership for spotty attendance. Among those dismissed was NAACP official Marvin Davies, who missed several consecutive meetings. Many educators and politicians, seeking to capitalize on the committee's popularity and the centrality of education in voters' minds, coveted appointments to the committee. They missed the point. Askew wanted a committee of, by, and for citizens to meet citizens' needs. He rebuffed many of these political appeals by explaining that they failed to recognize "the need for in-depth consideration which cannot be done in a quick and dirty atmosphere of special interests, partisan politics, or predetermined answers." Past committees, populated by lawmakers and education bureaucrats, had failed to produce results. Askew hoped a fresh approach and seriousness on his part would change the outcome.[8]

In January 1972, the CCE published its recommendations for reforming school governance. The highlight of these recommendations was a proposal to restructure the board of education. At the time, Florida had a cabinet board of education consisting of the members of Askew's state cabinet, all of whom were elected, including the state commissioner of education and the governor, who chaired it. That it was elected and not appointed allowed politics to stall efforts of any governor in setting educational policy. Florida's governors were left only with moral suasion to gain support from what could be an unfriendly board of education. The CCE proposed to change this structure. It recommended the creation of a lay board of education appointed by the governor and overseen by the cabinet board. Askew heartily endorsed this plan and announced that he had yet to find any recommendation by the CCE "which is not backed by solid reasoning." The time seemed right for the proposal. The legislature was meeting two months early in order to end the session before the 1972 election cycle began, and many members were determined to pass some form of restructuring, with or without the CCE's recommendations. Almost everyone agreed that the "planning and coordination" that was supposed to emanate from the cabinet board had been less than adequate in recent years.[9]

Floyd Christian, education commissioner since 1965, expressed grave reservations about Askew's plan. Popular among Floridians, Christian had proposed his own restructuring plan in 1971. Of course, he wanted to retain the elected commissioner, but he also proposed an appointive system similar to the CCE plan. Christian had argued that their primary cabinet responsibilities left members of the cabinet board little time to give to education. Since 1971, Christian had backed away from this proposal and had became a staunch defender of the cabinet board. The *St. Petersburg Times* had agreed with Christian then, calling his plan a "sound proposal." The *Times* was less enthusiastic about the CCE plan. The newspaper reasoned that not all Florida governors would be as progressive as Askew, reminding voters of the raucous Kirk administration. "If Florida learned one lesson from the chaotic years that Claude Kirk was governor," wrote the editors, "it was that checks and balances are needed on the powers of the chief executive." Richard Pettigrew attacked the proposal in the senate education committee. He called it a "ridiculous kind of organizational pattern" and stated that he was firmly opposed to creating another level of bureaucracy. Speaking before the committee, a visibly shaken Fred Schultz appealed for a second look: "Senator, I would hope you would rethink that position a little bit." Speaker Sessums warned Askew to expect major opposition to his restructuring plan.[10]

Along with his proposal to restructure the board of education, Askew also wanted to transfer responsibility for consumer protection and environmental safety away from the cabinet to other areas of state government. "You would be accused of seeking too much power by defenders of the cabinet system," wrote one Askew aide. Askew believed that greater accountability rested in the chief executive than with an education commissioner or any other cabinet position because the governor was the focal point for voter wrath or affection. Decisions by a cabinet of diverse political interests weakened the governor's influence over his own legislative program and policy recommendations. By removing such decisions from the cabinet, Askew also hoped to place responsibility in the hands of a trained civil service that would be more responsive to citizen needs. Whatever its result, Askew stood to gain from the proposal. Success signaled the end of a fragmented cabinet-governor relationship and cabinet-headed state agencies. Failure still placed Askew in good graces with "good government types and conservationists" and did not necessarily strengthen the cabinet system. The key question, though, was whether this ambitious suggestion would damage Askew's other education proposals. "In time," the aide told Askew, "everyone will come to recognize the correctness of your position. And every hard fight will weaken the cabinet system, not the office of governor."[11]

The legislature was not kind to Askew's restructuring plan. State senators Mallory Horne and Wilbur Boyd called the proposal "a royal hoax to sugarcoat a fight for political power as a meaningful solution to educational problems." Their problem was not so much with the governor, even though they believed he had a "thirst for power." Horne, Boyd, and a score of other legislators believed that restructuring removed from citizens their right to the ballot and threatened future generations with the "remote prospect of a runaway governor for the future." Although Askew's legislative allies claimed the proposal had the votes to pass, the bill came under "heavy fire." Speaker Sessums argued that the bill was a threat to the cabinet system, and state comptroller Fred Dickinson appealed to the senate to keep the cabinet involved in education. Askew's support quickly dwindled. Senate president Jerry Thomas, an Askew ally, announced that he knew the "pulse of the senate" and withdrew his support, calling the Askew plan "dead" for the session. "My colleagues came in and stepped on my conscience as a conservative," he explained. Thomas even suggested his own restructuring plan, but by that time no one favored weakening the cabinet.[12]

Askew's effort to restructure the cabinet died the following week. Richard Pettigrew declared the bill dead for the session. Pettigrew was an Askew ally and "strong supporter" of getting the cabinet out of education, but not with Askew's plan. He blamed Floyd Christian for the defeat. The education commissioner had lobbied hard against Askew's proposal, which would have in effect put him out of a job. Although many legislators favored some form of restructuring, they fell between Askew and Christian on what they preferred. The *Tallahassee Democrat* suggested that in the absence of a clear consensus, "it may be best for education in Florida" that Askew drop the plan. The newspaper reported that Askew "took his licking calmly." After his tremendous victory in passing the corporate income tax, Askew faced his biggest, and possibly most damaging, defeat. Had he simply proposed a separate elected board of education, Askew's restructuring plan might have met approval, given the dominant reform sentiment. He recovered quickly from this thrashing, graciously accepting the setback and asking the CCE to drop any more plans to restructure the cabinet.[13] He gave a pep talk to the committee, telling it that he shared its disappointment and then instructing committee members not to worry about the past but to look forward to greater reforms. Askew urged the committee to turn its attention to finance, teaching methods, and resources. Floyd Christian expressed visible relief: "Thanks to two votes in the house, and to almost the entire state senate, a very wise and deliberative body made up of very smart people, I'm still here and in one piece."[14]

Florida turned its attention to education finance in the summer of 1972 when the state released the first of its new "ratio studies." Under this system, the state made in-depth studies on a rotating basis of county property assessment. The report identified how far below full assessment counties collected property taxes. If a county was identified assessing property taxes below the minimum set by the MFP, it stood to lose state funds until it rectified the problem. In late June, the state released the first of these studies, which showed that assessment rates ranged from a high of 99 percent in Franklin County to 43 percent in Wakulla County against the 85 percent state average. One legislative aide declared that "this tells counties they're going to have to make some effort if they expect to get state handouts." The release of the studies caused "great wailing and gnashing of teeth."[15]

It also brought a lawsuit. Education commissioner Christian filed suit against the state, arguing that the ratio studies caused "fiscal chaos" because the state auditor did what Christian termed a poor job and turned the studies in after the deadline. This pushed the budgeting cycle back by three weeks. State attorneys did not see Christian's as a "friendly" lawsuit, one designed to settle illegalities before the state approved the studies. A year later the state supreme court ruled ratio studies unconstitutional in that they deprived schoolchildren of equal protection by withholding school funds from underpaying districts. State senator Bruce Smathers, a Republican from Jacksonville, blasted the decision, saying it was "inconceivable to me that our supreme court would become a Robin Hood in reverse by taking from the property poor counties to give to the rich counties." Although designed with the best of intentions, ratio studies hurt those they intended to help. The court told the state to consider total state assumption of school costs or find a better way to assess wealth. The MFP had financed schools by providing more money to poorer districts and less to wealthier ones. To determine district wealth, the state used property tax assessment. This formula depended on sound assessment, something Florida, and most southern states, sorely lacked. To correct the shortcomings in the MFP, the citizens' committee decided to heed Askew's advice to take bold steps.[16]

Less than two years into his administration, Askew had compiled quite a record with reforms in taxation, environmental protection, and state courts. An internal memo touted these steps and looked to the future. The memo reiterated the basic goals of Askew's administration: tax justice; a government responsive to its citizens; a commitment to "an open, fair political process"; and "a commitment to public education designed to meet the needs of Florida's present and future." Askew's legislative and public influence seemed to be peaking just when he needed it most, entering the 1973 legislative session with a major education reform package. Apparently, the cabinet restructuring fiasco had little effect on Askew's public appeal. "Our poll information," read one memo, "is that a substantial majority of the people of Florida see in Reubin Askew what we who are privileged to work with him see."[17]

The polls proved the governor's resiliency, and they also hinted that the time was right for reform. An August 1972 poll of teacher attitudes revealed that there was a statewide desire for far-reaching education reform. More than 70 percent of teachers surveyed favored having a greater role in developing school policy. They also favored investing in individual schools a greater role in administration and policy formulation. A vast majority also favored an independent state board of education as opposed to the cabinet board. Almost 71 percent expressed dissatisfaction with their salary, and just as many saw little hope for a raise. Even some schoolchildren became involved in the debate. A Dade County High School senior wrote to Askew of the "terrible conditions" at her school. Her school could only afford to provide textbooks for in-class use. A food and nutrition course had to stretch a budget designed for one class over five. She complained that her government class met in the school auditorium because of classroom shortages, that they had no text, and that each student had to bring a section of the Sunday newspaper each week to read in class. She begged Askew to help.[18]

In its quest to alleviate such problems, the CCE sought counsel from leading education advocates in the legislature. One of these, Democrat Bob Graham of Miami, was a power in the senate. Graham, according to committee aides, reflected a "big county" perspective. Most big counties in Florida contained a substantial urban area and were desperately in need of cost-of-living adjustments in state school funds because of a shrinking urban tax base. Graham stressed that "politically" the MFP was "engrained" [sic] and "accepted" in Florida. He did not oppose or discourage sweeping reform but suggested that it might be politically expedient to let reform fall under the rubric of the MFP. He explained that the easiest, most feasible way to implement reform would be to simplify the current program. Presented with a choice between funding on a per-pupil or instructional unit basis, Graham preferred to fund schools for each child, not in units. He also criticized recent tax ratio studies. Their flaw, he explained, was that they should have been conducted at the time tax rolls were certified by the state, not after taxes had been collected. County assessors under his suggestion were provided with a solid excuse to give irate taxpayers. Assessors could blame the state for forcing them to assess at 100 percent before tax rolls received approval. Graham also emphasized his underlying conviction that local school districts should be given "maximum local flexibility" in spending and policy formation. The CCE's general agreement with Graham's policy suggestions played no small part in the 1973 success.[19]

In 1972 the state received mixed news about how education fared in Florida. The Department of Education announced that the percentage of children taught by teachers with only temporary certificates (lacking college degrees) had fallen almost by half, from 6 percent in 1971 to 3.7 percent a year later. The greatest increase in certified teachers came in math, science, and elementary classrooms. The numbers of uncertified teachers in these fields fell from 12 to 7 percent, 11 to 7 percent, and 3 to 1 percent, respectively. In 1971, 99.2 percent of state teachers held at least a bachelor's degree, and 24.3 percent held a master's. Florida teachers had a median nine years' experience and a median age of thirty-seven years. Furthermore, thanks to sound financial management and an "extremely healthy" economy, Florida had its largest ever budget surplus, $157.9 million. Nonetheless, not everyone was happy. Florida Education Association (FEA) president Dorothy Davalt notified Askew that Florida schools were in a "dire situation." The MFP faced a $10 million deficit because the 1972 legislature had failed to appropriate sufficient funds. The current funding formula also prevented local districts from meeting all their educational and budgetary needs. As a partial result, local school construction had stalled, resulting in a huge backlog. "And what of Florida's teachers?" asked Davalt. Public instructional salaries had not seen a statewide increase since 1968. Since that time, Florida's national ranking in teacher pay had dropped from fifteenth in 1969 to twenty-fifth in 1972. "The message is quite clear," she concluded. "Florida's educational system is losing ground."[20]

Before it could enjoy success in the legislature, the CCE had to avoid pitfalls that had doomed previous groups' recommendations. Past study groups had tended to make overgeneralized recommendations for broad educational problems. They had offered neither practical solutions nor realistic cost estimates. The 1947 study group, which recommended establishing the MFP, had published a seven-hundred-page report that addressed almost every aspect of education in the state. The report was so large and extensive that legislators, lacking full-time legislative staffs, neither understood it nor had the time to digest it. There were so many recommendations that legislators had no idea where to start. Spurred on by its own professional staff, the CCE made herculean efforts to keep its focus and present an understandable, succinct, yet far-reaching conclusion. If it failed to do so, warned one staffer, "this committee may become as inefficient as the ones which were held under Bryant, Sims, and Kirk." An unfocused study was risky, the aide wrote. "If it comes out with simply a set of generalizations about what we want for education, it will have virtually no effect at all." Askew and his aides urged the CCE to limit its recommendations to items that were within the purview of the legislature. School boards were naturally resistant to change. Methods of combating legislative resistance included being able to "price out" costs for each recommendation and to accompany each recommendation with an economic impact study. CCE chair Fred Schultz also began carrying with him "vest pocket" economic analyses to use when "push [came] to shove" in the legislature. Most of Schultz's old legislative friends agreed that the legislature had to be educated fully about the CCE's recommendations to guarantee their success. By late 1972, early drafts of the citizens' committee report were long and "tiresome to read." The drafts also requested large sums of money with no corresponding recommendations of revenue sources. The CCE had only three months to shape up its report or risk having it thrown on the reform program trash heap.[21]

Between February 19 and 21, 1973, the Florida League of Women Voters (LWV) sponsored a "Citizens' Conference on Education" in Tampa. Several task forces at the meeting reached divergent conclusions. One recommended retaining the MFP with some modification. Another concluded that the MFP had to go. All disagreed on how best to determine enrollment and per-pupil funding for schools. Another task force endorsed scrapping the MFP and following the CCE's recommendations. Virtually everyone agreed that private schools, especially those built to escape integration, should receive no public school funds. More than 215 people attended, including 25 legislators. There was some criticism of Askew's committee, including an assertion that it was too limited in scope. Askew, perhaps miffed that another education advocacy group was confusing the public in name and substance, remained silent about the meeting. LWV president Betty Staton reported that "everyone seems enthusiastic about what the [LWV] committee has done except the governor! I have seen no word from him regarding our recommendations . . . or the conference or no regrets that he did not get here." Even though Askew education advisor Claude Anderson attended the meeting, Askew refused to endorse league recommendations for fear of undermining the CCE.[22]

In early 1973, an ebullient Schultz sent Askew the CCE's final report. "We believe that the Citizen's Committee Report, if properly implemented, can move education in Florida into a position of leadership in the nation." Schultz thought that his committee, with much help from Askew, had provided an unprecedented means of changing the state's education system. It was not merely education they were changing, he asserted, it was the entire state: "In the long run you can do more for the people of Florida by setting up a system which will meet their education needs than any other program." CCE reforms would leave Askew's mark on the state, posited Schultz. "Your administration so far has been characterized by greater equity in taxation and an emphasis on the quality of life. Your crowning achievement would be the implementation of a program which would represent a dramatic step forward in the effectiveness of education in our state. Without your leadership it will not happen."[23]

By early 1973, the MFP was on shaky ground. Nevertheless, it had served the state well. Developed in 1947 by University of Florida education professor Dr. Roe Johns, the MFP was revolutionary for its time. Its primary objective was to assure a minimum educational quality in each county in order that each child would receive an "adequate" education. Under its formula, the state paid a determined amount per instructional unit of twenty-seven students. Local tax revenue of seven mills was deducted from that amount, however. It behooved local districts to assess property low in order to increase the state's contribution and resulted in widespread underassessment. Differences between counties in assessment could be enormous. In Glades County, one mill equaled $76.71 per pupil. In Gadsden County, one mill amounted to a feeble $6.95. The MFP's author never assumed that assessment would be so abused or varied.[24]

The MFP also restricted local districts from educational innovation. The twenty-seven pupil instructional unit encouraged schools to pair that many students with one teacher, thereby restricting unconventional teaching methods. That the MFP was cost centered led schools to focus on financial concerns and incentives rather than educational output. Some schools padded their attendance numbers in an attempt to raise their state share of money. In short, the formula had become "unnecessarily complicated." It underestimated educational costs, inhibited experimentation in the classroom, and failed to account for variances in education brought about by disadvantaged or disabled students. The death knell for this formula came when its creator declared that the principles upon which it was based were no longer effective and that the state would do well to "liberate" schools from the instructional unit method of financing education.[25]

Two landmark 1971 school funding cases also placed on unsteady ground any system that relied on property taxes for the bulk of school funds. In California, plaintiffs in *Serrano v. Priest* argued that California's method of funding schools, sole reliance on property taxes, made quality education a function of the wealth of the county in which a child resided. In short, a child's education was determined by "the geographical accident of the school district." A disproportionate number of black children lived in poorer counties and were deprived of quality education. This, the plaintiffs argued, violated the equal protection clause of the U.S. Constitution.

After several dismissals, the California Supreme Court finally found California's system of education finance unconstitutional. Likewise, *Rodriguez v. San Antonio (TX) Independent School District* addressed property tax inequity. Plaintiffs argued that the Texas Constitution guaranteed quality public schools and that the state's reliance on an unfair tax system violated this right. *Rodriguez* made it all the way to the U.S. Supreme Court, which refused to reverse prior state rulings against the plaintiffs. The court did not reject the plaintiff's case, instead deciding that the problem could best be solved in the state legislature. *Rodriguez* temporarily relieved pressure on Florida's reformers, but the issue would not go away. Several state courts had rejected exclusive property tax funding of schools, including those of California, New Jersey, Michigan, and Minnesota. Although these decisions did not directly threaten the MFP in Florida, which was "basically sound" with respect to any *Serrano*-type lawsuit, officials were nonetheless uneasy because this formula had failed to correct fully the imbalance between poor and rich counties. Terrell Sessums confessed to Askew that he would be surprised if pupil-rich, tax-poor counties such as Duval and Hillsborough did not quickly file suit against the MFP. He urged Askew and the CCE to "get rolling" on corrective legislation.[26]

Released in 1973, the CCE's final report, *Improving Education in Florida,* was half the length of its 1947 predecessor at 342 pages but outshone the 1947 study in importance and innovation. On its cover, the report quoted Jonathan Livingston Seagull, "We're free to go where we wish and be what we are," as a theme for what it believed education should do for the state. An "enlightened citizenry" was empowered to do whatever it wanted. In most respects, the committee's recommendations reflected the lofty ambitions of the governor and the expectations of the rest of the state. The report, which read as if written by Askew himself, reported that Florida's education suffered from a crisis of confidence. In 1971, only 37 percent of the public expressed confidence in public schools, compared with 61 percent who had done so in 1966. The question was, "How do we restore lost confidence?" "Children are not alike," asserted the report. "They cannot be taught with mass production methods. The community must become a laboratory where young people can learn firsthand from the society rather than about the society. In summary, the committee believes the people of Florida must understand that education is the most important function of state government."[27]

The report posited several broad conclusions about Florida's educational system. In terms of education finance, the wide disparities in local property tax rates found in other states did not exist in Florida. In 1973, annual district budgets revealed that all but twenty-three counties were at the state-mandated ten mill limit. The remaining counties had a total of only 125,905 students who attended schools in a system funded under ten mills, only 9.8 percent of the state's average daily attendance. More than 90 percent of Florida's schoolchildren attended schools in districts "within a fraction of the ten mill state mandated property tax limit." Although Florida had no glaring problem with rates, assessment was a difficulty. The state ranked thirty-ninth in local school revenue contribution at 38.3 percent of total education funds. The U.S. average was 55.9 percent. Florida also ranked a surprising fifth among southern states in this category. Similar to South Carolina and Alabama in this respect, Florida's millage rates were quite acceptable, but assessment at anything near real market value of property was a fantasy. The CCE also concluded that the MFP would "probably" meet a *Serrano* court test. In short, Florida's system of assessment needed a "complete overhaul." The MFP was "needlessly complex," and the state could clearly do more to fund education adequately.[28]

Following three broad guidelines (simplicity, receptiveness to special education needs, and seeking output-oriented solutions), the CCE recommended radical change in Florida's education financing. First, property tax assessment had to be "substantially strengthened and improved." The committee recommended a joint state-local assessment program to ensure that assessment came at full- or near-market value. Cognizant of the fact that full assessment, or anything near it, was difficult to attain, the CCE recommended that in those cases where full assessment proved impossible, all properties in a given class should at least be assessed equally. For habitual underassessing counties, the CCE suggested the state adopt one or more of three options: state-ordered reassessment; mandated millage increases; or state takeover of property tax assessment until the problem was corrected. In fairness to poorer public school districts and to end a tremendous backlog of needed school construction, the CCE called for the state to assume full costs of new construction and to absorb debt service for districts with outstanding obligations from recent construction. The committee also advocated that the state assume all transportation and retirement costs for districts. The CCE also wanted the state to recognize the fiscal crisis that had wracked the state's urban areas in recent years. Government costs had skyrocketed as tax bases dwindled. To meet this special need, the committee recommended applying a cost-of-living factor to any state educational funds targeted for these troubled areas. The committee recommended cost adjustments for certain grade levels and educational areas. For example, some grade levels were seen as critical years in child development. Early education (kindergarten through third grade) was most critical for nondisabled students. As opposed to receiving a flat amount, K–3 should receive the standard per-pupil expenditure multiplied by a factor of 1.3. Likewise, urban areas would receive the same type of adjustment. Education for disabled students should receive even higher amounts.[29]

The committee also had nonrevenue suggestions. Reflecting national trends of devolution evident in President Nixon's "New Federalism," the citizens' committee prescribed more local involvement and control. Citizen participation, the report reminded, had long been an outstanding feature of American education. The committee suggested strengthening such participation by establishing School Advisory Councils (SACs) for each school. These groups, composed of citizens broadly representative of the community, would assist principals and boards of education in development of school budgets, policy, programs, and personnel. Their primary duty, however, would be in assisting school principals in drafting annual reports of school progress. Such reports were designed to require each school to undergo annual self-examination and suggest areas of improvement. Publishing these reports fostered accountability at the lowest levels of school governance. The CCE also called for making the school a servant to the community: "The schools will come to provide a variety of social services as the school plant will be used for more than just education." Adult education, career education, programs for the elderly, and teaching English as a foreign language to migrant farm workers were but a few of these services. Direct interaction among adults, parents, teachers, and students made education more valuable and, to Askew, more relevant for Florida's children.[30]

After the CCE's final report was published and submitted to the legislature, Askew's staff identified key players vital to the success of the education package. Bob Graham and Jack Gordon, both education committee leaders in the senate, and Speaker Sessums, William Conway, and Kenneth MacKay in the house would determine how many of Askew's proposals would become law. Sessums fancied the idea of allowing districts more control of their money, likening it to a "home rule bill" for education finance. The "lump sum" approach appealed to many legislators who approved of removing the state from control of local spending to an evaluatory and advisory position. MacKay commented that "this is the first time we have consciously addressed the education policy questions in this state." His endorsement was good news to Askew and the CCE. So was Dr. Roe Johns's approval. The author of the MFP himself had recently joined the CCE in calling for a replacement of the system he had created back in 1947.[31]

Askew's address to open the 1973 regular legislative session echoed his general outlook and vision for the state. Florida should be a national leader in "assuming a greater share of school costs at the state level and insuring equal educational opportunities for all children, regardless of where they happen to live." He challenged the legislature to preserve what was good about education in the state but not be afraid of correcting what was bad. "If you meet it as the talented, dedicated, and capable leaders that I know you are," declared the governor, "we'll have good government in our state. And you will have earned the faith of the people one more time." Bold steps were required to make Florida a leader in education and government service. Askew quoted the famous twentieth-century French writer Anatole France: "To accomplish great things, we must not only act, but also dream, not only plan, but also believe, not only follow, but also lead." He explained that to make Florida a national leader required a solid and progressive educational system, responsive to needs of the state's children. "Be assured that I stand ready to work with you as we plan and dream and believe together in a better Florida for all people for all time."[32]

Even before his idealistic speech, Askew had a clear notion of how his package might fare. To save time during the legislative session, many committees met before the session began. The house education committee voted unanimously to scrap the MFP, a system that had become so byzantine that many legislators confessed never having totally understood it. Three days after Askew addressed the opening session, the senate education committee unanimously passed the finance portions of the CCE's report. Legislators were clear about one thing: the instructional unit of financing schools no longer worked for Florida. The state would hereafter fund education by the student. The new and highly simplified formula was easy to understand. The amount the state set annually to spend on each child was simply multiplied by the number of children in a district. Thrown into the mix were cost adjustments that reflected the belief that certain grade levels were more important developmentally to children than others. Early childhood education received higher amounts of money than higher grades, for instance. Special education and urban areas also received more money from the state. It was a long overdue admission that not all children were alike and that many children in the state had special needs. Askew's dream of an educational system responsive to the needs of *every* child was one step closer to reality.[33]

The state supreme court's ruling striking down tax ratio studies had a greater effect than most imagined. When legislators got down to the business of determining how to encourage equalization and proper assessment, they realized it was hard to craft a plan that would stand legal challenge. House speaker Sessums told Askew that the legislature was "seriously impaired" in its ability to allocate state funds, "particularly to cause the substantial equalization of public school financing." The legislature had to correct that problem as well as try to pass reform measures. Both Sessums and Askew preferred that the Department of Revenue play a "more vigorous and meaningful role to assure fair assessment." Still, the speaker admitted that given the department's recent history, it might be asking too much to require it to do so. He doubted the department's interest in performing such a role. An examination of the department itself proved Sessums's misgivings correct. The division of ad valorem taxation was the smallest division of the Department of Revenue, with only 75 percent of its forty positions filled and employees facing a tremendous backlog. Sessums told Askew that the two of them were in accord as to the inadequacy of the Department of Revenue and the need for fairer assessment: "Our state can no longer ignore either the need for equity between taxpayers or the need for assessment at just value. Low and unequal assessment may not have been very important when we only required three mills of required local effort from school districts."[34]

The finance portions of the CCE's proposals may have enjoyed smooth progress in the legislature, but other portions faced substantial opposition. Legislation establishing SACs met firm opposition in committee and from interest groups. No one supported SACs in the house education committee except Kenneth "Buddy" MacKay and William Conway, who resolved to make them more acceptable to opponents. School boards and principals' groups saw SACs as a challenge to their legal authority and political influence. Parent groups wondered whether SACs might become objects of local political patronage and exclude blacks, the poor, and other minorities. They were not so much opposed to SACs as in search of assurance that such bodies would be "broadly representative" of the community. Once the bill was amended to mandate such representation, virtually all opposition disappeared, save from administrators and school boards, whose collective voice became quite small when compared with parents and students.[35]

The most important bill of the session was the Florida Educational Finance Program (FEFP), and the legislature almost ran out of time needed to pass it. After the state supreme court invalidated ratio studies, the legislature ground to a halt, suffering through what the *Tallahassee Democrat* called a "tizzy" over losing what many saw as the state's best chance to attain equalization. Sessums and senate president Mallory Horne, a Democrat from Tallahassee, agreed to extend the regular session by one week in order that the FEFP bill could come up for a vote. They needed the extra time not to cultivate votes for approval but to work out a compromise between house and senate versions of the FEFP, which were separated by $100 million. Part of the deadlock came over how much money the state planned to pay per pupil, what amount the state should assign to "catch up" school construction, and what cost-of-living rates should be applied to needy urban areas. The struggle between house and senate was typical of Florida politics, as the house proposed and the senate resisted. One house aide remarked, "It's our offense against their defense, and they've got the best defense around." In those last desperate hours, five legislative committees worked into the wee hours of the morning to "crack the tough nut" and reach agreement. That so many legislators worked so strenuously to replace an education finance system that many southern states wished they had was a testament to Askew's political and public appeal.[36]

After reaching compromise between "tax rich" counties (Dade, Broward, and Palm Beach) and "tax poor" counties (Brevard, Duval, and Hillsborough) over required local effort for schools, the legislature cleared a path for the FEFP to become law. The legislature needed only one day to reach agreement, but it was a long day. Speaker Sessums remarked that "it will take us a day or two just to find out what we did during the last two days." Eventually, the house passed the FEFP 102-13, and the senate followed suit, 34-4. The "historic bill" completely changed the way the state funded education and viewed children. Funding schools at a base state rate of $587 per pupil, the legislature approved an education budget totaling more than $1.1 billion, including $324 million in required local effort. This was a whopping increase of $200 million over the previous year's budget and more than Alabama spent on elementary and secondary education fourteen years later.[37]

The legislature also gave the state Department of Revenue more authority to force local tax assessors to update their tax rolls and assess nearer to market value. The Department of Revenue was provided increased authority to audit county assessments. Legislation also established an assessment administration review board to hear appeals from county assessors as to the adequacy and accuracy of their tax roles. The FEFP also had the ability to help equalize by state support those poorer districts whose yield per mill (after assessment equalization) was low. The bill narrowed the current millage yield range, which varied from $11 to $99 per mill, by supplementing the yield of poorer districts with state money. The FEFP "power equalized" millage yields among districts for every mill over seven. That is, the plan guaranteed each district the same yield per mill over seven mills regardless of local property values. This legislation was designed to decrease the gap between millage yields of poor and rich districts by bringing the average yield per mill in poor districts to about $40. It was a deliberate effort not to punish schoolchildren then enrolled by working toward future equalization.[38]

SACs survived and became a crucial part of Askew's reforms. They assumed heavy responsibility in assuring that the school or schools they served remained accountable to the public. The citizens' committee gave SACs four primary duties: assist in the selection of principals; establish criteria for employment of new teachers; assist principals and school boards in curriculum development; and help principals prepare an annual report of school progress. The annual report of school progress was perhaps their most important task. Submitted annually, these reports forced schools to judge their success at increasing pupil effectiveness, innovation, and fiscal responsibility. SACs assisted principals in the drafting of such reports, designed as much to publicize school progress as to force a yearly self-examination by schools. School-based management was the key to Askew's plans for reform. A state-centered approach to education did not lend itself to fostering local accountability. School-centered organization of instruction strengthened the managerial role of the principal, who had the authority and latitude to make key instructional decisions without relying on the approval of administrators in Tallahassee. Other nonfinance measures established leadership training for administrators and board members, provided ample funding for community schools, and expanded health education programs. In all, the legislature made sixty-two changes in educational law.[39]

Legislative leaders took special pride in their success. Terrell Sessums described the session as "great" and "terrific" and concluded that "this is perhaps, in the field of education, the most important bill this legislature or any legislature has ever passed." The *Tallahassee Democrat* was less exuberant, judging the session as "fairly productive." The *Democrat* did note that it was a unique session in that both houses and parties eschewed political gain in rejecting tax cuts for the sake of education reform. Sessums defended the session, calling it the "highlight" of his career and insisting that "if it had done nothing more than enact the Florida Education Finance Act of 1973, this legislature would have done more than many state legislatures do in decades." Sessums added that this legislation would "really crack the nut" of properly financing education. Bob Graham and his staff shared Sessums's outlook. A Graham legislative aide told senate president Mallory Horne that the "landmark" FEFP "should be considered one of the great accomplishments of this legislature" and joined many legislators in hailing the FEFP as a model for the nation. A positively giddy education commissioner Christian declared that the 1973 session would "go down in the books as one of the highlights of Florida education history, surpassing even the achievements of the 1947 session which enacted the minimum foundation program." In education, Christian declared, "Florida has come of age."[40]

All the back patting in the legislature seemed to ignore one vital component in the success: the governor. The *Tallahassee Democrat* judged the session only a mild success but declared Askew the "legislative winner of 1973." "Reubin Askew has been out of the State Senate for more than two years, but if last week's legislative output is any indication, he's still got to be ranked as one of the most powerful legislators in Florida." Aside from his educational reforms, Askew had won other successes, including a bill to purchase Big Cypress Swamp to create a wildlife preserve, creation of a "little FTC" to end deceptive trade practices in the state, new anti-obscenity laws, increases in workers' compensation, and establishment of a statewide grand jury. In short, almost his entire program became law. Askew remained behind the scenes during the session, not wishing to antagonize fellow Democrats or "strong-arm" his legislation through the legislature. To remarks that he was relatively inactive during the session, Askew explained, "It might not have been obvious, but I was active." For most of the session, Askew remained in his office, listening to senate proceedings from a "squawk box," occasionally making the trip up one floor to the senate chamber to discuss a bill with a former senate colleague. Moreover, even if Askew himself did not appear active, his aides did. During the critical closing days of the session, gubernatorial aides camped just outside the senate chamber, canvassing legislators. As many as four aides at a time were seen lobbying lawmakers during the last two days. Many solons chalked up the governor's subdued approach to political seasoning. In the past, they explained, Askew's aggressive style had caused adverse reaction among lawmakers. Others said it was because Askew did not want to antagonize fellow Democrats before his 1974 reelection campaign. Senator Kenneth Myers, a Democrat from Miami, credited Askew's political savvy: "He's a very sensitive and politically astute man."[41]

As pleased as the governor was with the results of the 1973 session, he knew there was little likelihood of a repetition of his success. Askew had benefited from the 1967 reapportionment that enabled many young legislators to come to Tallahassee. Many became education advocates in the state house. Still, the future of liberal legislative leadership looked bleak. In the reapportionment shuffle, more than a few veteran lawmakers lost their seats in the following election. In 1972 Askew had campaigned hard for a solid Democrat majority in the legislature. That majority was key to his success. The 1973 session, however, had forty-three new faces and a visible lack of leadership. The session was a success largely because of Askew's popularity and the leadership of a handful of remaining liberal legislators. One of these, house appropriations committee chair and Miami Democrat Marshall Harris, complained that seasoned lawmakers were lost "en masse" to recent changes. He predicted a bleak future in terms of legislative experience and leadership: "Growth patterns and reapportionment are going to make for a nightmare. The legislative mortality rate is going to increase." Not only were legislators were getting younger, they were also more conservative. Harris counted himself among only seventeen "liberals" in the legislature. The presence of a youthful component in the legislature may have been what made Askew so successful. Veteran lawmakers, usually more independent, might have been able to resist Askew's strategies.[42]

In the years following implementation of the FEFP, there was no shortage of analysis of its impact. A 1976 study praised SACs and annual reports of school progress for expanding citizen participation in education policy formation. It praised the state for how far it had come since Florida teachers had walked off their jobs in 1968. This "watershed" 1973 legislation, the study concluded, placed the state on the road to reform. A 1978 analysis conducted by an independent consulting group declared that Florida witnessed more change in education in 1973 than at any time since 1947. School-based management was "working effectively in several districts and exceptionally well within a few." By 1978, twenty counties still lacked SACs, but 66 percent of districts with student enrollment of less than twenty-five thousand had SACs, as did 88 percent of districts with enrollment more than twenty-five thousand. SACs were the key to Askew's reforms. Placing responsibility for important decisions in the schools, not in Tallahassee, made accountability and efficiency possible. School-based management promoted equal educational opportunity by allowing educators to tailor educational programs to individual student needs. Local school control became more meaningful. Nonetheless, development of this ideal was uneven, the study reported. Some district boards and principals displayed reluctance in sharing authority and responsibility with SACs.[43]

The study group found the FEFP to be "sound in theory" but concluded that it could be "improved in practice." The group discussed the word "efficiency," an oft-used term in education circles, which usually meant obtaining an adequate education as cheaply as possible. The people who threw that word around, asserted the committee, usually advocated "imposing spending limits, on the theory that, if restricted in the amount of money available, educators will use funds more wisely." Florida, in contrast, had increased appropriations while fostering efficiency. Askew had shown that efficiency did not require budget cuts or maintenance of the status quo. The FEFP also greatly increased the equity of Florida's educational system. Since 1973 and adoption of the FEFP, Florida had kept pace with national educational spending trends. The study group advised a little "fine-tuning" but recommended no major changes. The state needed only to step back and allow local districts time and assistance in implementing the spirit of 1973. Askew's citizens' committee succeeded in "nearly spectacular fashion." In short, the "Governor's Citizens' Committee on Education has had a substantial, essentially constructive impact on education in Florida." An even later study called the 1973 reforms "one of the most important pieces of education reform law" passed in the 1970s. In 1976, Dr. Roe L. Johns, author of the MFP, declared that Florida's educational finance system was "almost fiscally neutral," ranking Florida among the top six states in the nation in the extent to which educational opportunity was financially equalized. A 1977 dissertation called the FEFP the "model finance law in the nation today."[44] So much had been done for the state's public education system that in 1974 it no longer appeared as a priority in the governor's or the speaker's legislative priorities.

When compared with Alabama and South Carolina, Florida's FEFP and other education reforms appeared even more progressive. In 1969, Alabama governor Albert Brewer passed one of the most far-reaching education reforms that state had ever experienced. The system Brewer implemented, however, was quite similar to the 1947 Florida MFP Askew replaced in 1973. South Carolina's John West ushered in a period of economic prosperity unprecedented in his state. Brewer was able to keep Alabama twenty-six years behind Florida's educational curve, and West brought about a reform-dashing affluence to South Carolina. In terms of education reform, Askew clearly led this group of reformers.

For Reubin Askew, education meant everything. Coming from a poor single-parent family, the governor had used public education to make his life a success. His dream for Florida was to craft an educational system that left no one out, white or black, rich or poor, gifted or disabled. There was nothing more valuable to the state's future than its ability to educate its children. In 1973, education appropriations absorbed more than 68 percent of the state budget. More than one-third of the state's population was directly involved in education, whether as students, parents, teachers, or administrators. If Florida and the South were to lead the nation into a new age of prosperity and racial reconciliation, it had to be done through education, Askew believed. When the state legislature reassessed the 1973 reforms five years later, the consulting group hired to do the job was impressed by the effect. The consultants observed an "attractive optimism," as well as "vigor, active dialogue, and genuine commitment regarding education in Florida." The report was no surprise to Reubin Askew. After all, it was Askew's vision to create an educational system that prepared the state to meet its future with great expectations of success and prosperity. The 1973 education reforms pushed by Askew provided Florida a chance to do something even greater—to lead the region in education reform.[45]

Reubin Askew clearly enjoyed a moderate racial situation in his state and a political condition that was ripe for reform. Calmer than Alabama in terms of racial tension, Florida evaded the great tumult that erupted in Alabama during the mid-1960s. As a result, Askew was able to speak his racial conscience more freely than Brewer and South Carolina's John West. Florida's relatively moderate racial condition also allowed Askew to spend less time fighting racial battles and more time on reform. What sets John West apart from the others is that he had to fight both racial and budget battles in order to put his state into a condition that would accept reform and integration.

PART III

John C. West of South Carolina

In 1977, Jimmy Carter, West's good friend and fellow New South governor, appointed West the U.S. ambassador to Saudi Arabia, a position he held from 1977 to 1981. West was an ardent supporter of Carter's successful bid for president. Courtesy the John C. West Collection, Modern Political Collections, University of South Carolina.

5

Forging a "New South Carolina"

The Aftermath of Integration

In 1949 V. O. Key described South Carolina as a state dominated by the politics of race. It rivaled Florida in political factionalism, wrote Key, yet whites were united by this singular issue. The civil rights movement drastically changed this situation. The 1965 Voting Rights Act increased the number of black South Carolina voters from 58,000 in 1958 to 220,000 in 1970. No one benefited more from this increase than John Carl West. Winning the last overtly racial statewide campaign in South Carolina history, West defeated segregationist Republican Albert Watson by almost twenty-eight thousand votes, his margin provided by black voters. Indeed, West garnered virtually all the black vote, except for several thousand that went to a black protest candidate. The 1970 election was a "clear test of the politics of race." Race baiting may have worked in Alabama and ended Brewer's moderate administration, but it failed in South Carolina. West's was a victory for racial moderates in the state and served as a positive culmination of three turbulent years in South Carolina race relations. During these years, the state had suffered the massacre of several South Carolina State University students in 1968, court-ordered public school integration in 1969 and 1970, and an attack on several black students by two hundred whites opposed to integration in the small town of Lamar. During his term West addressed the effects of such events, including school dropouts and pushouts[1] and flareups of violence. When West entered office, racial tension had never been higher. By the end of his term, relations between blacks and whites had never been better. West's moderate course in office played no small part in this reconciliation. His effort to make integration work led South Carolina into a new day in race relations.[2]

West may have benefited from an increase in black voters in the late

1960s, but he also received help from his moderate predecessors. Former governor Ernest "Fritz" Hollings, one of West's closest friends, blazed the trail toward peaceful integration in South Carolina when he allowed Harvey Gantt to become the first black student admitted to Clemson University in 1963. In his final, and probably most famous, address to the state legislature, Hollings declared that the time for resistance had ended. "We have all argued that the Supreme Court decision of 1954 is not the law of the land," said Hollings. He continued:

> But everyone must agree that it is the fact of the land. Interposition, sovereignty, legal motions, personal defiance have all been applied to constitutionalize the law of the land. And all attempts have failed. As we meet, South Carolina is running out of courts. If and when every legal remedy has been exhausted, this General Assembly must make clear South Carolina's choice, a government of laws rather than a government of men. As determined as we are, we of today must realize the lesson of one hundred years ago, and move on for the good of South Carolina and our United States. This should be done with dignity. It must be done with law and order. It is a hurdle that brings little progress to either side. But the failure to clear it will do us irreparable harm.[3]

As early as 1962, Hollings concluded that segregation's end was near and that legal defenses would soon "fall like a house of cards." "You might as well start preparing for the inevitable," he said. "We are not going to secede." Later that year three black students enrolled in the University of South Carolina for the first time.[4]

West also profited from the actions and leadership of Robert McNair, governor from 1967 to 1971 with whom West served as lieutenant governor. By 1969, a mere twelve of South Carolina's ninety-three school districts had permitted token numbers of blacks to attend previously all-white schools. In 1969, federal courts ordered Darlington and Greenville Counties to desegregate fully by February 1970. Although he decried such orders for "instant school desegregation" and wished for a slower pace, McNair chose not to follow the defiant lead of other southern states. Instead, he appointed a fifteen-member advisory board to work with business and community leaders to ease the transition to a unified system. McNair ordered state legal officials not to intervene on behalf of local school districts. He even went on statewide television and "emphatically" told viewers that the law would be enforced regardless of the bluster-ing threats of defiance from Senator Strom Thurmond and Congressman Albert Watson. "When we run out of courts and time," declared McNair, "we must adjust to the circumstances." By the fall of 1970, the entire state was under desegregation orders. With only minor acts of violence and localized flare-ups of anger and tension, the state began integrating its schools. McNair's stand in the schoolhouse door—not to block it, but to keep it open—set South Carolina on a relatively peaceful course toward full integration, especially when compared with integration battles in Ala-bama and Mississippi.[5]

As lieutenant governor, West stood out for his role as mediator of ten-sions surrounding the Orangeburg Massacre, the killing by panicked po-lice officers of three unarmed black college students as they protested a segregated bowling alley. When a delegation of students from Orange-burg's South Carolina State College arrived at the capitol to present their grievances to McNair, the governor refused to see them for fear they wanted to create an incident. They took their protest to the legislature, where West presided over the senate. When they raised a ruckus in the senate gallery, West had the group removed and decried their tactics. Still, he advised one of the group's faculty advisors, Rubin Weston, of a more effective way to present their protest. As president of the senate, West could allow a reading of their grievances if the students would submit to him such a list. The grievances were printed in the *Senate Journal,* and in an unprecedented move, West assigned the list to all standing committees in the senate for consideration. He then commended student leaders for following legal procedures to have their complaints heard. He explained to student leaders that "although the process of the law sometimes may seem slow, human experience over centuries has shown it to be the only effective means of human betterment."[6] He reminded them that it was not in his power to drop any charges that may have been issued for dis-rupting the peace during their senate gallery protests, but if students is-sued a written apology West would urge the city to reduce or drop the charges outright. West then appointed a three-member senate committee, including himself, to visit the college and report on its needs. It was the first time in the college's history that state legislators had visited the cam-pus. After the visit, West recommended a major bond issue for capital repairs, later implemented at a total of $6.5 million.[7]

West's actions on behalf of South Carolina State College students left a lasting impression. The college's student government president, Robert Scott, thanked West for his "courageous support of our attempt to bring our problem before the lawmakers of the state." Some whites in South Carolina were perplexed, however. One citizen wrote West that newspaper reports of his actions had to be mistaken, asking how his office could commend "radicals" for "riotous" behavior. Others called West a McNair "patsy" and asked when had state capitol facilities, the governor's and the lieutenant governor's offices, been "made available to the weekly meetings of the NAACP communist niggers."[8]

West's racial moderation predated the Orangeburg incident. In 1958, then state senator West condemned the Klan after it had beaten a white bandmaster who taught music at a black school. Klansmen threatened West's life, at one time even attempting to force his wife's car off the road. Mrs. West countered the threat on her husband's life by telling the local Klan leader, who happened to be their neighbor, that if John was harmed, she would kill four Klan members before sunup and that he would be one of them. West's speech at a testimonial dinner in South Carolina for NAACP leader Roy Wilkins also caused many to question his racial orthodoxy.[9]

By most accounts, South Carolina's reaction to *Brown* was relatively peaceful. The state had a history of reform, having supported populist demagogue Ben Tillman, progressive moderate Woodrow Wilson, and New Deal liberal Franklin D. Roosevelt, but race had always determined the limits of reform politics. Although South Carolina by no means willingly endorsed the *Brown* ruling and did not move swiftly to implement it, the reaction paled to that in other southern states. In 1956, the state's Association of White Citizens Councils met in Columbia to plot defiance and hear speakers such as Senator Strom Thurmond and Sol Blatt, speaker of the state house. Events in other southern states dampened South Carolina's fighting spirit, however. Little Rock's school crisis and the attempted prevention of black enrollment in the Universities of Mississippi and Alabama caused many in South Carolina to reexamine their position. Although it took nine years to desegregate public education, South Carolina's response to integration was quite mild compared with other southern states such as Alabama. One scholar has written that South Carolina's "evolution from total segregation to even grudging acceptance by whites of measurable racial integration" in this period "constituted a transformation of extraordinary proportions."[10] West's education commissioner, Cyril Busbee, opined that *Brown* was a "reasonable" ruling, that in terms of "sheer human rights, to say nothing of civil rights, there was no other decision you could come up with." Nonetheless, said Busbee, the 1955 pronouncement of "all deliberate speed" was taken in South Carolina to mean "well, take your time . . . but begin to look to see if there's something you can do." West was not so positive. He recalled that all deliberate speed "meant a hundred years" in South Carolina. Still, the state's desegregation process remained peaceful, if slow.[11]

In his brief inaugural address, given on a cold January day in 1971 before six thousand people, West promised a new direction in state government. In the three hundredth year since the state's founding, the new governor called on citizens to "view the past and the future with a new degree of sensitivity and perspective." He proclaimed a new spirit of unity within the state and declared that the time had arrived for South Carolina to "break loose and break free of the vicious cycle of ignorance, illiteracy, and poverty which has retarded us throughout our history." West promised that his administration would strive to eliminate hunger and improve housing and health care delivery. Above all, "we can, and we shall, in the next four years, eliminate from our government, any vestige of discrimination. . . . We pledge to minority groups no special status other than full-fledged responsibility in a government that is totally color-blind." It was a new day in South Carolina and the South, said the governor. The politics of race had been "soundly repudiated" in the election. To move ahead and bring the generations and races together required more than a mandate from government. "Basic to all our hopes and aspirations," said West, "is the willingness of our people to accept change, and to gain a new respect for the opinions and the rights of all people." Any lasting racial reconciliation, he concluded, had to be accomplished with minimal government interference. West knew he could not mandate that blacks and whites get along, but he could create an atmosphere in which both races might lose their mutual fear and misconceptions.[12]

Reaction to West's fifteen-minute address was generally positive. The former state field director for the NAACP, I. D. Newman, called the speech an "emancipation proclamation" and "a clarion call to all citizens from all walks of life for positive participation in state government." John Harper, president of the black-oriented United Citizens Party, said the speech sounded as if it had been written by a member of his party, not a white man from South Carolina. Present at the speech were various dignitaries from other states, including Governor John Bell Williams of Mississippi; Rosalyn Carter, wife of Georgia's own New South governor; Illinois lieutenant governor Paul Simon; and South Carolina U.S. senators Ernest "Fritz" Hollings and Strom Thurmond. The "Dr. No" of American race relations, Thurmond reacted to the speech in a defensive and self-incriminating manner. "Democrats have been in power all these years," said the former governor and relatively new member of the Republican Party, "and if there is any discrimination, they could have eliminated it. I thought discrimination had been eliminated. Certainly, I'm not in favor of discrimination." A more supportive Hollings stated that West "really talked like a governor leading his people rather than like the head of a militia defending them against Washington."[13] The *New York Post* praised West's address and noted the symbolic contrast in Thurmond's presence. "A public commitment to racial justice," wrote the editors of the *New York Times,* was "novel for a Deep South governor."[14]

One particularly nasty racial incident had caused many in the state to rethink their devotion to defiance of integration. It also eased white acceptance of integration and directly contributed to West's election. West's opponent, Congressman Albert Watson, had given a campaign speech in Darlington County in which he had called for citizens to defy court orders and fight school integration. On George Washington's birthday, before twenty-five hundred people at a "Freedom of Choice Rally" in Darlington County, Watson tried to rekindle a revolutionary spirit. He told the highly sympathetic crowd that their forebearers "were men who did not give up without fighting." He quoted the South Carolina state motto, *Dum Spiro Spero* (While I breathe, I hope). Watson then decried federal involvement in what he believed was clearly a states' rights issue. He assured the crowd that he was working with them to end such intrusion into the South and wondered aloud why he was the only state or federal official at the rally. He further implored Lamar's citizens to fight court orders implementing integration. "Every section of this state is in for it," warned Watson, "unless you stand up and use every means at your disposal to defend [against] what I consider an illegal order of the Circuit Court of the United States." It was alright to stand up against such orders, explained Watson, because "right is on our side."[15]

Days later, a mob of two hundred whites in Lamar, a small cotton and tobacco town in the northeast part of the state, blocked the path of two school buses on their way to recently desegregated Lamar High School.

Whites had boycotted the school since an initial desegregation order two weeks earlier. Aboard the buses were fourteen black students. After stopping one of the buses, the mob attacked it with baseball bats, axe handles, chains, bricks, and sharpened screwdrivers. Women in the crowd pulled wires loose from the engine while men rocked the bus until it turned over. They threw bricks through windows, injuring several black children, and pummeled the outside of the bus with their clubs. It was the worst outbreak of desegregation-related violence since the Supreme Court had ordered desegregation—and it could have been prevented. Several U.S. marshals on the scene as the mob attacked the buses refused to intervene because they maintained that they "were there as observers." State police also were present and initially failed to act because, as one said later, "we didn't want any bloodshed." When the police finally intervened, tense moments passed as each group leveled guns on the other. Tear gas dispersed the crowd, but not before several rioters struck police officers with rocks. The students were not seriously injured, suffering only bruises, scrapes, and small cuts. "I was scared to death," one student said, "but I'm going back to school." Governor McNair closed the school for several days until peace could be fully restored. District school superintendent Clifton R. Severence said of the whole affair: "Actually, it wasn't too much of an incident."[16]

Police charged twenty-seven men with inciting a riot. One of these, Jeryl Best, chaired the Darlington County Freedom of Choice Committee but disavowed any responsibility for the incident. Best had spoken to the mob shortly before it attacked the buses and later explained that they were "just fighting communism." After arraignment, the defendants left the courthouse to cheers of local residents. Many doubted the group would face conviction. "Ain't gonna find 12 white men in this county who'd convict those fellows," said cotton farmer Tom Smith. Others hinted at further covert action. "I don't think there'll be any more trouble," said one local, "not on the surface leastways. Remember, the raccoon goes hunting at night." Another person agreed, opining, "My idea of a good nigger is Martin Luther King." When schools reopened three days later, students were escorted by state national guard, military helicopters, and 125 state police wielding shotguns. Authorities turned back another crowd of fifty-five protesters marching toward the school after classes resumed. Black students seemed to handle the situation better than whites. One student who had been trapped on the bus said: "I'm going to keep coming as long

as they let me." "The people around here," asserted another, "should realize we're human beings."[17]

That was exactly what John West hoped the jury in the case would understand, that these students of a different color deserved the same consideration under law and in society as white students. An all-white jury
convicted three men of inciting the riot and sentenced them on March 10,
1971, almost a year after the incident and shortly into West's term as
governor. Jeryl Best, James D. Marsh, and C. D. Kirven, who "double-
sweared" his innocence, received sentences of between twelve months and
two years in prison in addition to a $1000 fine. The judge in the case, Wade
Weatherford, also warned that they would serve the maximum sentence
if any jury member was harassed. West said the verdict proved that justice was indeed color blind. He welcomed the positive ending as an example of how far South Carolina had moved from its racial past. "All South
Carolinians," said West, "have repudiated violence as a means of protest to
accomplish an end." One year later conditions at Lamar High School had
vastly improved, verifying, as the *Columbia State* asserted, that "integration
can work." Students and teachers reported that "everybody just made
friends," and there was no animosity between races. One of the bus riders
blamed parents. "If it had been left up to the students," he concluded, "it
would have worked from the beginning." The incident caused many in
South Carolina to second-guess violent defiance of integration. Furthermore, it definitely turned the tide in the gubernatorial campaign. Many
saw the moderate West as the only reasonable candidate.[18]

Other positive racial developments made many South Carolinians believe that West was correct about the state's changing race relations. The
election of a black student body president at the University of South Carolina, the first black elected to that position at any Deep South university,
and the introduction in the general assembly of legislation to prohibit racial discrimination in public schools proved that times were changing. West
also created by executive order the South Carolina Council on Human
Affairs (SCCHA) to work in conjunction with the governor's office in
the transition to unified schools. Consisting of twenty-one members appointed by the governor, this body mediated disputes and sought solutions
to problems that arose in the aftermath of integration, such as school violence, dropouts, and pushouts. West also warned the fifty heads of state
agencies that if they did not cooperate with the SCCHA in ending discrimination in employment and promotion practices, he would recom-

mend that the U.S. Equal Employment Opportunity Commission intervene. Two years later, West again warned agencies that were resisting
cooperation with the council. At a quickly called meeting, he bluntly admonished agency heads to follow the lead of the council, saying: "I don't
like the idea of the federal government having to come down and tell us
to do what we know is legally and morally right." West warned that if
forced to, he would tell federal authorities that "this is your baby."[19]

Many South Carolina black leaders applauded such bold steps. Shortly
after his inauguration, West met with leaders of eight of the state's major
human rights organizations, including M. Hayes Mizell, state chair of the
American Friends Service Committee, who came away from the meeting
impressed. The field director of the state branch of the NAACP, Isaac Williams, was skeptical but supportive in the early days of the administration,
noting that West had "said nothing to make me think he will be a crusader
for black people, but he was honest and not elusive." A few months later,
Williams was effusive: "It is my feeling that John West has done exactly
what he said he would do. He is one of the few governors to stay by his
campaign promises. He may become one of the best governors in our
state's history or perhaps the best in the South."[20]

The good feelings did not last. Mizell, a community activist and newly
elected member of the Richland County District One School Board in
Columbia, sharply criticized West's SCCHA, charging that it was a "toothless" organization and no more than a "first tenuous step" toward human
rights. Part of the reason for this criticism was West's veto of a $97,000
federal grant for Mizell's own South Carolina Council on Human Relations (SCCHR) to create a center to promote "quality integrated education." West declined the federal funds because he believed the SCCHR
would only duplicate efforts of his own SCCHA and other private groups
working toward the same goal. A furious Mizell fired off a letter to the
chair of the U.S. Senate Committee on Equal Education, Walter F. Mon-
dale of Minnesota. Mizell accused West of killing the grant "because he
believes it will be something which he cannot control nor which he can
effectively monitor." The chairman of the proposed Citizen's Center for
Quality Education, Samuel Hudson, said that West's apparent reversal in
his support for human rights was puzzling. Hudson believed that West
wanted to solve problems arising from integration, and he "thought this
was one avenue of solving the problem." Believing that when it came to
human rights, the more organizations working for them, the better, many

groups that had supported West signed a letter of protest to the governor. The National Organization for Women, the South Carolina NAACP, the South Carolina League of Women Voters, and the Mizell-led American Friends Service Committee all cried foul over West's refusal to accept the funds.[21]

Mizell's SCCHR was an ambitious group. Founded in 1957 and located in Columbia, the organization sponsored several projects, of which the Center for Quality Education was but one. It wanted to start local human relations committees to keep an eye on school systems and ensure that blacks did not suffer discrimination. The organization planned to develop a training model for school administrators to recognize the needs of black students and potential dropouts and to end the "old patterns of racism and paternalism" in South Carolina. Mizell himself never shied from controversy. Vocal in support of integration as a member of the Richland County District One School Board, he also soundly criticized busing opponents by mocking a 1971 advertisement in the *New York Times* by the Champion Spark Plug Company that showcased spark plugs used by buses for a private school run by Charleston's First Baptist Church. Mizell called this school a "private segregation academy" and exposed the contradiction of parents who opposed busing in theory while allowing buses to transport their children to a private school. "It is clearly not busing which is upsetting the patrons of the First Baptist Church," concluded Mizell, "it is race." If West and Mizell disagreed as to how quickly the state should move to correct human rights violations, they nonetheless agreed that such violations should be corrected.[22]

Desegregation in South Carolina was only slightly affected by the U.S. Supreme Court's ruling in *Swann v. Charlotte-Mecklenburg Board of Education* (1971). The court held that busing, balancing ratios, and gerrymandered school districts were allowable methods to achieve full school desegregation. Speaking for a unanimous court, Chief Justice Warren Burger held that "all things being equal, with no history of discrimination, it might well be desirable to assign pupils to schools nearest to their homes. But all things are not equal in a system that has been deliberately constructed and maintained to enforce racial segregation. . . . In these circumstances, we find no basis for holding that local school authorities may not be required to employ bus transportation as one tool of school desegregation."[23]

The order was expected to have very little impact on South Carolina, where ninety-three school systems were either under court order already or were using approved desegregation plans. Still, *Swann* meant that busing was no longer a last resort for desegregation. Reminiscent of Albert Brewer and *Davis v. Board of School Commissioners* in Alabama, West attacked this ruling. A supporter of neighborhood schools, he saw that avenue as the only one through which quality education could be achieved. During the campaign, West briefly attacked busing as a means of achieving racial balance and criticized the "social experimentation" and "short-sighted tyranny" of the Department of Health, Education, and Welfare. He also accused the federal government of usurping local authority and praised efforts in the 1970 general assembly to make busing illegal in South Carolina. West even argued that the state had to "fight to prevent the massive disruption of our public school system." Many of these outbursts came in response to Albert Watson's increasingly negative campaign. West wanted to show that he was not the liberal Watson depicted him to be. Later, West abandoned the court-baiting strategy because, as he told his aides who urged him to continue the strategy, if he "had to yell 'nigger' to get elected governor, he didn't want the job."[24]

West, like Brewer, feared other *Swann* consequences, the most dangerous of which was decreased public support of education. Already inadequately financed and in need of substantive reform, South Carolina public schools had taken quite a hit from the growth of private schools. In the fall of 1970, 11,400 students enrolled in forty-one new private schools in South Carolina. More than thirty-five thousand children attended the state's 139 private schools, 61 more than existed in 1964. By the 1971 school term, eighteen thousand more students had abandoned public education for fifty new private schools, with another two thousand estimated to follow in 1972. In Charleston, 12 percent of the school-aged population attended the city's thirty-one private schools. Public school enrollment there had actually fallen from 60,901 in 1968 to 59,812 in 1972. Enrollment in "segregation academies" (save for a handful of parochial schools) had increased to 8,421 in 1971, up from 6,906 in 1968. In Columbia, Richland County District One reported that 1,760 fewer whites attended the district's public schools. One school, Lyon Street Elementary, had become 77 percent black although it had been projected under desegregation orders to be 52 percent white.[25]

This was not good news for West in his search for a peaceful transformation to an adequately funded, unified school system. With South Carolina public school funding based on average daily attendance (ADA), decreases in enrollment only diminished state funding of local school systems. This meant trouble in South Carolina, one of the nation's five poorest states in 1972. Even without white flight, the effort to increase school funding was no easy task. The white exodus merely compounded the problem. A 1972 state educational finance study concluded that any undertaking to increase revenues was politically handicapped by "the flight from public schools in some of the communities of the state. Those making tuition payments to private schools are not enthusiastic supporters of taxes for public schools."[26] Private school development in South Carolina was nowhere near the "virtual abandonment" of public schools reported in Louisiana and Mississippi and fell well below Alabama, Florida, and Texas in the number of "segregation academies." Still, West considered white flight a "real danger." Claude Kitchens, Richland County District One superintendent, maintained that the issue was not a district problem but a community problem. "Combating white flight," said Kitchens, was "like trying to fight a wildfire." Like West, Kitchens believed that if white children fled from public schools, everyone suffered. Not only would resegregation occur (when a school became 30 to 40 percent black and would "tip" to all black) but also urban areas would lose their tax base. Because many blacks held lower-paying jobs, urban decay resulted. The way to combat white flight and its devastating results, concluded West and Kitchens, was to ensure that integration occurred peacefully and that educational quality improved after integration.[27]

The one consolation West and state officials took from *Swann* was that it added little to South Carolina's desegregation efforts.[28] There was a good chance that no further busing would be required, and the state would not face the threat of another Lamar riot. Because integration had become a matter of fact in the state, West's duty became clear. He did not have to convince the state that integration was necessary. Rather, his task was to make integration work, to guarantee that after blacks and whites arrived at the same school, nothing more than learning took place. He helped manage the way the state dealt with the aftermath of integration.

Integration in the Richland County District One school system with its thirty-eight thousand students highlights postintegration problems. That Columbians accepted the inevitability of school mixing without much protest was a major feat in itself. Still, a whole new set of problems faced West, parents, students, and administrators: how exactly should integration be implemented? Which schools should be closed and why? How did officials reconcile the vastly different educational experiences of white and black students? In enforcing court orders, HEW allowed Richland One to integrate in whatever manner it chose, as long as the ratio of white to black students remained 55:45. In an effort to make the transition as smooth as possible, the school board solicited suggestions from district parents. Two opposing parents' groups quickly formed and offered divergent plans, each designed to preserve as much of their neighborhood school as possible. "Parents for Pairing" represented white parents and students from Lower Richland High School. They suggested a pairing plan that demoted traditionally black Hopkins High School to a junior high school and left Lower Richland as the sole high school serving the district. According to its authors, this plan prevented school zone lines from being drawn across black and white sections of the district, which would have, in effect, sent half the white students to Lower Richland and the other half to Hopkins High. In short, the plan prevented white students from having to attend the black school, while forcing black students to abandon their school for the white one.[29]

Parents at Hopkins High rejected this plan, which forced students to abandon their school and its traditions, mascots, and memories. PTA president Alexander McRant said that he neither wanted an all-black school nor desired the maintenance of segregation, but he did want to preserve Hopkins High for the sake of his community, which had worked hard to improve it aesthetically and educationally. Integration was important, remarked McRant, but so was preserving neighborhood schools. McRant's group favored a zoning plan that not only preserved both schools and their ancillaries but also met the needs of a growing population in the area. Parents for Pairing president Sam McGregor replied that to keep both schools open and have zoning would only result in "white and black flack."[30]

District superintendent Kitchens was in a bind. Faced with the need to create harmony among both groups, he had several other problems to think about before recommending either option to the board and HEW. Kitchens realized that whites had left the district in large numbers, and if forced to send children to a formerly black school, even more would flee. On the other hand, black parents had accused him of favoritism toward whites, to which he responded that even though there was a hemorrhage in the white population, he had no intentions of "giving anyone a break." Still, Kitchens did not want the school district to "tip" and become all black, a sure result if the board accepted the zoning plan. The board, then, voted four to three for the pairing plan. Hopkins became a feeder school for Lower Richland High School. In response, a group named Parents for Displaced Students formed to represent the displaced children. The group contained a mixture of black and white parents, those from Hopkins High who had been moved to Lower Richland High and others, mostly white, who had been moved out of their schools and into formerly black schools such as Booker T. Washington High School in Columbia. Their appeal of the board's decision failed.[31]

The *Columbia State* lamented such a sweeping plan and reminded readers that even though the white group got what it wanted, a 55:45 ratio did not guarantee educational success or quality. Because the board trusted white Columbians to accept the plan, the *State* remarked, "they credit white Columbians with a far greater tolerance of massive integration" than seen elsewhere. The newspaper feared an exodus of white students and a loss of the "leavening influence" of racial diversity that had served Columbia well for so long, not to mention a decrease in tax base and property value. The *State* also pointed out that one of the unmentioned effects of school pairings and closings during this period was the loss of black high school traditions and culture. "There seems no logical reason," wrote the editors, "to erase the traditions of such former Negro high schools . . . by substantially diluting their student bodies with numbers of white students burdened with unhappiness." Although the *State*'s complaint was more about white unhappiness and less about concern for black school tradition, the paper made a point that blacks recognized as well. All too often when schools were paired, black schools suffered disestablishment or demotion. Black students were increasingly forced to give up mascots, team colors, fight songs, alma maters, and other traditions. In many instances, black students had to relinquish their traditions, assimilate into white schools, and accept white school traditions, even when those traditions celebrated the Confederacy. It was a major cause of unrest. Black high school traditions and customs were obliterated "for the sake of conservative whites' feelings." Black students had become intruders at worst, unwelcome guests at best, in these formerly white schools. In Greenville County three black high schools were closed, two others were demoted to junior high schools, and the black student population was forced to assimilate into a hostile atmosphere.[32]

A white high school student from Columbia, Richard Gergel, blamed white administrators for the problems experienced by black students. Active in Mizell's American Friends Service Committee, Gergel argued that many administrators were biased against black students, depicting them as hoodlums or educational ne'er-do-wells. At his high school in 1971, the first day of school was marred by a fight between blacks and whites. Administrators labeled the incident a "premeditated racial assault" and expelled the black students but declined to punish the whites. Gergel blamed both parties. Administrators at his school also changed extracurricular activities to daylight hours or canceled them altogether. Some schools in Columbia canceled proms to prevent mixing black and white students. Even more devastating, many black students were grouped by ability in the classroom and not given the educational attention they needed in order to succeed. "Tracking," as such performance segregation was termed, was a form of intellectual segregation. Gergel reported that in the summer before the integrated school year, many white parents filled their children's heads with old racial myths and sexual misconceptions that made an already tense situation worse. At the same time black parents were either communicating inferiority to their children or telling them not to "take anything" from whites. Effects of the dual system gradually caught up with those black students who were lucky enough to survive initial integration. What resulted were dropouts and pushouts.[33]

In January 1971, West explained his view of "quality education" for the *South Carolina Education Journal.* He wrote that in the nostalgic "never-never" days, education was simple: the three "r's" ruled, and if one were not academically inclined, then there was a plethora of low-skill jobs. West declared this nothing more than educational fiction. The only system of education he knew about included segregated schools that "wound up rejecting more students than [they] served." This type of education believed in "the best education for the best student." As late as 1968, more than half the students who started first grade in South Carolina failed to graduate. West believed that public education could no longer serve primarily the best and brightest; it had to become more inclusive. In short, West argued that quality education had to include "the best education for all students, whatever their capabilities and inclinations." By 1969, though West reported that the dropout rate had fallen below 50 percent for the first time in state history, integration jeopardized the decline. Inability to meet the needs of disadvantaged black students in a hostile atmosphere was the most pressing problem because they were more apt to leave school for lack of educational tutelage.[34]

In 1971, West started a major effort to decrease dropout rates. Just a year before, the state had witnessed more than twenty-five thousand dropouts directly related to the elimination of dual educational systems. State graduation rates had improved but still barely rose above 50 percent. Many of the more recent dropouts lived in rural areas, and a high percentage, approximately 75 to 90 percent, were black. Many of these were female. They had either dropped out or had been pushed out of schools because of disciplinary problems. They were victims of the state's general "maladjustment" to the needs of integration-era students. "The young person (usually black) who is permanently expelled from the public school," said West, "will unquestionably become a social outcast. He is the future criminal, rioter, and trouble maker, or at best, a future welfare recipient." To meet this crisis, West began Project Helping Hand, coordinated by South Carolina State College in Orangeburg, site of the 1968 student massacre.[35]

With $90,000 seed money provided by HEW, West started the pilot program in the summer of 1971. An intensive six-week effort to return students to the classroom, the program allowed them to make up missed work and also deal with their personal and discipline problems. Project Helping Hand had three simple objectives: allow students a chance to earn (or make up) up to three credits toward graduating; provide them with a stronger sense of self-worth and self-identity; and ensure that a majority of the students returned and remained in school. Three colleges participated in the pilot program that summer: Columbia College, which served thirty-two live-in students; the College of Charleston, which taught seventy commuter students; and Sumter's Morris College, where sixty-six live-in and commuter students received instruction. The dropouts came from four surrounding counties, Kershaw, Clarendon, Sumter, and Lee. For a short time Wofford College considered participation but finally declined on grounds that the time and money necessary to set up such a program was lacking and that other institutions might be better suited for such service. Wofford president Paul Hardin II told South Carolina State College dean A. I. Mose as much when he recommended that black colleges "may be able to gear up for this kind of program much less expensively."[36]

To save money on instructional staff, West used teachers already scheduled for summer training. The summer pilot program was a great success, as all 168 (103 female, 65 male, 34 whites) students returned and remained in school the next year after receiving instruction in social studies, math, and English. The only drawback associated with Project Helping Hand was a lack of money to fund the program. More than 585 students applied for the pilot program, which originally planned to accept 400 per year. Funding problems limited the pilot program to only 166 students. In September 1971, West appealed to HEW secretary Elliot Richardson for $370,000 in additional funds for the project. Richardson explained that HEW had a total of only $420,000 available for the entire state. Instead, Richardson awarded Project Helping Hand about $100,000 in HEW grants for the next two years. At the 1971 Southern Governors' Conference, West hailed the program as one way of addressing postintegration problems. It was important that public education meet the needs of all students during the difficult period following integration. Effects of the dual system would be seen for years to come and would continue until the state adapted to particular problems of disadvantaged students. "We cannot, and we must not," said West, "give up on a student simply because he, or the system, fails to come to terms in their first encounters." West told fellow governors that dropout problems were just as dangerous as segregation itself because an integrated public school system was no good if it could not retain its students. Said West, "We cannot afford to have them expelled to a life of mediocrity."[37]

Project Helping Hand was a classic example of how West planned to help the state move to a unified educational system. It was considered "the South's most progressive remedial education" program. Not everyone praised him for it, however. Some accused the governor of not doing enough. One critic in particular, M. Hayes Mizell, ridiculed the phrase "quality education," likening it to another overused but meaningless expression, "law and order." Mizell said both phrases were nothing more than empty clichés meant to assure whites that schools would not suffer from integration. Mizell accused the state of failing to address issues that caused black students to drop out in the first place: ignorance of black needs; discipline that always seemed to fall heaviest on blacks; and an assumption that black students had not the capability to learn nor contribute to society. Mizell criticized the state for reacting to problems instead of preventing them.[38]

West tried to address these issues in part by starting Project Helping Hand and by organizing the state's first human affairs commission. Mizell misunderstood West's commitment to maintaining order and discipline. It was a key component in West's efforts to sustain an orderly integration process. He believed that blacks had to have confidence that their children would not be attacked as in Lamar. In addition, whites wanted assurance that so-called hoodlums and militants, whom they characterized as black, would not disrupt "quality education." In many respects, strict discipline countered the arguments of integration foes, many of whom believed that segregated schools had no discipline problems. Opponents of integration argued that teachers in a segregated system need not waste their instructional time in order to break up fights between black and white students, that teachers could not teach and maintain order at the same time. Guaranteeing law and order was West's attempt to remove this justification for leaving public schools.[39]

West also criticized busing as a means of school integration. As lieutenant governor, West had supported legal appeals of desegregation orders that mandated busing. During his gubernatorial campaign, he had confused many as to his position. On one hand, West had condemned busing. On the other, he decried Watson's Darlington County speech and the subsequent Lamar riot. He had explained that appealing a court ruling was a "far cry from the events which transpired in Lamar." Nevertheless, he did not want the state to "willingly surrender to unreasonable demands of Washington bureaucrats." West had supported integration strongly but was "completely against busing except where it is an absolutely necessary tool." Nor did he support bombastic attacks on federal courts after they had made a decision. West's reputation became sullied outside the state among busing opposition groups because of his moderation. He walked a fine line between court bashing and total acceptance of integration.[40]

Many people wrongly equated West's moderation with outright liberalism. A group of mothers from Mobile, Alabama, walking their way across the South toward Washington D.C., stopped in Columbia on October 11, 1971. Representing an anti-busing organization called Concerned Citizens of Mobile, they wanted West to sign their anti-busing petition. Dressed in red, white, and blue, they were stopped by state police upon entering the state house and told that their signs and placards were not allowed in the governor's office. Upon entering the governor's office, they learned that West was out of town. They asked press secretary Kelly Jones to sign for the governor. When he refused, they asked him to sign as a private citizen. Jones declined on the grounds that the petition was first offered to him in an official capacity. The leader of the group, Edna Wade, turned to her fellow walkers and asked, "Would you girls believe you just got a lot of political double talk?" One responded, "I think it's snowing in South Carolina." Through Jones, the women learned that a sympathetic West had a policy of not signing petitions, believing that such overtures and protests only diverted him from upholding the law and tended to foster dissent and disruption in schools. He refused to join Lester Maddox, Jimmy Carter, and George Wallace in signing the petition.[41] The women suspected as much, they said, as they had been told before leaving Alabama that South Carolina had "the most liberal governor in the South."[42]

At the September 1971 National Governors' Conference in San Juan, Puerto Rico, several southern governors (including Wallace, Carter, and Winfield Dunn of Tennessee) offered resolutions condemning busing and calling for impartial treatment of the South in desegregation. Two resolutions were brought up in committee, one by Wallace and a moderate resolution cosponsored by Jimmy Carter and the Republican Dunn. West supported the Carter-Dunn resolution because it "called for impartial treatment throughout the U.S. and affirmed the sense of what all responsible governors wanted." It also advocated an end to discrimination, but not through busing, and a defense of the neighborhood school concept. West's use of "responsible" was a dismissal of Wallace's more militant resolution. His own resolution, said Carter, "would not embarrass any governor." Neither made it out of committee.[43]

In November, at the Southern Governors' Conference in Atlanta, Wallace and Carter again submitted resolutions condemning busing. The Carter resolution, which included a proviso that praised a recent resolution passed by the U.S. Congress that sought to ban federal funds to bus students, was voted out of committee. Maryland governor Marvin Mandel suggested that this resolution be amended to rephrase the proviso of praise. He explained that some school districts were under strict court orders to bus and that such a resolution would be unfair to them. At West's suggestion, they amended the resolution to say that Congress's action was a good "first step" in the restoration of neighborhood schools. They also stated that the act would be meaningless if enacted in the absence of a "single national policy" for desegregation "uniformly applied by all branches of the federal government." This subdued resolution reflected the governors' desire not to repeat the conference splitting that busing caused in 1969 and 1970. It also represented a mood shift in southern politics away from blustering about busing to more substantive issues. Most of the resolutions proposed at the 1971 conference were passed, even some of Wallace's, to which he remarked: "I'm not used to that."[44]

Despite continued pressure on West from anti-busing quarters, he continued in his moderation. If asked, West agreed that busing was not the right way to desegregate.[45] Yet in the end, he argued, the law was the law, and he would enforce it. West committed himself to doing all within his power to preserve school order. But he refused to jump on Wallace's soapbox and make an issue out of something that had long been decided. He agreed with Hollings that South Carolina had run out of courts and time. The only thing left to do was make the transition peaceful.[46]

Nowhere was West's commitment to order and nonintervention more evident than in his reaction to violence in Columbia schools during the spring of 1972. By many accounts, racial conditions in public schools had improved after 1971. Only occasional outbreaks of violence occurred. At Lower Richland High School in 1972, however, what started as a black student protest erupted into an all-out racial incident. Black students complained about a lack of due process given one black student after he allegedly made "ugly comments" to a white girl. Although it was later discovered that the white girl had provoked the incident, the black student remained expelled. Black students refused to go to class, congregating in the lunchroom until the principal heard their grievances. According to one black student, as they discussed their problem with Principal J. C. Bales, ten to fifteen white students entered the lunchroom with sticks. White students explained that they only wanted to watch and that a black student had brandished a knife at them. Whatever the cause, a scuffle ensued. At the same time, four black students at Dreher High School in Columbia were charged with attacking a teacher. Both schools were closed until the situations improved. Rumors spread to other Columbia schools that blacks from the closed schools were milling about on other campuses. The board of education closed all schools until passions cooled. At Keenan High School no such tensions arose, for the student body had established "rap sessions" weeks earlier to prevent such incidents.[47]

West responded firmly and swiftly to the disorder by personally appealing to students to "cool it" and help "restore a spirit of harmony within our schools." "There must, and will be," declared West, "order in our schools." He then met for two hours with the SCCHA to determine how best to restore order and maintain discipline. After concluding that the disorder was not part of a planned disruption, as many thought, members of the advisory group decided to stand aside until local authorities asked for help. The committee decided to survey those schools that had suffered no disruptions to determine a solution that might help disrupted schools. West announced that "while the basic responsibility for education, including the maintaining of order, is a local responsibility the full power of the state stands ready . . . to preserve order in our schools." The *Charleston Evening Post* hammered West for allowing the Council on Human Affairs to address school disruptions. It was like letting the fox guard the chicken coop, explained the *Evening Post*. The black chairman of the council, George D. Hamilton, would devise solutions "so heavily laced with black chauvinism even Mr. West may not be able to stomach them." Schools remained closed for the remainder of the week and opened the following Monday with no disruption. Such disturbances, concluded West, were merely growing pains associated with the end of dual educational systems. For the governor to become directly involved would have only heightened the exasperation of the moment and made a minor problem a statewide concern. The next fall, schools opened relatively peacefully and quietly, just as state leaders expected. Local disruptions that newspapers reported regularly on the first day of school in past years had all but disappeared by 1974.[48]

By the end of West's term in office, race relations in South Carolina had never been better. Despite persistent rumors of black militancy, knifings, extortions, violence, and victimization—all the standard racial stereotypes—South Carolina schools integrated peacefully. Desegregation in South Carolina occurred rather quickly once it actually began. In 1969, only 15 percent of black students were enrolled in white schools. By 1971, 93 percent of black students attended formerly all-white schools, and 99 percent of white students attended desegregated schools. All over the state, the racial reconciliation West had predicted in his inaugural had actually taken place. Many schools picked new fight songs, mascots, and colors to replace Confederate symbols. One high school changed emblems on class rings from the rebel flag to the state seal. In another case, a group of black parents that had vehemently protested the name of Strom Thurmond High School in Edgefield dropped its objections. If anything, concluded the

Charleston News and Courier, this singular incident revealed a maturation of race relations and a sign of Thurmond's growing popularity among blacks, something he began to cultivate after his 1970 embarrassment. Several circumstances made integration in South Carolina smoother than in other states. First, West's predecessors, Robert McNair and Ernest Hollings, had made the initial assaults on segregation and had appealed to South Carolina's conscience. Next, West's commitment to retaining order assured blacks and whites alike that the law would be enforced. He was helped by state law enforcement director J. Preston "Pete" Strom, who seemed to always know what the Klan and other militant groups were up to before many in the groups knew themselves. Strict law enforcement was an important factor in keeping tensions low, for parents and students could reasonably assume that shenanigans on either side would not be tolerated.[49]

John West's role in fostering a new day in South Carolina race relations was crucial. In 1970, the state faced a crossroads. It could choose either to follow George Wallace's path by electing the segregationist Albert Watson or to continue in its racial moderation. Voters realized that to elect Watson meant that incidents such as Lamar might become the norm. South Carolina took a bold step, helped in large part by newly registered black voters, and sent a racial moderate to the capitol in Columbia. Although considered one of the weaker governorships in the nation in terms of the prerogatives of state power, South Carolina under West followed a commonsense approach. He did not let emotions rule the day and preserved as much as possible the separation of state and local governments. West realized that he could not mandate racial harmony from above. Solving integration problems and improving race relations required a local effort. West stayed out of the picture unless needed. In the meantime, he proposed solutions to help those who had been pushed out of the public schools because of integration and guaranteed that schools would remain safe for both races. He enjoyed no small success in both endeavors.[50]

Still, by 1974, West was criticized by some of the same people who had praised him in 1971. Isaac Williams said that West's administration was "marked with rhetoric and tokenism." He accused West of demoting staffers who took strong advocacy positions and of being generally unsympathetic to blacks. Those blacks whom West had appointed to prominent positions had been relegated to the background and ignored, charged Williams. "The ebony suite is now the lily-white flower garden," he complained. Williams's criticism was shortsighted and failed to acknowledge

West's willingness to let the state Council on Human Affairs devise its own solutions to school disruptions, his commitment to end poverty and inadequate housing among South Carolina's poor, and his record on race.[51]

In 1974, West reflected on the move to unified schools. "If anything," he said, "our experience in adapting to the unitary school system has expanded our horizons, and broadened our concept of the educational function." He touted Project Helping Hand as one new way of solving problems inherent in unifying schools. West was proudest of improved racial relations in the state and marked this development as one of his greatest accomplishments. In the past, he said, blacks would come to his office to discuss what the state could do to help poor blacks. Now, he said, they wanted to discuss how to help middle-class blacks. What made West proudest was that such improved relations were not the product of a federal or state mandate. They came through a process of acclimation, through working out problems in local schools, city hall, and civic clubs. Racial harmony developed without his direct intervention, and it convinced him that because it had developed at such a personal level, this goodwill would last a long time.[52]

As he left office, West was generally praised for his moderate approach. Normally Republican and conservative, the *Columbia State* exalted South Carolina's move from the Solid South to the New South, giving much credit to West. "We much prefer this New South thinking and goals," wrote the editors, "to the moonlight, magnolias, and political hell-raisin' that characterized the old Solid South." Under West, reported the *State*, South Carolina had made "major advances in the economy and race relations." A close friend of West's and publisher of the *Kershaw County Record*, Fred Sheheen, broke a self-imposed policy of not commenting on the political fortunes of friends. He could not help but "salute a friend who has demonstrated superior moral courage and political fortitude that must not go unheralded." He praised West for exhibiting a notable "display of leadership and conscience among government officials." West was successful, said Sheheen, because he chose to abide by his deep personal convictions, "for who can quarrel with a man who listens to his conscience?"[53]

West's last address as governor, one day before his successor, Republican James Edwards, took office, spoke of the past and looked to the future. "As we have broken that cycle of human deprivation," reported West, "so we are now moving to free the spirit of South Carolina from the bondage of limited expectations." The state had advanced because of "partnership, teamwork, and mutual understanding," which had become the "heart of progress at all levels" between races, sexes, generations, and classes of the state. Such was the essence of West's governing style. He chose to let people work out problems on their own, to leave matters in local hands, unless state intervention was absolutely necessary. He stood ready to provide support and encouragement, or the state police, when situations dictated. It made him proudest that such progress and social change were not forced "but came instead as the natural creation of a state at peace with itself." He then predicted what his administration would be remembered for: "If there is a legacy to which this administration and this generation can be said to leave to future South Carolinians, I like to think that it is a new South Carolina, forged from the efforts of all, excluding the rights of none, and respecting the individual dignity of each individual citizen."[54]

West was not the most progressive New South governor. In many respects he matched the restrained moderation of Albert Brewer rather than the outspoken racial views of Reubin Askew. Both West and Brewer advocated neighborhood schools and disliked busing, whereas Askew supported busing. All wanted to move beyond the politics of race. West and Askew had the benefit of moderate predecessors to make their task easier; Albert Brewer clearly did not. John West's moderate style perfectly suited South Carolina's changing political nature. In one respect, West personified South Carolina's transformation from secession leader to peacefully integrated state. In another respect, West's administration was a major stimulus of that change. One thing is clear. West helped usher in one of the most peaceful and prosperous periods in South Carolina history.

6

Sunbelt to the Rescue

Education Reform in South Carolina

John West believed South Carolinians should work out their race problems for themselves, but he thought differently about education reform. A vocal advocate of what he called quality education, West wished to make South Carolina education worthy of its citizens and suitable for the state to attract industrial investment. The state, said West, had to develop "the best education for all students." It also had to pay its teachers better. West was hamstrung by the past, however. Before leaving office, his predecessor, Robert McNair, had cut the state budget by 6 percent to prevent an expected $16 million budget deficit for the first part of 1971. West had also campaigned on a no-tax pledge that he soon found harder to keep than promise. He was faced with increasingly militant teachers and an equally obstinate legislature, and his hopes for significant educational reform seemed doomed. He found deliverance in the state's industrial development, which provided enough revenue during his term to fund education properly without painful tax increases. Yet the windfall that resulted from industrial development also dampened interest in significant reform. Because the state seemed inundated with new wealth, many believed property tax and education finance reform could wait. The surge in revenues prevented him from tackling the state's glaring educational deficiencies. West became the only one of the three New South governors in this study not to implement, or propose, substantial educational reform. Albert Brewer and Reubin Askew passed breakthrough reform legislation; John West simply made his state unbelievably affluent. Not until the mid-1980s did education in South Carolina undergo a major reform effort. Then, it came at the hands of Democrat Richard Riley, a member of a second generation of "New South" governors. Even though West did not completely address all of South Carolina's education problems, he at least set the stage for future successes by helping turn the state's economy around.[1]

In 1971, the state's educational system was in bad shape. Chronically underfunded, South Carolina schools also suffered high dropout rates. In 1969, the state's dropout rate finally fell below 50 percent for the first time in state history. Nonetheless, integration threatened to make that figure climb again. Expenditures per pupil in South Carolina ranked below most states and were 25 percent below the national average. South Carolina teachers were also underpaid. In 1971, South Carolina teacher salaries on average fell 25 percent below the national average and 10 percent below North Carolina and Georgia. As in Alabama, many teachers trained in South Carolina universities left the state for greener pastures. The University of South Carolina reported that 54 percent of recent teacher education graduates left to work in other states, and more than 13 percent of current teachers left the profession in 1970 and 1971 because of low pay.[2] It was clear, one state study concluded, that as one of the five poorest states in the nation South Carolina was "economically disadvantaged" and could not hope to fund education as its neighbors had.[3]

The reason for this economic quagmire lay in the state's tax structure, which taxed its citizens lower than the national average and below even its neighbors. In 1971, South Carolina collected forty-one dollars per capita in taxes, only 1.3 percent of personal income, against a national average of sixty-nine dollars. Sales taxes, especially those on food (4 percent), were oppressive, the ninth highest in the nation. Property taxes were the most "conspicuously underdeveloped and glaringly abused element in the South Carolina revenue system." State officials might have found it easy in nonelection years to raise sales taxes, but few dared even to suggest reforming state property taxes. The only local source of revenue for local governments, the antiquated property tax system had been studied in past years by the legislature.[4] Indeed, committees formed in 1920, 1930, 1948, 1951, 1952, 1957, and 1958 by the general assembly all had reached the same conclusions: property taxes in South Carolina were underassessed, and inequities from county to county were significant. Nearly all the committees had concluded that the state needed some centrally established and supervised authority to aid in property assessment and real property taxation. In 1960, the general assembly had created the State Tax Commission to review these recommendations but failed to give it power to force equalization. Even with its toothless mandate from the legislature, the tax commission had authority to review assessments and valuations on appeal, but the commission had never acted on its own initiative. The commission did try in 1967 to encourage assessment at 10 percent of market value statewide in an effort to equalize taxes. The state constitution called for property to be assessed at 100 percent of market value. But the 1967 overture, like many others before, fell on deaf ears.[5]

Because most assessment and review systems existed at the local level, local tax assessors bore most of the blame. Local assessors faced several factors that prevented them from equalizing or fairly assessing property in their counties. Largely undertrained and understaffed, local assessors also could not, or would not, handle the wrath of taxpayers whose assessments they increased. They were also unprepared to respond to the state's rapidly changing economic landscape from agriculture to industry, the growth of state infrastructure, and increased business development. It was no wonder that South Carolina's average assessment of real property was the lowest in the United States. In the state capital, Columbia, the effective tax rate on real property was 1 percent.[6] In 1962, the national average for property assessment reached 30.6 percent. In South Carolina, that rate was only 5.8 percent, making it one of three states in the nation with an assessment average of under 10 percent. A 1938 Clemson University study revealed that property with an acreage value of ten dollars or less was assessed at 52 percent of market value, whereas property worth more than a hundred dollars an acre was taxed at 12.7 percent. Not much had changed since that study and the 1970s. Ironically, for all its deficiencies and desperate need of reform, the property tax played a minor role in funding schools. Because the state funded some 70 percent of school costs, South Carolina was not threatened by recent court rulings in California and Texas that ruled that disparate property taxes were an unconstitutional method for school funding. South Carolina's deficient property tax system symbolized a missed opportunity for increased school funding, something that did not go unnoticed by education advocates.[7]

The most pressing and visible education problem during West's years was teacher salaries. In 1970 he campaigned long and hard on the need for quality education, focusing his attention on teacher salaries as a particularly conspicuous example of the state's reform needs. West did not want to raise taxes to accomplish this goal, however. Ruling out tax increases left several other options for raising teacher salaries. In a position paper he sent to South Carolina Education Association (SCEA) executive secretary Carlos Gibbons, West highlighted three plans, including earmarking for education a large portion of funds expected from President Nixon's proposed revenue-sharing plan (almost $50 million). He also wanted to establish a system of regular salary increases based on a combination of cost-of-living adjustments and the natural growth of the state economy. This system, said West, would keep teachers from having to beg for more money each year. He also desired to earmark funds from his proposed escheat law that would claim dormant bank accounts and unclaimed property. West believed that with "proper leadership" South Carolina could both improve education and go well into the decade without raising taxes.[8]

West withheld one bit of information from Gibbons. During the McNair administration in the late 1960s, several industries had relocated to South Carolina, attracted mainly by low corporate tax rates (6 percent), "tax honeymoons" of up to five years, and an aggressive state industrial development board established by McNair. West realized that many of these tax honeymoons were fast approaching their end and that a deluge of new tax revenue was set to fill state coffers. West hoped to use much of this windfall for education reform. Still, he needed time for the money to roll into Columbia, something South Carolina teachers were not willing to concede.[9]

Early in 1971, Gibbons and the SCEA turned up the pressure on state leaders by announcing an ambitious legislative program. The plan called for almost $52 million in increased funds for education, including $40 million in salary increases, property tax equalization, and more money for the state's fledgling kindergarten program. The SCEA also wanted to change the way the state funded schools. As it stood, school boards formulated budgets based on average daily attendance (ADA). Too volatile a gauge for funding schools, ADA was prone to cause underbudgeting. Determined by taking the average number of students present in school over a given period, ADA was subject to fluctuations due to absences caused by illness, school disorder from integration, and suspensions. Gibbons wanted the state to use average daily membership (ADM), or the average number of students enrolled in school for a given period (a figure that was not affected by absences). More stable, ADM meant higher budgets. In 1969, ADA was only 94.3 percent of ADM. In a state as poor as South Carolina, this difference was significant.[10]

That 45 percent of beginning teachers left the state and that more than fifteen hundred people living in South Carolina had master's degrees in teacher education but chose not to teach led Gibbons to conclude that South Carolina suffered from an educational crisis. He called for the general assembly to end the hemorrhage by raising teacher salaries by $1,500. In waiting for the state to bring education into the seventies, Gibbons warned, teachers had developed a "threadbare patience." Between 1958 and 1968, the state had increased teacher pay by almost 80 percent, ranking thirteenth nationally in a ten-year effort at funding schools. Inflation made the real effect of this increase only 38 percent, however. A 1970 survey revealed that 64 percent of state teachers believed that they should have struck for higher pay in 1969. More than 80 percent of them blamed the legislature for their salary woes.[11] In the past, complained Gibbons, legislators had used "evasive tactics" to stall meaningful reform, such as requiring teachers themselves to suggest alternate methods of financing raises. In 1971, the SCEA came prepared. Gibbons deluged legislators with revenue suggestions, including an escheat law that would raise $25 to $40 million, income tax increases of $23 million, sales tax increases of $50 million, cigarette taxes worth $8 million, a gasoline tax hike of $8 million, and property tax equalization that would net untold amounts. He also proposed eliminating sales tax exemptions for special interests, including agriculture. This last step alone would net more than $31 million, claimed Gibbons. South Carolina teachers had fired the first shot in what would be a nasty war for raises during West's term.[12]

West proposed level funding for state agencies in order to garner funds for a raise of $500 to $600. If he could have gotten the legislature to go along, West might have netted about $20 million for a raise. His plan, however, far exceeded an increase in funding that had been approved in the last session of the legislature, which would only have provided teachers a $200 raise. House speaker Soloman Blatt, a powerful Democrat from Barnwell in his fifteenth term as speaker, balked at West's plan. Citing an expected budget deficit, Blatt said he would work to hold level all spending, including education. Although sympathetic to teacher woes, Blatt laughed at calls for a $1,500 raise because it required $37 million that the state did not have. He maintained that "you can't ride in a Cadillac when you can only afford a Ford."[13]

Blatt and other legislators also bristled at SCEA tactics in forcing the issue. Gibbons announced that groups of fifty teachers planned to picket the state house each day for two weeks to display their seriousness. They wore pins and carried signs that read "Teachers care. Do you?" R. James

Aycock, chair of the House Ways and Means Committee, criticized the "militant" campaign for pay raises. "We'll do what we can again this year," said Aycock, "but if we can't afford it, I won't lose any sleep over it." Teachers admitted that their tactics constituted a "calculated risk" but explained that their limited protest was designed to prevent a more massive gathering. Teachers and supporters also inundated West's office with letters of support for raises.[14]

In his first address to the general assembly in 1971, West lamented the state of the national economy that caused shortfalls in the state budget. The national recession caused the state to end the previous fiscal year with an $8 million deficit, and it looked as if such a deficit might recur. Still, West thanked McNair for moving quickly to slash $15 million from the budget, which he said would leave a budget shortfall of only $1 million. Moving to teacher salaries, West expressed concern. The average South Carolina teacher made $6,933, almost $700 below the southeastern average. West took pride that the state ranked sixth in the nation in state support of teacher pay but complained that local support ranked forty-fifth. West asserted that he had worked long and hard to find innovative ways to raise pay but that the recession did not allow him to raise salaries any further without tax increases. This he was not prepared to do "when so many of the working people are actually taking home less money than they were one year ago." West called for $7.5 million for an average teacher raise of $250. He also invited the assembly to pass an escheat law and approved of Nixon's revenue-sharing plan, the proceeds of which he recommended be earmarked for education. Regretful that the amount could not be higher, West asked teachers to accept what he termed a "meaningful" raise.[15]

State teachers considered West's proposal a disappointment. Sumter High School principal Bob Matthews said the state had to improve its offer or else. "I'm afraid we're going to see some teachers starting unions," he lamented. Carlos Gibbons was less subdued, labeling the proposal a "pittance." He announced that "South Carolina has the ability to do better." West simply did not have teacher concerns at heart, argued Gibbons. Many teachers felt cheated. In 1968, with the state experiencing an industrial boom, Governor McNair had promised that salaries would match the southeastern average by 1971. Nevertheless, by that time, even with $1,000 in raises in 1968 and 1969, teacher salaries still had not risen above the 1969 southeast average.[16] Still, the new administration and legislature had run on firm promises not to raise taxes—promises they were not ready to break so soon. It was enough to make some teachers consider a walkout. The Richland County District One Teachers Association met soon after West's speech. Almost 900 of the 1,350-member body voted to request the SCEA to call a work stoppage on February 18. "Displeased" with West's proposal, the association announced that whether the SCEA followed suit or not, they planned to walk out. The group soundly defeated a motion to unionize, deferring that option to a last resort. "When we reach the point when we need Jimmy Hoffa types telling us what to do," said one teacher, "then it's time for us to seek employment elsewhere." More angry at Blatt than West, the group doubled its membership after this meeting.[17]

Nor was unrest restricted to Columbia. Gibbons received sixty-seven petitions from teachers statewide in favor of a walkout. Sumter County teachers announced solidarity with their Columbia colleagues and promised to walk out on the same day. Many teachers said West's proposal for so small a raise made them only more militant, like a "carrot in front of the donkey." Not all teachers supported the protest, however. By no means in lockstep to begin with, state teachers were divided by a generation gap. Older teachers argued that they had no right to walk out, whereas a majority of their younger colleagues favored a work stoppage. This same younger group threatened to leave South Carolina if necessary.[18]

The *Columbia State* condescendingly warned teachers not to "dissipate goodwill" by throwing a "temper tantrum." The newspaper agreed that teachers deserved a "substantial increase" but warned that militant behavior was not proper. Teachers had always enjoyed broad-based public support, but militancy would only harm their reputation and cause, the editors argued. Editors also chastised state authorities for not working hard enough to help teachers: "The state has been chasing that elusive southeastern average so long it's getting embarrassing." Several days later, the newspaper tempered its earlier criticism with ebullient praise. South Carolina teachers were due more than money, wrote the editors; they deserved the "gratitude of all citizens for keeping the public school system afloat." Of course, the *State* confessed, "words of praise and appreciation buy no groceries and pay no bills, but for whatever balm it may bring to troubled school minds and hearts, the *State* extends its thanks to the public school teachers of South Carolina."[19]

Sol Blatt's bellicosity did not ease tensions. He declared that anyone who participated in a work stoppage should be not only fired but also banned from teaching in South Carolina. State education secretary Cyril Busbee suggested that teachers find more effective means of obtaining larger raises. Even West warned that a walkout would be "ill-advised" as he reiterated his grave concern for their needs. He then encouraged teachers to support some of his reforms that might ease the tension: cost-of-living adjustments, free tuition for summer college work, and courses to help teachers study for the National Teacher Exams (NTE) on which salaries were based. Gibbons tried to soothe tensions. He praised West for the way he "stuck his neck out" for teachers. He also supported a one-day work stoppage, fearing that anything longer would only cause "backlash." Teachers followed his advice. On February 18, teachers statewide walked out of work. Although not overwhelmingly supported, the action sent a message. In Columbia, 851 of the district's 1,931 teachers stayed home, closing twelve schools.[20]

West responded in part to the walkout by calling for local authorities to increase school funding. If new money was to come from sources other than new taxes, it was to be found here. Local support of schools comprised only 29 percent of the total school budget, well below the national average of 56 percent. The state contributed more than 60 percent of school costs, exceeding the national average. In addition to West's request for increased local support, some advocated total state funding. Such action would have eliminated local support altogether, thereby erasing local deficiencies. Still others demanded property tax reform. The leader of this last group, Representative Isadore Lourie of Richland County, proposed a statewide uniform tax assessment ratio. Pointing to gross inequities in the current property tax system, he conceded that property taxes had no chance of ever being assessed at 100 percent of fair market value as mandated in the state's constitution. Instead, Lourie suggested that the state mandate that all counties assess property at 10 percent. Such a uniform ratio would reveal those counties that had underfunded education even if it lowered assessments in other counties.[21]

In the meantime, over Blatt's objections, the House Ways and Means Committee boosted West's original $250 proposal by $50. West praised the committee for the increase, confessing that he knew $300 still was not enough, but "in a year of austerity" it had to do. Gibbons was also thankful but demanded more. Soon after, the general assembly held a rare joint session of its education committees so Gibbons and teachers could argue their case. On March 17, 1971, the committees "grilled" Gibbons and the SCEA. Much of the interrogation focused on statistics Gibbons had used to make the case for pay raises. He had claimed that only sixty-one of the state's teachers made more than $9,000 a year. Democratic state senator John Drummond of Greenwood doubted the validity of these numbers. In a tense exchange, Gibbons responded that "if you doubt our statistics, don't doubt the motives." He told Drummond that the figures came directly from the state education department. State senator Anthony Harris, a Democrat from Chesterfield, pressed Gibbons further on the figures by asking him to recall his salary comparisons of South Carolina, Georgia, and North Carolina. When Gibbons could not respond directly, explaining that he did not bring the numbers with him, Harris accused him of evading the question. Gibbons asked Harris if the senator could recite from memory the recent appropriations bill, to which Harris replied, "I'm not the one quoting the unforgivable statistics that you have." Boos fell from the visitors' gallery as teachers reacted angrily. In an effort to save face, Blatt ordered Harris to apologize. Representative Thomas B. Bryant III of Orangeburg then asked Gibbons about a recent SCEA press release that said teachers held the assembly in low regard. Gibbons credited that appraisal to a pattern of low salaries over several years and notified legislators that $800 would be the bottom limit for a "substantial" raise. Anything lower necessitated further action.[22]

Action was on the agenda when the SCEA annual convention met in Columbia in late March. Gibbons outlined options for teachers. They could first issue a statewide sanctions alert, giving legislators until April 5 to make "satisfactory progress." If this failed, the SCEA could enact statewide sanctions. Sanctions involved gaining the help of the National Education Association (NEA) to discourage teachers nationwide from taking jobs in South Carolina. Likewise, the SCEA could ask business and industry to consider not relocating in the state. If sanctions failed to achieve the desired end, Gibbons could recommend that the SCEA ask the NEA to investigate the state and file a status survey on the state of education in South Carolina. A strike was a last, desperate resort. Gibbons argued that a strike could backfire on teachers by destroying any remaining goodwill among the public, legislators, and teachers. Other states had followed this course with mixed success. Utah and Oklahoma had enacted sanctions in recent years. So had Florida in 1967. The following year, however, Florida teachers struck with "no immediate success." No statewide raise followed until well after the strike, and state-teacher relations suffered.[23]

The SCEA placed the state on sanctions alert, threatening to impose sanctions if given an unacceptable raise. Before the vote, though, a rash of negotiations occurred among West, the legislature, and the SCEA. West sent SCEA president Claude Kitchens an urgent letter promising to call a special session for teacher pay if any of three scenarios occurred: congressional approval of revenue sharing; plausible revenue suggestions from a newly appointed legislative committee on teacher pay; or increased state revenues. West reiterated his concern for at least providing teachers with a raise that equaled the cost of living. He worried about legislative inability or unwillingness to provide a substantial raise in the current session and all but asked Kitchens to give him more time. Many teachers bristled at West's "wait-a-little-longer" stance. Many believed they had waited long enough. Kitchens refused to read West's letter before the convention. Nevertheless, he did attend a press conference at the general assembly at which West and legislative leaders announced income tax collection revisions designed to bring increased revenue of $10.5 million, much of which would go to education. No guarantee was given that any of this money would be used for instructional salaries.[24]

After his backstage tactics failed to produce results, West appealed directly to the convention. He cautioned teachers that any work disruption would severely damage education and would be "inconscienable [sic]." Appealing to their concern for education, West told teachers that their only loyalty should be toward "furthering the total educational opportunities for all citizens of this state."[25] Education secretary Cyril Busbee followed West. Whereas West appealed to teacher professionalism and concern for education, Busbee told them to behave. In a biting and unfair judgment of the profession and recent actions, he notified teachers that "professional performance would certainly suggest professional pay."[26]

Gibbons personally appealed to West for help. Having grown fond of playing mediator between teachers and state government, Gibbons told West that teachers needed to see "significant achievements" from the general assembly. Easing West's fears about a strike, Gibbons told the governor that he knew work stoppages were a double-edged sword. On one hand they could hasten increased funding; however, they could also "inflict wounds that take years to heal." "I am going to gamble my professional status," Gibbons told West. At the next SCEA delegate assembly, he planned to call for a moratorium on full-scale sanctions. "In doing so," he notified the governor, "I run the risk of 'soft-pedaling' and failure to give positive direction to a very disenchanted organization." Gibbons had been accused of "pussyfooting" before, he said, and his next gambit would surely result in the formation of several chapters of a teacher union, the American Federation of Teachers (AFT). All this could be prevented by the future actions of West and the legislature. In a brilliant political move, Gibbons forced West to make a choice. What did West want to see less: a full-scale teacher strike and the rise of unionization within the ranks of the state's public school teachers or a tax raise to give teachers a meaningful increase in salary?[27]

State power brokers soundly criticized Gibbons and the SCEA. Sol Blatt warned Gibbons that threats did not work with him. Gibbons had "gone too far," Blatt declared. "I will not be forced to do something wrong by demands." Others interpreted Gibbons's "deliberate charting of a collision course" with state government as "inciting the public school teachers to rash action." Sanctions did nothing more than threaten the "good name and economic posture of the state," said the *Columbia State,* which notified its readers that as bad as teachers needed a raise, South Carolina's "depressed economy" could not take the strain. Teachers had to face "hard facts" and give up their chase. Local government also had to contribute more, wrote the editors. Statewide property tax equalization was the first step in ending this madness. The SCEA, concluded the *State,* had missed the real culprit in its ministrations: local authorities and their "woeful" school support. Letters to the editor were divided. One man wrote that teachers should be given a raise only after the "misfits" were fired. One teacher noted a double standard. Why was it, she asked, when other state employees received raises it caused no controversy, but when teachers asked for raises they became the scapegoat? "Why should I be punished by a low salary," wrote the teacher, "because I want to help South Carolina grow educationally?"[28]

Teachers were not without allies in the general assembly. A growing coalition of youthful legislators, called "young Turks" by some, had entered office in recent years. Led by Representative Alex Sanders, a Democrat from Richland County, they attempted to double the proposed $300 raise. Their bill would have reduced taxes for South Carolinians in the lowest tax bracket, those earning below $400 a year, and raised them in the highest bracket. Branded "robin hood" by its opponents, this legislation failed in the house, 77-34, defeated by Blatt and his forces. Another group of lawmakers from the state's Pee Dee region attempted to pass legislation designed to raise half a million dollars for pay raises. This bill standardized fines for criminal and traffic violations, earmarking a portion for education. Although unsuccessful, both proposals revealed a growing base of teacher support.[29]

All the talk of austerity and inability to afford Cadillacs reeked of hypocrisy when the house passed an appropriations bill that raised the salaries of constitutional officers by $10,000 and state agency heads by $1,500 to $3,500. West asserted the raises were "well deserved" but criticized the timing. To his credit, he donated his $10,000 to the state's fledgling kindergarten program, which funded 1.5 new kindergarten units per year. The *Columbia State* agreed with West. It was "poor psychology" to offer raises, wrote the editors, especially when state leaders wished to forestall teacher militancy. Democratic senator Walter J. Bristow of Richland County noted the legislative hypocrisy. "We are saying this is a year of austerity and yet there are increases in salary in some areas of state government," said Bristow. "How do you think the teachers and parents of school children feel when we give these raises?" He then offered the "young Turk" amendment that had been defeated in the house. Blatt's senate allies led the opposition with similar results. Another bill, submitted by future governor Richard Riley of Greenville and Kenneth Rentiers of Charleston, would have raised taxes between 1 and 3 percent in the highest tax brackets. This, too, lost in the senate 26-16. Senate Finance Committee chair Rembert Dennis accused reformers of using teachers as a "political football" in a venture to raise taxes. Others criticized this plan as "piecemeal tax revision." Either way, these failed amendments represented the SCEA's "last gasp" for a meaningful raise in 1971.[30]

Gibbons did not wait until May to urge a delay in militant action. In a hastily called meeting of the SCEA delegate assembly in April, Gibbons blinked first in what the *Columbia State* dubbed "brinkmanship." Placing his hopes in revenue sharing, Gibbons concluded that education could not be financed out of "confrontation and discord" and convinced delegates to delay any vote on sanctions or any other aggressive course from May 15 until October 1. Many in state government sighed with relief. The *State* expressed hope that this was the beginning of a more positive ending to the situation. Perhaps, the editors observed, South Carolina would not be plunged deeper into the "bottom of the heap where the nation seems to view it already." West appreciated Gibbons's gift of time, which he proposed to use to right the state's economic woes.[31]

Although most legislators believed that opposing teacher raises was akin to "talking against motherhood," they concluded there was little they could do short of raising taxes. Nor did they support slashing other agencies' budgets to help teachers. Although West announced he was "optimistic" about the prospects of the state economy for the next six months, there was little money to provide the type of raise teachers wanted. Nevertheless, the state economy had stopped its downward slide and had begun to grow. State tax commissioner Don Wasson announced that the state ended the fiscal year "safely in the black." A 6 percent budget proration and a slight increase (2.7 percent) in seasonal nonmanufacturing jobs and tax collections helped the state evade the projected $16 million deficit predicted just six months earlier. The looming specter of teacher militancy tempered West's reaction to such welcome news.[32]

At the end of what many considered a "dismal" legislative session, teachers had their $300 raise and not much more. The assembly passed about half of West's proposals, making the session a successful one for the new governor. Gibbons took the opportunity to congratulate the governor and remind him of prior commitments. He informed West that he promised to call a special session if necessary and that teachers were watching to see how he would solve this educational crisis. He told the governor that SCEA members would not rest until they fulfilled their aims. Such gentle encouragement and praise was limited only to his private correspondence with West.[33]

Gibbons may have moderated his tone in private, but publicly he never eased up. He reminded lawmakers that the delay did not mean that the threat of sanctions had disappeared. The only "acceptable" raise for teachers would be $800. "There is no way the teaching profession can survive in this state," declared Gibbons, "without a tremendous financial effort by the General Assembly. We have got to have some new taxes. It's just inevitable." The legislature, judged Gibbons, was not very "education friendly." State senator Rembert Dennis demanded that Gibbons tone down his rhetoric and stop making "inflammatory statements."[34]

Many hoped a special legislative committee on teacher pay would find a solution. Composed of fifteen appointed members, five each from the house and senate and five gubernatorial appointees, the committee was created by the assembly in 1971 to hold hearings across the state on how best to address problems of teacher pay. West appointed Claude Kitchens; Agnes Wilson, new SCEA president and 1970 state teacher of the year; the editor of the *Spartanburg Herald;* a Columbia accountant; and a Charleston attorney. Legislative appointments included "young Turk" leader Alex Sanders and Gibbons's foe Anthony Harris, along with the chair of the senate education committee, James Mozingo. West told the group that its recommendations "may well guide the future tax and educational policies of our state in the years to come." In the interim, the committee's recommendations would have "considerable influence" over the next legislative session. "If this group cannot come up with a reasonable solution to the problem of teacher compensation," confessed West, "I don't know anybody in the state who can." Unfortunately, by March 1972, the committee had met only four times, none in public, and reported to the assembly two months late with few constructive proposals.[35]

In August 1971, President Richard Nixon launched his New Economic Policy (NEP). Designed to fight inflation and revive a flagging economy, the NEP was dramatized by a wage and price freeze. Nixon wanted to show that he took inflation seriously. This policy provided the national economy with the "shot in the arm" it needed, but in South Carolina it was not welcome. Although it lasted only ninety days, the wage freeze strained relations between teachers and state leaders. Frustrated at Nixon's unintentional torpedoing of his $300 teacher raise, West declared that unless enjoined by legal action the raises would go through. State comptroller Henry Mills supported this position. He ruled that raises actually went into effect the day the new fiscal year began, in July, thereby predating the freeze. The state also had a federal precedent. In Washington, D.C., a Cost of Living Council, created by the NEP to set price and wage levels, had cleared a path for states whose teachers negotiated statewide teacher contracts. If one teacher worked under a new contract before August 15, then all teachers under the same contract received raises. South Carolina quickly adopted this "golden sheep" provision. Education Secretary Busbee said he knew of no school district where such was not the case. Busbee also declared that any teachers who worked in preparation for the next year, even if they had not "officially" started work, would get the raise. The controversy seemed easily handled.[36]

On September 4, the Cost of Living Council ruled that only those specific teachers who had started work prior to August 15 were eligible for raises, in effect closing the golden sheep loophole. West unsuccessfully appealed to the council twice. In doing so, he learned more bad news. The council also set a fixed percentage on any future raises. Not only did South Carolina teachers not receive their "pittance" but also future increases promised to be far below their desires. West admitted that teachers were bound to be "mad as fire, and I don't blame them." Appeals to the council on their behalf by West, the state attorney general, the SCEA, and even U.S. senator Strom Thurmond all failed. Desperately in search of a solution, West appealed directly to Treasury Secretary John Connally for a "hardship exemption." He argued that because South Carolina teachers were among the lowest paid in the nation and because the most recent raise was barely enough to be considered a cost-of-living adjustment, then grounds existed for an exemption. Connally declined.[37]

Although the wage and price freeze hurt teachers' chances at a raise, it had a positive impact on the state economy. Tax commission chair Don Wasson announced that the freeze had a "major stabilizing effect." He also reported that for the first quarter of the 1971-72 fiscal year, tax revenues had increased 12.3 percent over the same period the year before. State sales taxes were 13.2 percent higher, as were corporate income taxes, which had increased a whopping 23 percent, their first increase in eighteen months. By October, South Carolina saw a tiny budget surplus of $5.2 million, almost a million dollars higher than predicted. West's calls for austerity, midyear spending cuts, and Nixon's freeze had all contributed to the gains. Wasson predicted a "sound economic climate."[38]

The good news came at a relatively inopportune moment for budget makers in South Carolina. It was that time of year when state agencies paraded before the Budget Control Board to ask for increases in their new budgets. Teachers were no exception. News of economic gains only whetted budgetary appetites. The major issue, of course, was a teacher pay raise. The state board of education asked for $45 million in budget increases, which included almost $35 million for a $1,200 per teacher raise. Raises under this proposal were not across the board but were instead based upon length of service and merit. Busbee argued that such large raises were necessary in order to keep South Carolina "reasonably competitive" with other states. West considered the $1,200 raise reasonable, but he declined to commit himself to that goal. Still frustrated with "gobbledy-gook" from the Nixon administration over the length of the freeze, West insisted that unless he received more definitive answers, he would give teachers the previous year's raise. He eventually proposed a $35 million increase to provide the $1,200 raise asked by teachers and suggested by the board of education. He also wanted money to fund other educational reforms, including increased funds to the state's kindergarten system, the implementation of a five-year plan by the board of education to alleviate a variety of deficiencies, and money to increase teacher retirement benefits. The budget board reminded West and other state agency heads in search of more funds that the economic gains of the previous six months had not provided enough money to meet all their requests. Taxes had to be raised to satisfy them all. Because the state was in an election year, these requests would be all the more difficult to push through the general assembly.[39]

Amid the unfolding budget battle, teacher frustration reached a peak. The October 1 deadline had come and gone, and nothing significant had been accomplished by the state. Gibbons warned state leaders that the breach in ranks evident at the sanctions alert vote was not as wide as it seemed. There was another tactic that teachers and administrators were considering. Gibbons foresaw the establishment of Political Action Committees for Education (PACE) as had been formed recently in North Carolina. PACE formed branches in each county and worked to elect education-friendly legislators. Administrators, a clear three-to-one minority in the SCEA delegate assembly, favored this plan. Teachers favored more militant action. South Carolina would not see the end of some form of militant action for the foreseeable future however future votes on sanctions went.[40] West warned teachers that education would be "substantially damaged" by sanctions. Whichever way the delegate assembly voted, West reminded teachers, his commitment to education remained firm. "Anything you can do to avoid sanctions would be a tremendous help and would help our efforts to improve education," pleaded West. "The educational climate of this state would not be helped by an NEA investigation." SCEA legislative committee chairman F. E. DuBose told West his words "might take the steam out of the sanctions vote." West certainly hoped so. He feared the "distasteful" effect an outside investigation might have.[41]

On October 23, 1971, a "bitterly divided" SCEA delegate assembly ignored West's pleas and voted 181-132 to request an NEA investigation of South Carolina education. The vote was the first step in moving toward a full sanctions vote. The NEA required an investigation before issuing nationwide sanctions. The vote almost did not occur. A motion further to delay the vote failed in a 156-156 tie. The result disturbed DuBose. "It is going to hurt me in my efforts to work with the legislature, knowing the political climate and knowing the people of South Carolina as I do." Gibbons put a positive spin on the result, saying that an investigation was not necessarily a bad thing. "Fact finding," he explained, "is as basic to American government as apple pie." He also argued that if the state had been investigated earlier, maybe it would not be in the midst of such a crisis.[42] In its formal request to the NEA for an investigation, the SCEA listed several areas of deficiency. Among the more important were low per-pupil spending, the lack of a fully developed statewide kindergarten system, "gross inequities in property valuation and assessment," a reduction in the total percentage of the state budget appropriated to education over the previous ten years, low teacher salaries, and state use of the NTE to determine teacher pay scales. It was quite a list. One teacher explained that the $300 raise "was just a drop in the bucket" compared with other problems, and "it evaporated before we got it."[43]

A "quite distressed" West claimed that the vote would hinder his search for teacher pay hikes in the next legislative session. "The overwhelming consensus from the legislature," said West, "is that the action . . . will serve no useful purpose and has endangered the cause of education in South Carolina." Senate Finance Committee chairman Edgar Brown (D-Barnwell) concluded that the vote "was an affront to the people of South Carolina." As reprehensible as Brown believed it was, it would not hamper his efforts at helping teachers. Still, he reminded the SCEA that legislators were miffed because "they don't like outsiders interfering." Given the state of the economy and teacher agitation, House Ways and Means Committee chairman R. J. Aycock (D-Sumter) said he did not see "a chance in the world" for a $1,200 raise unless taxes were increased. Furthermore, he was not about to vote for that. Most legislators, though clearly angered by the vote, restated their commitment to pay reasonable increases so long as they did not "gouge the taxpayers." The *Columbia State* accused "militants" in the SCEA of trying to "blackmail" the state, something that would surely diminish goodwill. Lecturing teachers not to bite the hands that fed them, the editors asserted that teachers displayed "an unseemly degree of impatience and a singular lack of appreciation of what has already been done at great expense." What purpose would be served, asked the newspaper, by subjecting the state to investigation by a group of outsiders with a "pre-conceived bias?"[44]

Upon West's first anniversary in office he paused for reflection. Clearly, he admitted, the "low point" was the SCEA's sanctions vote. What irked him and caused "keen resentment" among legislators was continued teacher bellicosity even after state leaders had promised to work for higher pay: "One of the most disappointing things has been the attitudes of the teachers in asking for an investigation by NEA in the face of my commitment to them, publicly and privately, that we should give them a substantial raise next year." He added, "I can't see any useful purpose that can be served" by sanctions. Not only would relations between teachers and legislators suffer further strain but also bad publicity had already damaged the state's reputation. Formal sanctions only compounded bad publicity.[45]

The clash between educators and West was a case of ill-timed teacher aggression and general misunderstanding. Teachers had run out of patience waiting for what they clearly deserved. Dealing with integration and a whole new set of variables in the classroom fed an increasing desire for higher pay. To wait two or three more years for compensation that might never come, depending on who held office, was not an option. Yet West needed that time to allow South Carolina's economy to recover through increased tax collections and new investment. West believed that teachers had all but called him a liar by not taking him at his word, and he became frustrated at teachers' inability or unwillingness to realize the long-term effects of an NEA investigation and sanctions. West believed that industry begat industry and that sanctions disrupted that cycle. Teachers denied him their trust. As sincere as he was, West was not the only politician in the state. One teacher explained to the governor that an inherent mistrust of public officials necessitated the sanctions vote. "Our representatives take trips everywhere, do not attend meetings we pay for, and take home desks and chairs that cost more than we take home in a month," wrote the educator. Yet that was the least of it. "Our legislators even tried to raise their own salaries! They find money for the things they want to do! Do you see why the teachers are mad? Thank you for not accepting your raise. That was a magnificent gesture!"[46]

Although the SCEA demanded $1,500 raises the next year (the $300 dollar retroactive raise and a new raise of $1,200), West initially suggested a more reasonable $700 or $800. This suggestion still required tax increases. For the first time in his administration, West seriously considered breaking his no-tax pledge. Although he had only promised not to raise taxes in 1971, he had hoped to get through four years without doing so. The industrial tax revenue windfall was still months away, however, and West was in a bind. He could risk further teacher unrest by arguing for patience but doing so threatened his plan to turn the state's economy around and enable the state to raise public employee pay. Steering the state further on a course of austerity risked sanctions and harming South Carolina's industry-friendly reputation.[47]

West had few options for raising taxes in his rather poor state. The area of "greatest neglect" was the property tax, but it was most impervious to reform. To equalize property taxes for the short term would cost the state more than $15 million initially, a hard figure to justify, even if reform meant greater revenues and a fairer tax structure for the future. Besides, Sol Blatt opposed equalization. Cigarette taxes were a prime target because only six states had cigarette taxes lower than South Carolina, and each cent taxed per pack garnered $2,820,000. Tobacco farmers in the Pee Dee region made a strong opponent, however. South Carolina taxed alcohol at one of the highest rates in the nation, and that left little room to add new taxes. Any addition to the gasoline tax drew the attention of the highway department, which claimed such revenues as one would a birthright. Nonetheless, the South Carolina Supreme Court had ruled in 1941 that gasoline tax revenues could be used for the general fund and not exclusively for highways. Carlos Gibbons threatened the highway commissioner that he would go after any increased gasoline tax revenues. West also considered adding brackets to the state's income tax. Adding two brackets would bring in $52,300,000. West could impose a "bad medicine" strategy to raising taxes. To raise the income tax rather than a number of smaller taxes would certainly be more politically expedient, something akin to taking bad-tasting medicine all in one gulp. To West, the problem with that strategy was whether one general income tax increase provided enough money for his programs.[48]

West entered his most difficult political position in January 1972. He faced an "increasingly adamant" SCEA, legislative resistance to increased taxes, the beginning of an election year in which all 170 seats in the house were up for grabs, and an impending NEA investigation of his state's educational system. Many capitol watchers said that 1972 would be West's "make or break" year. The governor decided to take bold action. Tax increases, he decided, were the only way to provide for teacher raises, which most citizens considered the most pressing issue. West had to abandon his no-tax goal to "put down militancy," as the lieutenant governor phrased his dilemma. Many legislators agreed with the governor. He had to act or risk increased disruptions by teachers. Hesitant to raise taxes in an election year, many legislators agreed with West that the repercussions of antagonizing the state's twenty-eight thousand teachers any further were even greater than voter anger over a tax increase.[49]

West invited small groups of legislators to discuss his ideas for revenue measures, finding that many agreed to go along with his increases only if he took the brunt of responsibility. While discussing a 10 percent raise for teachers, about $600, West received advice from Gibbons, who told West that teachers would more willingly accept rejection of a sizeable pay increase by the federal pay board than compromise on the lower figure. In short, Gibbons wanted West to pass a large raise and then see what the pay board said. It was a clever political move on Gibbons's part. He did not plan to allow state leaders to hide behind Nixon's economic policies. Although $600 raises would be a "step in the right direction," said Gibbons, they were still "inadequate to solve the problem."[50]

In West's second state-of-the-state address, he proclaimed that South Carolina's economy had recovered, announcing a $5 million budget surplus, but warned that the extra money was not enough to cover the state's needs. Moreover, he could not allow South Carolina to suffer three consecutive years of austerity, which might "seriously jeopardize the quality of state services." He asked the legislature to join him in his quest to "free the spirit of South Carolina from the bondage of limited expectations." To do this, West requested tax increases totaling $75 million, including $18 million for teacher raises of $600, $3 million for vocational education, $1.5 million for kindergartens, and $900,000 to help provide equal opportunity to education for children with disabilities. West called for a 1 percent increase in the income tax to generate $42 million and an additional two cents in cigarette taxes, which would bring in $5.6 million. Such hard choices were necessary, West explained, if South Carolina wished move closer to "the ultimate unleashing of the full energies and capabilities of our people." Legislators interrupted him with unexpectedly warm applause seven times during the speech, the loudest coming after West asked them to join him "in a resounding rejection of simply maintaining the status quo." Sol Blatt praised West for effectively highlighting the state's problems but predicted more than a few objections to raising taxes. Blatt was right. Legislators representing the Pee Dee region's tobacco farmers announced their intentions of fighting such "unfair" taxes. Gibbons mildly praised West for offering half of the SCEA's suggested raise.[51]

The *Charleston News and Courier* blasted West. "And all of the time they have been telling us the Wild West was a thing of the past," wrote Hugh Gibson. "Scratch that myth off your list. The wildest West of them all— Gov. John C.—is alive and well in Columbia, South Carolina." Gibson predicted that "realistic" legislators would soon take to "hauling West's pie out of the sky."[52] The *Charlotte Observer* rhapsodized over West's "courageous" address that "didn't duck the hard issues, that pointed the way to the high road." By and large, reaction to the speech fell between these two extremes. Blatt and other leaders admitted that West enjoyed growing support in the legislature. This support lasted only as long as the governor stuck his neck out along with theirs.[53]

Before the general assembly could act on West's revenue proposals, tax commission chair Wasson released new data on the state's economic recovery. In January, Wasson reported that tax revenues ran 13.1 percent ahead of the previous year. South Carolina saw increases in construction, building supply, a 14.1 percent rise in income tax payments, a 3.7 percent increase in corporate income taxes, and a jump in auto sales. Thanks to belt-tightening, Nixon's economic policies, and South Carolina personal income growth, which outpaced the rest of the nation by 20 percent, Wasson reported, South Carolina was on track to enjoy a $15 million surplus at the end of the current fiscal year. Less than seven weeks later, Wasson updated his earlier report. In February 1972, state tax revenues reached their highest one-month total in state history, $53 million. Wasson amended his earlier projections and announced that South Carolina could end the fiscal year with a surplus of more than $22 million. So confident was Wasson of these numbers that he told the House Ways and Means Committee to use them in planning the budget. By the end of April, tax collections ran 16.3 percent ahead of 1971. South Carolina's annual growth rate in March was a whopping 14.4 percent. There was no question that the economy was booming. The new data also provided legislators the opportunity to table tax legislation until receiving further reports from Wasson.[54]

The astounding economic growth and tax revenue increase in South Carolina resulted from a variety of causes. One was an ingenious suggestion by West to change the frequency with which state taxes were collected. Instead of quarterly, the state made monthly collections. The increase in interest on these payments brought in twenty-five million dollars. West also carried out an aggressive campaign to lure international and national industry to the state. Thanks to former governor McNair, West inherited a strong and ambitious state development board. By the time he took office, the board had gained valuable experience attracting industry to South Carolina. West and the board implemented a three-phase plan to attract investment. First, and probably most important, West concerned himself with projecting a positive state image. If investors failed to see the state as an attractive place to live and work, they would not want to invest. South Carolina could no longer afford to be seen as the leader of the secessionists. "Projecting an image" had several layers. The state's overall image as a hospitable place, peopled by friendly folks, had to be the dominant impression for those visiting the state. South Carolina's image was also reflected by its traveling citizens. West himself succeeded marvelously when he traveled abroad by using his good humor, modesty, and toleration. Yet the first two levels pale in comparison to the most important factor that new industry wanted: daily "quality of life" issues. A progressive state government constantly in search of areas of improvement, with a strong education system and economy, impressed future investors.[55]

West traveled to Europe and Asia, selling his state as a sound investment. In his first ten months in office, he visited Europe three times. In 1971 he visited the International Trade Fair at Basle, Switzerland, to push South Carolina products. On one whirlwind trip between June 25 and July 8, 1971, West visited New York, Paris, Cologne, Assmannhausen, Wurzburg, Rothenburg, Baden Baden, and Zurich before returning to South Carolina. Visits to West Germany, Japan, India, and an international textile exposition in France all paid dividends. Japanese and German companies built plants in Orangeburg and Spartanburg, producing petrochemicals, steel, and synthetic fibers. By 1972, West Germany had invested more money in South Carolina than in any other state, with $377.4 million, followed by Great Britain with $335.6 million and the Netherlands with $50 million. So enamored with Germany was West that he took an overnight trip to West Germany to give a speech. He made the trip on the promise by German officials that he would have a personal audience with the directors of various German firms, several of whom wished to discuss expanding investments in Georgetown, South Carolina. The French built a Michelin tire plant in Greenville. Michelin's tire plants in Greenville and

Anderson Counties, their first such U.S. investments, at more than $200 million, comprised the largest single initial foreign investment in the state's history. The Anderson mixing plant employed four hundred workers, and the Greenville tire plant put fourteen hundred South Carolinians to work. West opened state offices in Brussels in 1971 and three years later started ones in Tokyo. Strategically located in the capital of the European Common Market and in the most industrial and prosperous nation in the Far East, these offices steered money and industry to the state. West also opened an office in Washington, D.C., to garner federal grants.[56]

Such efforts produced "unprecedented success" for the state. Between 1971 and 1973, more than 470 new industries and plants located in South Carolina, creating 41,383 jobs and a total investment of $2,205,600,000. In 1972, foreign investment in South Carolina comprised 10 percent of the total foreign investments in the United States for that year. The state was so successful in attracting investment that other states patterned their development boards after South Carolina's. In 1973, Colorado sent a group to study the system, and a year later Rhode Island announced it had adopted South Carolina's methods.[57]

To meet the demand for skilled workers, West strongly supported the establishment of Technical Education Centers (TECs) across the state to teach noncollege-bound high school graduates. Technical education began in the state as early as 1961 but remained small in scale and underfunded until the early 1970s. In 1972, the state established the State Board for Comprehensive and Technical Education, replacing an older advisory council. This new body was given broader powers for program development and authority over the state's technical education system. By 1974, TECs, located in areas such as Greenville, Spartanburg, and Orangeburg, enrolled more than eighty-one thousand people in sixteen centers statewide. In twenty-three years South Carolina's technical education system provided training to almost a half million workers. West credited this progressive system of technical education for helping triple per-capita income in the state between 1960 and 1973. TECs became West's biggest selling point on his international trips. His goal for TECs was to have workers 65 percent efficient by their first day on the job. West believed that such programs were a greater attraction to new industry than tax incentive "giveaways," which he believed were merely "short run gimmicks."[58]

West also emphasized tourism. Past South Carolina governors had placed special emphasis on casting the state as a vacation paradise. West was no different. During his administration, appropriations for the State Commission on Parks, Recreation, and Travel more than doubled from $1.6 million in 1968 to almost $3.9 million by 1973. Funding for development of tourist-attracting activities quadrupled, rising from $1.3 million to $5.8 million during the same period. The twenty-eight million people who visited the state spent more than $675,000,000, creating more than ten thousand new jobs and making tourism the state's second largest industry in 1974. To West, all these issues were related: education, industry, tourism, taxation, and progressive state government. Forming a circular relationship, each factor fed the other. Left undisturbed, the cycle could pay great dividends for the state. Sanctions, NEA investigations, and general teacher unrest, though understandable, threatened the stability of the cycle. West lamented that teachers failed to see the long-term effects of their actions, however warranted they might be.[59]

As ominous as an NEA investigation sounded when first requested by teachers, many in the state changed their minds and greeted it as an opportunity to improve education. The *Columbia State* welcomed the committee and looked forward to its recommendations for improvement. Arriving in South Carolina in April 1972, the investigation committee announced that it had decided to refocus the investigation in light of recent developments. Since the initial request from the SCEA, the state had taken appropriate steps to correct low salaries and high dropout rates, the lack of a kindergarten program, and low per-pupil expenditures. The State Board of Education's Five Year Plan for Education laid out goals to correct these deficiencies. Satisfied that the state's intentions were sound, the committee decided to focus only on job-related teacher concerns, the area of "sharpest disagreement" between teachers and the state.[60]

The committee held public forums statewide, interviewing teachers, administrators, and state leaders. Although the investigation concluded that underfinancing of education was a "major obstacle to teaching effectiveness," it credited the state for taking steps to correct funding deficiencies. Still, there was a dangerous tension between educators and leaders. Summing up the strained relationship, committee chair Dorothy Massie described state attitudes as "paternalistic." Teachers were "treated like the children they teach," she complained. Of the governor, Massie spoke kindly. His quick reaction to the SCEA's demands and his obvious interest in addressing their concerns impressed her. West, she concluded, "seemed to have a keen recognition of the fundamental problems of education, he seemed to have a concerned attitude about them, and seemed to be very open in his discussion with us."[61]

Massie's evaluation was not without harsh criticisms. The investigation expressed singular displeasure with the state's use of the NTE for determining certification grade and pay scales. Since 1945, the state had used the NTE as a basis of pay. For twenty-five years, the test determined what grade certificate was issued. This grade determined the amount of pay a teacher received. In 1968, the U.S. Supreme Court ruled in *Green v. County School Board* that southern school districts had to convert immediately to unitary school systems. Three months later, the state board of education met to revise NTE requirements. It eliminated different grades for certification, in effect leaving only two: professional certification and warranty certification. Warranty certification allowed a five-year period for teachers to increase their NTE score or face termination. The net effect of this more stringent revision was the termination of scores of teachers. A disproportionate number of these terminated teachers were black. Although the NEA could not prove that the revision was the result of racial discrimination, it condemned its net effect. Aside from the racial effects of the exams themselves, the state had used them in a manner that violated the guidelines for their use published by the company that administered the exams, the Educational Testing Service (ETS). The ETS urged that their tests be used only as a means of assuring minimum academic competence, not as a forecasting tool for teaching performance or to determine pay. Since 1969, the state had terminated scores of black teachers with low scores on the NTE even though they had years of satisfactory service in the classroom.[62]

Legal decisions supported the NEA's conclusions. The U.S. Court of Appeals for the Fifth Circuit affirmed in June 1972 that the Columbus, Mississippi, Municipal School District's use of the NTE in the same manner as South Carolina violated the equal protection clause of the Fourteenth Amendment. The SCEA threatened to file suit if the state did not change the way it used the NTE by June of 1973. When the ETS learned that only experienced teachers would receive the salary schedule and that new teachers would continue to be salaried by the NTE scores, it threatened to withhold scores from the state as well. The state relented and stopped using the exam as a basis for salary determination. It retained the test for its intended purpose, as a means of testing cognitive development.

The board of education designed a four-year phaseout and implemented a new salary schedule based on years of service. This decision successfully ended a three-year correspondence by the ETS and the SCEA on NTE abuses and alleged discrimination.[63]

With the NEA investigation over and an SCEA president who strongly supported West's plan to "low key" the results of NEA's investigation, the governor concentrated his attention on spending the money that was flowing into the state. National economists predicted that the state would lead the nation in industrial development and tourism in 1973. Indeed, South Carolina enjoyed over a half billion dollars in new and expanded industry, its lowest unemployment in ten years, personal income increases of 11 percent, tax collections growth of 19 percent, an 18 percent increase in consumer spending since 1971, and an overall economic growth rate of 14 percent. The state seemed ready to fund West's progressive platform without raising income taxes. The state enjoyed a $70 million surplus thanks to "staggering" revenue, which had increased 26.3 percent over the previous year. That figure later ballooned to $83.5 million with the arrival of federal revenue-sharing money. Carlos Gibbons even ended the sanctions alert in hopes of showing the legislature that he was ready to make a deal.[64]

West hailed the onset of "the most productive, the most progressive, and the most prosperous period" in South Carolina history. South Carolina had become a perfect example of the new "Sunbelt South." And John West had been at the helm. Celebrating the two years during which his state moved from dire financial straits to having money in the bank, West said that the state had an opportunity to use the $83 million surplus to move ahead. He called for an expansion of kindergarten, vocational and technical education, and special classes for students with disabilities and gave special priority to another raise for teachers, an average of $500. To stave off future fiscal problems, West also suggested the establishment of a $25 million reserve fund. After two years of austerity and hard work at industrial development, West said, the state had achieved its goals. "The greatness of South Carolina" said West, "has been diminished only by the frustration of unfulfilled human promise." It was time, he said, to tap the potential of each citizen. In education, this task was clear: teachers had to receive better pay, children with disabilities should be given opportunities to learn, dropouts had to drop back in, and the state's preschool children needed more kindergartens to prepare them for elementary school. The state had to pursue a noble but simple goal, said West, "the goal of human understanding, human concern, and full human development."[65] In a brief legislative session, much of the governor's legislative package was easily passed. Teachers received a $500 raise, kindergartens received a $1.5 million increase in funds, another $1.4 million went to facilities for children with disabilities, and more than $18 million went to an expansion of technical and vocational education.[66]

The following January, West announced that South Carolina's boom had peaked. In 1973 alone, the state enjoyed $1.2 billion in capital investment. The textile recession of 1971 had ended, and employment and payrolls in the state's largest industry were at all-time highs. West gleefully announced that he would end his administration without having to raise taxes. Proposing a record budget of $912 million, West called for yet another teacher raise, this time 4 percent. By the end of the legislative term, this figure had doubled, to about $700. Another $1.4 million went for kindergarten expansion. By 1974, tensions between teachers and the state had all but evaporated. West had brought average teacher pay even with the southeastern average, at about $9,340 per year. Moreover, it was done exactly the way West envisioned when he took office, with heavy emphasis on investment and industrial development. The onset of the Sunbelt phenomenon in South Carolina was the reason why West could provide so much money for education.[67]

Unable to succeed himself in office, West only had four years to turn the state around. By most accounts he achieved his goal. Nevertheless, his was not an administration without shortcomings. One glaring example was the lack of any true property tax reform. West had considered such reform but decided that it was too difficult to accomplish in four years. Recent U.S. Supreme Court rulings that held unconstitutional the use of property taxes as a major source of education funding meant little to South Carolina because property taxes accounted for a smaller percentage of school monies than other taxes in the state. West failed to provide any long-term solution to education finance, instructional quality, or school governance. Still, this failure was balanced by his ability to raise the state's contribution to education through industrial development. Powerful opposition prevented him from doing more. So did South Carolina's constitution, which prevented him from serving consecutive terms. After the industrial boom, West had no chance of convincing legislators to tackle serious reform. One of the weakest state chief executives in terms of legislative influence, South Carolina's governor had little more than moral suasion as an instrument to push reform. When the boom came, legislators were spared the task of tax reform. By escaping the need to raise taxes, West also evaded the type of bitter rural-urban fight over their dispersal that Brewer witnessed in Alabama. The Sunbelt phenomenon may have brought South Carolina out of the economic doldrums, but it also covered a multitude of educational sins.

Upon leaving office, West reflected on his four years. In a period of unprecedented racial harmony, he said, the state witnessed the greatest period of economic growth in its history. During his term, almost three billion dollars of new and expanded industrial development came to South Carolina, creating more than sixty thousand jobs. At a time when the nation suffered severe economic recession, bragged West, his state enjoyed better-paying jobs than at any time in history. International firms spent more than $750 million in the state as South Carolina became a pioneer in industrial development with its technical education system and aggressive state development board. South Carolina became the first state to recognize and exploit overseas investment and markets, especially in the Far East. What made West proudest, though, was the manner in which such fiscal rewards were used to meet the "human needs" of his state.[68]

Conclusion

Nevertheless, if it can be said there are many Souths, the fact remains that there is also one South.

—W. J. Cash, *The Mind of the South*

No man's South was the same as another's.

—Michael O'Brien, *The Idea of the American South, 1920–1941*

Perhaps Cash's quote applies, but in a different order, regarding New South governors and what they meant to their South. Albert Brewer, Reubin Askew, and John West proved that although there is one New South, there also exist many new political Souths. Each governor shared common beliefs, characteristics, goals for office, and, at times, similar results. Nevertheless, their individual experiences were quite different, and so was the political dynamic within each state. Without question they were alike in many ways. They held a common desire to move beyond the divisive politics of race. Young, well educated, and business oriented, each governor sought to expand political, economic, and educational opportunity for all the citizens of their states. Each saw education reform as a vital step in the South's economic and social reconciliation with the North following the turbulent civil rights era. They hoped that with improved educational opportunities came a better-educated workforce and perhaps an end to the fear and ignorance that had driven racism in the region for so long. Active in their local churches, often as deacons, Brewer, Askew, and West drew on a strong religious conviction. Each credits religion as a formative influence in his commitment to moderation and racial justice. In varying degrees they advocated centralization and streamlining of state government, businesslike management, state planning, fiscal conservatism, and delegation of decision making to experts.[1]

These governors mark a watershed in southern politics, but their successes and failures came in no small part because of the recent political pasts of their states. In short, the state political dynamic dictated just how much of what they believed in became reality. Albert Brewer's Alabama was a far cry from Askew's Florida or West's South Carolina. Still mired in racial politics, the state did not allow moderation to develop without difficulty. Alabama did not elect a New South governor. It still had not by the end of the century. One was thrust upon it in 1968 following Lurleen Wallace's death. When examined against Askew's successes, Brewer's claim to New South status appears dubious. Still, Brewer's New South was as "new" as his state would allow. With the overbearing presence of arch-segregationist George Wallace and no silent moderate majority to call on, Brewer found himself flanked by the state's segregationist past, through which he rose to office, and the need to move the state forward. When he lost in 1970 to Wallace, the state failed to appreciate his call for a more progressive course.

While in office, Brewer represented a marked albeit brief change from the recent past. He ushered in a period of fiscal responsibility in govern-ment, refused to stand in any schoolhouse doors, and gave the state a chance to enter the new political South. Even though Brewer did not al-ways appear to embrace school integration in the style of Askew, he marked a radical departure from the events of the turbulent Wallace years. Although Brewer legally appealed federal court rulings ordering integra-tion, he did so in generally nonthreatening tones and never called for defiance of the final decisions of the courts, instead appealing for the adop-tion of school choice as a means of integration. His education program was one of the most progressive Alabama had ever witnessed. The Brewer reform program of 1969 was remarkably similar to the 1947 Minimum Foundation Program replaced by Askew in 1973. Nevertheless, for Ala-bama, it was no small step forward.

Reubin Askew was a true southern liberal. His outspokenness on race and his advocacy of busing as the only effective means of desegregating schools proved that he was a different kind of southern politician. In ad-dition, his populistic appeals for tax justice reminded many of past Popu-list governors. During Askew's fight to implement a corporate income tax, one of his corporate opponents called him "a nut with a Huey Long out-look." Many questioned his sanity as he fought on the losing side of the busing amendment referendum. His ability to rebound from that crushing 1972 defeat on busing and make Florida a national leader in education just one year later indicates his broad appeal to Florida voters, even if many disagreed with some of his views.[2]

Askew had certain advantages that West and Brewer lacked. His state had the smallest percentage of blacks in the population in 1970, only 15.3 percent compared with Alabama's 26.4 percent and South Carolina's 30.5 percent. V. O. Key had correctly predicted that Florida's small black population might contribute to the easier development of two-party politics. The state's population was also less southern. Only 37.6 percent of Floridians in 1970 were native born, whereas 76.6 percent of South Carolinians and 80.7 percent of Alabamians were born in the state in which they resided, giving Florida a population that was less inclined to cling to the notion of a segregated South.[3]

Askew also had the clearest vision. He tried to fulfill the "burden" of the New South. He shared a hope with C. Vann Woodward that the South could learn from its mistakes and help the nation cope with rapidly changing notions of race, economics, and liberty. Askew wanted more. He believed the South could lead the nation, not merely teach it. In some ways, Askew's desire for the South was naive. He correctly thought that whites and blacks could unite to fight economic injustices, that southern decency and morality could defeat racism. Yet so had others before him with little result. Three decades later, racism remained a problem in the South, albeit in a more subdued form than in 1970. Nevertheless, Askew was the most articulate of these southern governors in expressing a vision of what the South could become.

John West's South Carolina probably underwent the greatest transformation during this period. Whereas Alabama and Florida exhibited minor changes in racial politics, South Carolina underwent a veritable revolution. West's 1970 victory ushered in a racial transformation of his state, illustrated by Strom Thurmond's courting of black voters after 1970. The era of racial politics in South Carolina was over. Unlike Brewer and Askew, West had to deal with what followed integration. He addressed post-integration problems such as dropouts, pushouts, and student tension. In addressing the needs of educationally marginalized black students, West revealed that there was more to integration than just placing blacks and whites in the same classroom. He also provided his state with alternative methods of reform that stepped out of the conventional changes offered by other governors. Although West's vision was not as clearly elucidated as Askew's, it still focused on helping southerners whose needs had not been met.

Brewer and Askew clearly outpaced West in traditional education reform. Like Alabama, West's state was poor. South Carolina per-capita income in 1970 was $2,936, forty-seventh in the nation. Alabama's was slightly lower at $2,853 (forty-eighth), whereas Florida at $3,642.50 ranked twenty-sixth. In 1970, South Carolina had neither the will nor the funds to undergo drastic education reform. Standing by a promise not to raise taxes, West set about making his state a full member of the new Sunbelt South before undertaking significant and traditional education reform. Under West the state experienced an economic recovery unprecedented in South Carolina history. But affluence came at an ironic price. South Carolina's prosperity dashed the very reform West hoped eventually to carry out with the newfound wealth.[4]

As members of the first generation of New South governors, Brewer, Askew, and West also played the role of trailblazer in their states. Like the moderate governors who preceded West and Askew, this group made initial assaults on economic and racial injustice in their states that a second generation of New South governors in the 1980s would take advantage of to pass even more extensive reform measures. Their administrations accomplished two things that fostered the success of the next generation. First, their moderate stance on race and their victories in 1970 against segregationist foes proved that it was possible to run successful campaigns against racist candidates. Even Brewer's narrow loss to Wallace exhibited a flourishing of black political activism that would eventually spell the doom of overtly race-based campaigns. The new coalitions of black voters and moderate-to-liberal middle-class whites that formed to elect the first generation remained and grew stronger, later helping elect the next generation. These governors proved that class-based politics would not always lose to race in the post–civil rights years. The lone exception in this group was Albert Brewer's Alabama. Unable to overcome the master of racial politics, Brewer lost to George Wallace in 1970. Partly because of this situation, Alabama remained behind the Atlantic Seaboard South in political development due to the "Wallace freeze." Nonetheless, Brewer's strong performance showed Wallace that racial rhetoric would not always work in the South's changing political environment. His close victory over Brewer in 1970 revealed to Wallace that he could no longer cry race and win. Indeed, after 1970 Wallace began to court Alabama's black voters who, thanks to the 1965 Voting Rights Act, became a mainstay in the state's Democratic Party.[5]

This group also planted the seeds for future reformers. John West's failure to enact substantive traditional education reform was not without a positive result. He made his state a model for the rising industrial "sun-belt South." Its dramatic recovery from recession and budget deficits in the early 1970s and subsequent prosperity may have stalled reform during his term, but not forever. In 1984, Governor Richard Riley, who had been a young legislator during West's administration, enacted South Carolina's Education Improvement Act. The act made South Carolina a national education reform leader, just as Askew's 1973 reforms had made Florida a leader eleven years earlier.[6] Still, West's contribution to the state in his concern for the needs of marginalized students and the importance of righting his state's economic fortunes made Riley's success possible. Albert Brewer showed his state that there existed the possibility for fair and responsible government after the Wallace years, that the state could become something other than a bastion of segregation. As the first Florida governor to be elected to consecutive terms, Reubin Askew set a standard by which future Florida governors would be judged. He restored integrity and professionalism to the governor's office while speaking bluntly about the American crisis of race.[7]

Following Askew and the "class" of 1970 came a second generation. Richard Riley was not alone. Men such as Robert Graham in Florida, George Busbee in Georgia, Louisiana's David Treen, Mississippi's William Winter, South Carolina's Richard Riley and Carroll Campbell, Lamar Alexander of Tennessee, Virginia's Charles Robb, Arkansas's David Pryor and Bill Clinton, and the North Carolina triumvirate of James Holshouser, Jim Hunt, and Jim Martin all followed the path struck by first-generation New South governors such as Brewer, Askew, and West. Since 1970, every southern state save Alabama had elected at least one New South governor; most have had two or more.[8]

Brewer, Askew, and West each brought something "new" to their states. Michael O'Brien best describes their contribution to the region. In political terms, to paraphrase O'Brien, no governor's South was the same as another's. Each brought something "new" to the politics of their state. For Brewer, it was a hope for what politics in Alabama could be after the Wallace era. He demonstrated that a racially moderate, reform-minded governor could succeed in Alabama. No Alabama governor has yet matched his education reform successes or skill in handling the state legislature. West represented the death of segregationist politics in South Carolina, embarking the state on a new course of postintegration technical training and industrial investment. Florida under Reubin Askew became a national education model. Fulfilling Askew's desire to lead the nation, Florida government committed itself to racial and tax justice. All three proved to blacks that white southern governors could govern all the people, not just whites.

In the wake of Jimmy Carter's election to the presidency, *Time* magazine devoted an entire issue to the South in 1976. Something had definitely happened in the region, the editors posited. Carter's southern roots, and his legacy as a New South governor in Georgia, caused *Time* to examine "Carter Country," including its politics, culture, society, and economy. *Time* went to perhaps the best person to explain the 1970s South and what the future might hold, Yale historian C. Vann Woodward, who summarized the region's past in an effort to forecast its future. He predicted that the "bulldozer revolution" would end southern distinctiveness as the region knew it then but foresaw the persistence of southern distinctiveness in a manner yet to be defined in 1976, even if it would be state of mind. Woodward also maintained hope for the region's future. Reiterating his arguments from *The Burden of Southern History,* Woodward predicted that if the South received another opportunity to serve as a leader or example for the nation, it might fare better with the apparent removal of the burden of being southern. No longer would southerners, he believed, have their origins and history working against them as much as in the past.[9]

Time also interviewed other "eminent Southerners," including Florida governor Reubin Askew, author Walker Percy, *Alabama Journal* editor Ray Jenkins, and political scientist Alexander Heard. Each agreed that the South had changed for the better following the civil rights movement and rise of two-party politics, and they all expressed a guarded optimism about the South's future.[10]

In its examination of the South in 1976, *Time* also celebrated the rise of a "remarkable group of southern governors." The magazine remarked that this "new class" reflected a paramount change in southern politics caused by the civil rights movement and the abatement of racial tension in the region. It did not go unnoticed that the South's old racial guard had learned the lessons of 1970—by 1976 George Wallace and Strom Thurmond had each moderated their views on race and began to court black voters openly. Much had changed in the South, and the class of New South governors elected in the 1970s played a key role in the transformation of Jim Crow South to Sunbelt South. If, as Askew asserted, education reform, school integration, and southern politics in general was a question of justice, then this group did as much as any other in striving toward that goal. The region had not undergone such a transformation since the end of World War II, when the old agricultural South became modern and mechanized. If the South became economically "new" following World War II, then this group of New South governors contributed substantially to the rise of a new political South. To all three governors, their actions reflected a desire to make the region something better, to bring the South a small portion of the prosperity enjoyed by the rest of the nation. To Askew, West, and Brewer, it was a question of justice for the South and its people.[11]

Notes

INTRODUCTION

1. James Clotfelder and William R. Hamilton, "But Which Southern Strategy?" *South Today*, April 1971, 6; quoted in Numan Bartley, *The New South, 1945–1980* (Baton Rouge: Louisiana State University Press, 1995), 399. For more on the economic transformation of the South after 1945 see Gavin Wright, *Old South, New South: Revolutions in the Southern Economy since the Civil War* (New York: Basic Books, 1986) and Gilbert C. Fite, *Cotton Fields No More: Southern Agriculture, 1865–1980* (Lexington: University Press of Kentucky, 1984); David Goldfield, *Promised Land: The South since 1945* (Wheeling, Ill.: Harlan Davidson, 1987), 172–79; David Goldfield, *Black, White, and Southern: Race Relations and Southern Culture, 1940 to the Present* (Baton Rouge: Louisiana State University Press, 1990), 178–81.

2. Numan Bartley and Hugh D. Graham, *Southern Politics and the Second Reconstruction* (Baltimore: Johns Hopkins University Press, 1975), 18–19, 184–90; V. O. Key, *Southern Politics in State and Nation* (Knoxville: University of Tennessee Press, 1984).

3. Richard L. Ergstrom, "Black Politics and the Voting Rights Act, 1965–1982," in *Contemporary Southern Politics*, ed. James F. Lea (Baton Rouge: Louisiana State University Press, 1988), 83–106; Earl Black and Merle Black, *Politics and Society in the South* (Cambridge: Harvard University Press, 1987), 99.

4. Ergstrom, "Black Politics"; Larry Sabato, "New South Governors and the Governorship," in *Contemporary Southern Politics*, 194–213; Alexander Lamis, *The Two-Party South*, 2d ed. (New York: Oxford University Press, 1990), 4–5.

5. Sabato, "New South Governors." For more on business progressivism, see George Brown Tindall, *The Emergence of the New South, 1913–1945* (Baton Rouge: Louisiana State University Press, 1967), 224, 232, 368.

6. It is John Boles who asserts that the South suffered from "regional bipolar disorder," voting moderate governors into office while also supporting Richard

Nixon. See John B. Boles, *The South through Time: A History of an American Region* (Englewood Cliffs, N.J.: Prentice Hall, 1995), 507–8. For other examples of the scant survey attention paid to "new South" governors, see Dewey W. Grantham, *The South in Modern America: A Region at Odds* (New York: Harper Perennial, 1994), 291–93, and Bartley, *New South,* 467–68; Morgan Kousser has argued that watersheds not only can be deceiving and artificial but also can skew the historical record. See J. Morgan Kousser, "Comments on Michael Perman Paper at the Southern Historical Association" (paper presented at the 66th Annual Meeting of the Southern Historical Association, Louisville, Kentucky, November 8–11, 2000), copy in possession of author.

7. Albert P. Brewer, interview by author, tape recording, October 15, 1997, Birmingham, Alabama, tape in possession of author; *Alabama Journal,* January 8, 1963; Brewer biographical information, Albert P. Brewer Papers, Box 42, Alabama Department of Archives and History, Montgomery (hereafter cited as Brewer Papers).

8. The "Wallace man" label went only so far in Brewer's case. Brewer once commented on Wallace's race baiting when he described a discussion with the former governor over a tax cut Wallace had failed to pass: "He looked at me in silence for a moment and said, 'I'll just holler nigger and everybody will forget it.' And he did. And they did. I was thirty-three years old and speaker of the house and was never so disillusioned in my life." Quote from Jack Bass and Walter De Vries, *The Transformation of Southern Politics* (New York: Meridian, 1977), 58; *Montgomery Advertiser,* May 7, 8, 19, 1968; *Birmingham Post-Herald,* May 8, 1968; *Mobile Register,* May 25, 1968.

9. Bass and De Vries, *Transformation of Southern Politics,* 58; Robert Ingram, *That's the Way I Saw It* (Montgomery: B and E Press, 1986), 3; Brewer interview; James Glen Stovall, Patrick Cotter, and Samuel H. Fisher III, *Alabama Political Almanac,* 2d ed. (Tuscaloosa: University of Alabama Press, 1997), 88–93; Lamis, *Two-Party South,* 76–92.

10. In select precincts Askew, Brewer, and West polled similar numbers from the black community in the 1970 elections. In Miami and Jacksonville, Askew averaged 94 percent of the black vote. In Birmingham and Montgomery, Brewer garnered 98 and 89 percent respectively, and West won 95 percent and 94 percent in Charleston and Columbia. For each, the African American vote was crucial in the success of their campaigns, and in Brewer's case it made him a technical winner in the first primary, though he failed to win 50 percent of the vote, forcing the ill-fated runoff against Wallace. Numan Bartley and Hugh D. Graham, *Southern Elections: County and Precinct Data, 1950–1972* (Baton Rouge: Louisiana State University Press, 1978), 348–49, 358, 386–88.

11. Allen Morris, *The Florida Handbook,* 2d ed. (Tallahassee: Peninsular Press, 1997), 337–38; Reubin O'D. Askew, interview by author, transcript, September 2, 1997, Tallahassee, Florida, recording in possession of author; "Reubin O'Donovan Askew," *Current Biography* (April 1973): 3–5.

12. Alexander Lamis asserts that the 1970 elections were critical to the development of a two-party system in Florida. He noted that Democrats were in disarray, Republicans were on the ascendancy, and the race issue was at prime strength. Lamis, *Two-Party South,* 184–85; Askew interview; Larry Vickers, "Governor Askew in Profile," *South Today,* November 1972, 1–4; *Tallahassee Democrat,* September 30, October 27, 30, November 10, 1970; Howell Raines and Robert Hooker, "Reubin Who?" *Floridian,* February 12, 1978, 7–10; see also Askew campaign files, RG900000, MSS, M83–8, Florida State Archives, Tallahassee; Bass and De Vries, *Transformation of Southern Politics,* 126; Earl Black, *Southern Governors and Civil Rights: Racial Segregation as a Campaign Issue in the Second Reconstruction* (Cambridge: Harvard University Press, 1976), 97.

13. John C. West, interview by author, tape recording, August 20, 1997, Camden, South Carolina, transcript in possession of author. Biographical information on West in Box 33, William D. Workman Jr. Papers, Modern Political Collection, South Caroliniana Library, Columbia (hereafter cited as Workman Papers); Walter Edgar, *South Carolina in the Modern Age* (Columbia: University of South Carolina Press, 1992), 121; Key, *Southern Politics in State and Nation,* 150; *Columbia (S.C.) State,* June 27, 1970.

14. Lamis contrasts Mississippi and South Carolina, "sister states of the Old South." The difference, he wrote, was political leadership. South Carolina had tremendous leadership in leaving race behind; Mississippi did not. Lamis, *Two-Party South,* 44–64. Billy B. Hathorn, "The Changing Politics of Race: Congressman Albert William Watson and the South Carolina Republican Party, 1965–1970," *South Carolina Historical Magazine* 89 (October 1988): 227–41; Edgar, *South Carolina in the Modern Age,* 121, Walter B. Edgar, *South Carolina: A History* (Columbia: University of South Carolina Press, 1998), 547.

15. The 1970 South Carolina gubernatorial election was a watershed for the Republican Party in that state. It forced the party eventually to court black voters and fought the race issue between two parties, not within the Democratic Party, as in Alabama. See Lamis, *Two-Party South,* 75. *Columbia (S.C.) State,* November 1, 4, 5, 1970; *New York Times,* April 25, 30, 1971.

16. Fred Sheheen, undated editorial manuscript, in Albert Watson vertical file, Modern Political Collection, South Caroliniana Library, Columbia, South Carolina; Cole Blease Graham, *South Carolina Politics and Government* (Columbia: University of South Carolina Press, 1994), 93–95, 151–55.

17. Black, *Southern Governors and Civil Rights,* 16–21; Brewer interview; West interview; Askew interview.

18. Sabato, "New South Governors."

19. Ibid., 5–6, 229–31.

20. Diane Ravitch, *The Troubled Crusade: American Education, 1945–1980* (New York: Basic Books, 1983), 119–22. Black per pupil expenditures as a percentage of white

per pupil expenditures struggled to reach 50 percent across the South. In 1931 the figure was 29.6 percent, in 1941, 44 percent, and in 1945, 55.8 percent. Tindall, *Emergence of the New South,* 501.

21. See Tindall, *Emergence of the New South,* for further information on southern school reform in the early twentieth century. The standard work on business progressivism remains George Brown Tindall, "Business Progressivism: Southern Politics in the Twenties," *South Atlantic Quarterly* 42 (winter 1963): 92–106; Lawrence A. Cremin, *American Education: The Metropolitan Experience, 1876–1980* (New York: Harper and Row, 1988), 213–26; Goldfield, *Black, White, and Southern,* 55.

22. David Goldfield provides an excellent discussion of the etiquette of race in his book *Black, White, and Southern,* where he defines it as a manner in which blacks were to act when around or addressing whites. This included such things as averted eyes, addressing whites as "sir" or "ma'am," and smiling continuously. Whites would address blacks as "boy," "uncle," or "aunty."

23. Cremin, *American Education,* 256–64, 270–72.

24. Ironically, white southern businessmen are due partial credit for some successful desegregation efforts. David R. Colburn and Elizabeth Jacoway's edited work, *Southern Businessmen and Desegregation* (Baton Rouge: Louisiana State University Press, 1982), examines how white businessmen in the South gave in to, and sometimes led, desegregation efforts rather than lose potential business and profits. They also needed a minimally educated workforce and hence their support for education reform in many cases. Cremin, *American Education,* 258–60; Goldfield, *Black White, and Southern,* 55; Numan V. Bartley, *The Rise of Massive Resistance: Race and Politics in the South during the 1950s* (Baton Rouge: Louisiana State University Press, 1969) is an excellent treatment of the South's defiance in the face of *Brown.*

25. Cremin, *American Education,* 263–65. An excellent study of the role of federal judges in enforcing *Brown* is Jack Bass, *Unlikely Heroes: The Dramatic Story of the Southern Judges Who Translated the Supreme Court's Brown Decision into a Revolution for Equality* (New York: Touchstone, 1981).

1. "DEEPER THAN A BUS RUNNING DOWN A ROAD": THE INTEGRATION OF ALABAMA'S PUBLIC SCHOOLS

1. Brewer interview; Ira Harvey, *A History of Educational Finance in Alabama, 1819–1986* (Auburn, Ala.: Truman Pierce Institute for the Advancement of Teacher Education, 1989), 239.

2. Brewer interview.

3. Robert J. Norrell, *Reaping the Whirlwind: The Civil Rights Movement in Tuskegee* (New York: Knopf, 1985), 137–39; Jack Bass, *Taming the Storm: The Life and Times of Judge Frank M. Johnson, Jr. and the South's Fight over Civil Rights* (New York: Doubleday, 1993), 207. The Mobile case was officially styled as *Birdie Mae Davis, et al and U.S. v.*

Board of School Commissioners, Mobile County, Civil Action no. 3003-3063, U.S. District Court for the Southern District of Alabama. Joseph W. Newman and Betty Brandon, "Integration in the Mobile Public Schools," in *The Future of Public Education in Mobile,* ed. Joseph W. Newman and Howard F. Mahan (Mobile: South Alabama Review, 1982), 45–54; see also Tinsley Yarbrough, *Judge Frank Johnson and Human Rights in Alabama* (Tuscaloosa: University of Alabama Press, 1981).

4. One such newly founded segregated institution, Macon Academy, was established shortly after Johnson's order. Located in an empty mansion just across from Tuskegee High School, the school received a great deal of support in its early months. By the end of its first month more than $25,000 had been donated to the school, including $2,000 solicited from state employees by Governor George C. Wallace. Norrell, *Reaping the Whirlwind,* 150–51, 195; Newman and Brandon, "Integration," 45–48, argue that integrating the schools with the twelfth grade first caused more tension than integrating lower grades first. The order to desegregate on this basis is found in *Davis v. Board,* 333 F2d 53 and *Davis v. Board,* 322 F2d 356.

5. The pupil placement law actually passed an early constitutional test. Federal judge Rivers of the Northern District of Alabama upheld the law as constitutional "on its face" in his decision in *Shuttlesworth v. Birmingham Board of Education,* 162 F. Supp. 372 (1957). The Supreme Court allowed this ruling to stand in 1958. Bass, *Taming the Storm,* 212–13; Norrell, *Reaping the Whirlwind,* 139; William Warren Rogers, Robert David Ward, Leah Rawls Atkins, and Wayne Flynt, *Alabama: The History of a Deep South State* (Tuscaloosa: University of Alabama Press, 1994), 547–49. For a study of Alabama's early reaction to *Brown* see James Tyra Harris, "Alabama Reaction to the *Brown* Decision, 1954–1956" (D.A. diss., Middle Tennessee State University, 1978).

6. Bass, *Taming the Storm,* 213–14.

7. Ibid. The NAACP decided not to fight the *Briggs* decision because the organization was short of funds, having just fought and won *Brown.* It also feared that loss of such an appeal would have given greater legitimacy to freedom of choice.

8. *Davis v. Board,* On Writ of Certiorari to the U.S. Court of Appeals for the Fifth Circuit, Brief for the Board of School Commissioners of Mobile County, in Brewer Papers, Box 3; Newman and Brandon, "Integration," 45–48.

9. Newman and Brandon, "Integration," 45–50; *Davis v. Board,* 322 F2d 356, 333 F2d 53, and 364 F2d 896.

10. Bass, *Taming the Storm,* 222, 225; telegram from Wallace to Brewer, no date, ca. 1966, Brewer Papers.

11. Bass, *Taming the Storm,* 228–29.

12. Indeed, some local boards of education investigated freedom of choice applicants. In Crenshaw County in 1965 and 1966, for instance, school officials recorded criminal records and illegitimate births. Hugh Maddox, legal advisor to Mrs. Wallace and Brewer, kept a file of such information to be used when necessary. Basing freedom of choice on investigations of illegitimate births and criminal records made it

clear that the intent of such action was to deny blacks access to previously all-white schools. The state's defense of *Lee v. Macon* attempted to capitalize on perceptions of black inferiority and white fears of radicalism. The defendant's deposition questions included such interrogatories as "Do you think Negro teachers are just as qualified as white teachers?" "By 1956 weren't there a total of seventy-seven top officials of the NAACP alleged to have been involved in pro-Communist activities?" "Didn't W. E. B. DuBois finally join the Communist Party in his old age?" "Does your organization contend that a Negro child can get a better education merely because he is sitting by a white child?" Notes on a Saturday conference on Crenshaw County desegregation, no date, ca. 1966; "Interrogatories Propounded under the Provisions of Rule 33, Federal rules of Civil Procedure," *Lee v. Macon,* Civil Action No. 604-E; both in Alabama Governor Legal Advisor files, Hugh Maddox Papers, SG 20051, Alabama Department of Archives and History, Montgomery (hereafter cited as Maddox Papers).

13. Brewer's fears were correct. Between 1965 and 1975 public school enrollment declined by one-third whereas nonpublic school enrollment grew by 80 percent. James D. Thomas and William Stewart, *Alabama Government and Politics* (Lincoln: University of Nebraska Press, 1988), 120–24. Between 1967 and 1971, more than fifty thousand white children enrolled in private schools. Between September 1970 and September 1971, eight thousand to ten thousand white children enrolled in such schools. John William Heron, "The Growth of Private Schools and Their Impact on the Public Schools of Alabama, 1955–1977" (Ed.D. diss. University of Alabama, 1977). Transcript of press conference, May 22, 1968, Brewer Papers, Box 41; *Mobile Register,* September 1, 1968.

14. *Montgomery Advertiser,* August 23, 1968; see also Fred Gray, *Bus Ride to Justice, Changing the System by the System: The Life and Works of Fred D. Gray* (Montgomery: Black Belt Press, 1995).

15. Judgment of the court in *Annie Yvonne Harris v. Crenshaw County Board of Education,* August 8, 1968, Civil Action No. 2455-N; Preliminary Writ of Injunction, *Harris v. Crenshaw County Board of Education,* September 23, 1966; Civil Action No. 2455-N; both in Brewer Papers, Box SG 20051.

16. Speech before the Alabama Bar Association, Tuscaloosa, July 19, 1968; speech before Jacksonville State University commencement, July 26, 1968; speech before the Alabama Association of High School Principals, Montgomery, Alabama, July 29, 1968; all in Alabama Governor, Speeches, Albert P. Brewer, SG 12678, Reel 3, Alabama Department of Archives and History, Montgomery (hereafter cited as Brewer Speeches). For a copy of the speech before the high school principals also see Brewer Papers, Box 9; *Birmingham News,* July 20, 1968; *Montgomery Advertiser,* August 23, 1968; Brewer interview.

17. Bass, *Taming the Storm,* 222; *Montgomery Advertiser,* August 29, 1968; *Alabama*

Journal, August 29, 1968; *Green v. New Kent County, Va. School Board,* 391 U.S. 430 (1968); see also Davison M. Douglas, *Reading Writing and Race: The Desegregation of the Charlotte Schools* (Chapel Hill: University of North Carolina Press, 1995).

18. The seventy-six systems under the order had a total of 102,641 students. *Birmingham News,* August 29, 1968; *Alabama Journal,* August 29, 1968; *Montgomery Advertiser,* August 29, 1968. Years later Brewer admitted that Johnson's closing of the black schools to force integration was "clever. He was pretty creative with some of his orders." The two later became close friends. Brewer interview.

19. *Montgomery Advertiser,* August 26, 29, October 3, 1968; *Birmingham News,* October 8, 1968; Brewer interview.

20. *Birmingham News,* September 5, 24, October 3, 1968; *Birmingham Post-Herald,* September 5, 14, 1968; *Alabama Journal,* September 27, 1968; *Trial Brief of the United States, Lee v. Macon,* 267 F. Supp. 464, 469.

21. *Montgomery Advertiser,* September 5, 13, 1968; *Birmingham Post-Herald,* September 14, 19, 1968; speech before the Alabama Association of School Boards, October 4, 1968, in Brewer Speeches, SG 12678, Reel 3; Brewer interview.

22. Brewer Speeches, SG 12678, Reel 3.

23. In Baldwin County, forty-two parents of black school children filed a petition with Johnson to keep open their neighborhood school because they feared overcrowding and the loss of sixteen teaching jobs held by black teachers. *Montgomery Advertiser,* October 26, 1968; *Mobile Register,* October 27, 1968; Brewer to Dewey Woods, October 30, 1968, Albert P. Brewer Administrative Papers, SG 22459 (hereafter cited as Brewer Administrative Papers); *Montgomery Advertiser,* October 2, 1968.

24. The nineteen noncomplying county systems included fifteen counties (Baldwin, Calhoun, Chilton, Clark, Clay, Geneva, Henry, Limestone, Marengo, Monroe, Morgan, Pickens, Shelby, Sumter, and Walker) and four cities (Decatur, Demopolis, Florence, and Piedmont). *Montgomery Advertiser,* October 15, 1968; *Mobile Register,* October 19, 1968.

25. *Montgomery Advertiser,* October 16, 1968.

26. *Birmingham News,* November 22, 1968; *Montgomery Advertiser,* November 24, 1968, February 19, 1969.

27. Address before the Alabama Education Association, Birmingham, Alabama, March 13, 1969, Brewer Speeches, SG 12678, Reel 3; copy of speech in the Brewer Papers, Box 9; *Montgomery Advertiser,* March 14, 1969; Brewer interview.

28. Address before the Alabama Education Association, Birmingham, Alabama, March 13, 1969, Brewer Speeches, SG 12678, Reel 3; copy of speech in the Brewer Papers, Box 9.

29. Brewer was distressed at the merger of the Alabama State Teachers Association and the Alabama Education Association because the former had been involved in the desegregation suits. He felt that AEA was opposed to such litigation. AEA president

Raymond Christian agreed with Brewer and included himself in the group opposed to the litigation. Brewer to Raymond Christian, May 20, 1969; Christian to Brewer May 23, 1969, both in Brewer Administrative Papers, SG 22459; *Montgomery Advertiser,* March 14, 1969; *Alabama Journal,* March 17, 1969.

30. The *Alabama Journal* once wrote of the Sovereignty Commission: "The very name of the State Sovereignty Commission conjures up the smell of moldering, leather-backed volumes of the Confederacy, commissioned by the U.D.C. to further mythologize lost causes and slain generals." *Alabama Journal,* July 18, 1968; Brewer to G. E. McNabb, June 17, 1969; Kenny Jenkins to Brewer, July 22, 1969; Brewer to Jenkins, July 24, 1969; P. D. Sadlera to Brewer, May 3, 1969, in Brewer Administrative Papers, SG 22459; Hugh Maddox memo to Brewer, May 1, 1969; State Attorney General MacDonald Gallion to Brewer, June 16, 1969, both in Maddox Papers; Reverend Edward Sheppard to Brewer, July 30, 1969, Brewer Administrative Papers, SG 22639; letter to the State Sovereignty Commission from Marion County Board of Education Superintendent Fred Hubbard, May 19, 1969; Hugh Maddox memo to Brewer, May 22, 1969, both in Brewer Administrative Papers, SG 22652; unpublished history of the State Sovereignty Commission, no date, in the Papers of the Alabama State Sovereignty Commission, SG 13842, Alabama Department of Archives and History, Montgomery (hereafter cited as Sovereignty Commission Papers).

31. *Alabama Journal,* March 18, 1969; Financial Summary of the Alabama State Sovereignty Commission, September 30, 1972, Sovereignty Commission Papers, SG 13842.

32. Maddox memo to files, June 13, 1969, Maddox Papers, SG 20057; *Montgomery Advertiser,* September 12, 1968.

33. *Montgomery Advertiser,* September 12, 1968; *Davis v. School Commissioners, Decree on Suit,* August 1, 1969, Civil Action No. 3003-63; Maddox notes from phone conversation with Abe Phillips, August 4, 1969, both in Maddox Papers, SG 20057.

34. Many of the hundreds of letters and telegrams to Brewer opposing court orders can be found in the Brewer Administrative Papers, SG 22639; R. W. W. to Brewer, January 13, 1970, Brewer Administrative Papers, SG 22459; Mildred Ball to Brewer, October 16, 1968; *Mobile Register,* July 14, 1968; *Montgomery Advertiser,* October 1, 1968; Canes Club of Mobile resolution, July 23, 1969; Exchange Club resolution, July 30, 1969; Robert L. Pellein to Brewer, July 26, 1969; James Jones to Brewer, June 3, 1969; Louise Hand to Brewer, no date, ca. 1970, RC 2, G 404; and Jim Cooper to Brewer, January 15, 1970, both in Brewer Administrative Papers, SG 22459; flyer of the Citizens' Political Action Committee, spring 1969, Brewer Administrative Papers, SG 22639.

35. League of Women Voters-Mobile president Ruth S. Perot to Brewer, January 23, 1970; Ralph Gustafson to Brewer, October 1969; all in Brewer Administrative Papers, SG 22639.

36. See carbon copies of Brewer responses to protest letters, Brewer Administrative Papers, SG 22639; Brewer to Ralph Gustafson, October 10, 1969, Brewer Administrative Papers, SG 22637; Brewer to John W. Turner, August 28, 1969, Brewer Administrative Papers, SG 22459; press conference transcript, May 22, 1968, Brewer Papers, Box 41; John and Gladys Scott to Brewer, July 24, 1969, Brewer Administrative Papers, SG 22459; Brewer interview.

37. Lester Maddox to Brewer, July 30, 1969; Brewer telegram to Maddox, August 6, 1969; Ernest Stone to Brewer, August 19, 1969, all in Brewer Administrative Papers, SG 22459; *Alabama Journal,* August 6, 1969.

38. Martha B. King to Brewer, September 2, 1969; L. O. Ingle to Brewer, August 21, 1969; J. W. Park to Brewer, August 19, 1969; G. E. McNabb to Brewer, August 13, 1969; Brewer to Edward Ford, August 29, 1969, all in Brewer Administrative Papers, SG 22459.

39. *Alabama Journal,* September 5, 1969; *Montgomery Advertiser,* September 5, 1969.

40. The senate voted 23-11 and the house voted 85-5 in favor of the resolution. *Montgomery Advertiser,* September 5, 1969.

41. *Montgomery Advertiser,* September 6, 1969; *Alabama Journal,* September 4, 1969; Joe Payne to Brewer, September 11, 1969, Brewer Administrative Papers, SG 22459.

42. *Alabama Journal,* September 15, 1969.

43. *Alabama Journal,* September 15, 1969; Dewey Bartlett memo on busing resolution; resolution submitted by Governor Marvin Mandel of Maryland; "Report of the Resolutions Committee to the Southern Governors' Conference, September 14–17, 1969," all in Brewer Papers, Box 2; *Nashville Tennessean,* September 18, 1969; Brewer notes on busing resolution, Brewer Administrative Papers, SG 22461.

44. *Montgomery Independent,* October 16, 1969.

45. Transcript of Brewer press conference, October 15, 1969, Brewer Papers, Box 41; *Alabama Journal,* October 29, 1969; *Montgomery Advertiser,* October 16, 1969.

46. *State of Alabama v. Robert Finch,* motion of leave to file complaint, Supreme Court of the United States, October term 1969, in Maddox Papers, SG 20058.

47. Brewer's appeal to the U.S. district court was styled Civil Action No. 70-82, Maddox Papers, SG 20058; *Alabama Journal,* February 3, 4, 1970; *Montgomery Advertiser,* February 3, 1970; *Birmingham Post-Herald,* February 5, 1970; *Montgomery Independent,* January 29, 1970.

48. Before the Mobile meeting was finalized, the southern governors and congressmen were invited to a large rally scheduled in Birmingham on the same day. The sponsors, Concerned Parents for Public Education, scheduled the rally to start a petition drive to protest court-ordered integration. Governor Williams wanted assurance that the rally would not in fact be a Wallace rally before he would attend.

Birmingham News, February 4, 6, 1970; *Mobile Register,* February 8, 9, 1970; Brewer handwritten notes for the meeting in Mobile, February 8, 1970, Brewer Administrative Papers, SG 22641.

49. *Montgomery Advertiser,* February 21, 1970; *Birmingham Post-Herald,* February 21, 1970.

50. *Birmingham News,* February 24, 1970; *Montgomery Advertiser,* February 24, 1970; Brewer address to special session of legislature, February 23, 1970, Brewer Papers, Box 14, and Brewer Administrative Papers, SG 12678, Microfilm Reel 3.

51. Representative Bob Ellis of Jefferson County tried to pass all three measures in a "Concerned Parents Package" of legislation. *Birmingham Post-Herald,* February 26, 1970; *Birmingham News,* February 28, 1970; *Alabama Journal,* February 25, 1970; *House Journal, Alabama, Special Session 1970; Senate Journal, Alabama, Special Session 1970; Summary of Laws and Resolutions Enacted during the Special Session of the Alabama Legislature which Convened February 23, 1970* (Montgomery: Legislative Reference Service, March 17, 1970).

52. Brewer interview.

53. *Montgomery Advertiser,* August 23, 1968.

2. "WHY NOT THE TEACHERS?": EDUCATION REFORM IN ALABAMA, 1968–1970

1. *Montgomery Advertiser,* May 12, September 4, 1968; flyer from the American Association of University Women, 1968, in Brewer Administrative Papers, SG 22458; National Education Association press release, 1968, Harry M. Philpott Papers, Box 5, Special Collections, Ralph Brown Draughon Library, Auburn University Archives (hereafter referred to as Philpott Papers); Ira Harvey, *A History of Educational Finance in Alabama: 1819–1926* (Auburn University: Truman Pierce Institute for the Advancement of Teacher Education, 1986), 238–41; National Education Association, *Rankings of the States, 1970* (Washington, D.C.: National Education Association, 1970).

2. *Preliminary Report of the Alabama Education Commission, 1919* (Montgomery: N.p., 1919), and *Report of the Alabama Education Commission, 1959* (Montgomery: N.p., 1959), both in Auburn University Special Collections. The *Report of the Alabama Education Study Commission* (Montgomery: N.p., 1969) provides good summaries of preceding studies; Harvey, *A History of Educational Finance in Alabama,* 236–37.

3. *Preliminary Report of the Alabama Education Commission, 1919.*

4. *Report of the Alabama Education Commission, 1959.*

5. Ibid.

6. Alabama Education Association, "Better Education Essential to Alabama's Expanding Economy," 1957, Special Collections, Auburn University.

7. *Report of the Alabama Education Study Commission.*

8. Alabama Education Association, "Better Education"; Alabama Education As-

sociation Research Division, "Research Report," January 1968, Philpott Papers, Box 5; *Report of the Alabama Education Study Commission.*

9. Brewer speech before the Alabama Association of Secondary School Principals, July 29, 1968, Brewer Speeches, SG 12678, Reel 3; Brewer press conference transcript, May 22, 1968, Brewer Papers, Box 41; *Montgomery Advertiser,* April 24, July 18, August 1, 1968; *Alabama Journal,* June 15, 1968.

10. Brewer speech before commencement exercises at Northeast Alabama State Technical School, June 1968, Brewer Administrative Papers, SG 7036.

11. *Geneva Reaper,* August 15, 1968; *Montgomery Advertiser,* July 31, August 1, 1968; *Lowndes Signal,* August 8, 1968; *Birmingham News,* August 9, 1968; *Birmingham Post-Herald,* August 2, 1968.

12. *Auburn Bulletin,* August 1, 1968; *Alabama School Journal* 86 (May 1969): 40.

13. Brewer's bold reform stance differed from his lukewarm acceptance of integration.

14. Brewer speech at Troy State University commencement, August 9, 1968, Brewer Speeches, SG 12678, Reel 3; *Alabama Journal,* September 12, 1968; transcript of Brewer interview on WSFA-TV, Montgomery, Alabama, August 20, 1968, Brewer Speeches, SG 12678, Reel 3.

15. The Special Education Trust Fund was the primary funding source for education. Funded by sales and income taxes, it was especially sensitive to fluctuations in the economy. More often than not, shortfalls in revenue collections required proration of the state education budget. *Birmingham News,* August 25, October 2, 1968; *Montgomery Advertiser,* October 3, 1968; *Birmingham Post-Herald,* August 22, 1968.

16. *Montgomery Advertiser,* September 4, 12, 1968; Sarah L. Stewart to Brewer, October 7, 1968, Brewer Administrative Papers, SG 22458; Anne Permaloff and Carl Grafton, *Political Power in Alabama: The More Things Change. . . .* (Athens: University of Georgia Press, 1995), 281; *Alabama School Journal* 86 (October 1968): 4–5.

17. Associated Industries' arguments had merit. Alabama's state support for schools in 1967 was among the highest in the nation at 62.3 percent. Only New Mexico, Hawaii, North Carolina, South Carolina, and Maryland were higher. The national average was 39.1 percent. Associated Industries of Alabama represented 1,039 member companies and their 736,000 employees located in sixty-four of Alabama's sixty-seven counties. Only Pennsylvania with 6 percent; Kentucky, Mississippi, and Rhode Island with 5 percent; and Florida, California, and the District of Columbia with 4 percent had a higher sales tax than Alabama. Statement of Associated Industries of Alabama before the Educational Study Commission, November 7, 1968, Montgomery, Alabama, Brewer Administrative Papers, SG 22459.

18. *Montgomery Advertiser,* October 18, 22, 1968; Grover Talbot Jacobs, "Constitutional, Statutory, and Judicial History of Property Tax as a Source of Support for Public Education in Alabama, 1819–1976" (Ph.D. diss., Auburn University, 1976), 87, 92; Permaloff and Grafton, *Political Power in Alabama,* 287.

19. Assessment was so low that in 1967 the Louisville and Nashville Railroad sued the state for assessing its land at 40 percent while the rest of the state paid on average 20 percent. See *Louisville and Nashville Railroad Co. v. State of Alabama,* Montgomery County Circuit Court, nos. 36397, 36642, and 36936 (April 4, 1967); Jacobs, "Constitutional, Statutory, and Judicial History," 49; *Mobile Register,* October 18, 1968; Statement of the Birmingham Area Chamber of Commerce before the Education Study Commission, November 8, 1968, Brewer Administrative Papers, SG 22459; Permaloff and Grafton, *Political Power in Alabama,* 286–87.

20. *Birmingham Post-Herald,* September 24, 1968; Ernest Stone to Brewer, October 8, 1968, and October 16, 1968, Brewer Administrative Papers, SG 22458; Brewer speech to the Capital City Jaycees, October 4, 1968, Montgomery, Alabama, Brewer Administrative Papers, SG 22458.

21. Some of Alabama's most powerful legislators attended the Birmingham rat pack meeting: Mobile's Bill McDermott, Stewart O'Bannon of Florence, J. J. Pierce from Montgomery, Alexander City's Tom Radney, Ollie Nabors of Gadsden, C. C. "Bo" Torbert of Opelika, and Woodrow Albeen of Anniston. *Birmingham Post-Herald,* December 10, 17, 1968; *Birmingham News,* December 22, 1968; *Phenix City Citizen-Herald,* December 26, 1968.

22. *Birmingham News,* December 17, 1968; *Birmingham Post-Herald,* December 22, 1968; *Alabama School Journal* 86 (May 1969): 5.

23. *Birmingham News,* January 3, 1969.

24. H. C. Sikes to Brewer, February 17, 1969; Rosemary Carter to Brewer, February 11, 1969; Jean Smith to Brewer, February 14, 1969; Joe Parish to Brewer, January 28, 1969; Ernest Stone to Brewer, February 25, 1969; see also scores of letters to the governor, all in Brewer Administrative Papers, SG 22458 and SG 22459.

25. *Alabama Journal,* February 20, 1969; *Opelika Daily News,* January 28, 1969; *Montgomery Advertiser,* January 24, 1969.

26. *Montgomery Advertiser,* January 24, 1969; *Alabama School Journal* 86 (April 1969): 18–19.

27. *Birmingham News,* January 4, 1969; *Brewton Standard,* December 26, 1968; *Decatur Daily,* January 28, 1969; *Montgomery Advertiser,* February 15, 19, 1969; Brewer press release, February 5, 1969, Brewer Papers, Box 39.

28. *Alabama Journal,* February 19, March 15, 1969; *Montgomery Advertiser,* February 19, 20, 1969; Brewer speech before the Alabama Education Association, March 13, 1969, Birmingham, Alabama, Brewer Speeches, SG 12678, Reel 3.

29. *Montgomery Advertiser,* March 23, 1969.

30. Ibid; Permaloff and Grafton, *Political Power in Alabama,* 282–86.

31. *Huntsville News,* April 5, 1969; *Montgomery Advertiser,* March 23, 1969; *Anniston Star,* April 2, 1969.

32. *Montgomery Advertiser,* March 25, 1969; *Huntsville Times,* March 23, 1969.

33. Brewer address to special session of the Alabama Legislature, April 1, 1969,

Brewer Speeches, SG 12678, Reel 3, and Brewer Papers, Box 14; *Alabama Journal,* April 2, 1969; *Alabama School Journal* 86 (April 1969): 3–4; Harvey, *History of Educational Finance in Alabama,* 239–41.

34. Brewer address to special session of the Alabama Legislature, April 1, 1969, Brewer Speeches, SG 12678, Reel 3, and Brewer Papers, Box 14.

35. *Birmingham News,* April 11, 28, 1969; *Birmingham Post-Herald,* May 2, 1969; *Montgomery Advertiser,* April 23, 24, 25, 1969; *Mobile Register,* April 24, 1969; Brewer press release, April 23, 1969, Brewer Papers, Box 39; *Alabama School Journal* 86 (April 1969): 3–4; *Alabama School Journal* 86 (October 1968): 9; *Alabama School Journal* 86 (May 1969): 5.

36. See editorials in the *Tuscaloosa News,* May 4, 1969; *Decatur Daily,* May 5, 1969; *Opelika Daily News,* May 6, 1969; *Baldwin Times,* May 8, 1969; *Birmingham News,* May 12, 1969; *Montgomery Advertiser,* May 18, 1969; *Sand Mountain Reporter,* May 17, 1969; and the *Auburn Bulletin,* May 8, 1969; *Alabama School Journal* 86 (May 1969): 5.

37. Permaloff and Grafton, *Political Power in Alabama,* 280; Brewer message to the legislature at the close of the 1969 special session, no date, ca. May 8, 1969, Brewer Papers, Box 14; Brewer address to annual meeting of the Alabama Education Association, Birmingham, Alabama, March 12, 1970, Brewer Speeches, SG 12678, Reel 3; *Auburn Bulletin,* May 8, 1969; Brewer press release, April 16, 1969, Brewer Papers, Box 39; WSFA-TV editorial, Brewer Papers, Box 19; AEA executive secretary Paul Hubbert to Brewer, July 24, 1969, Brewer Administrative Papers, SG 22459; *Alabama School Journal* 87 (September 1969): 17–18.

38. *Montgomery Advertiser,* October 5, 1968; *Birmingham Post-Herald,* October 12, 1968; *Huntsville Times,* January 26, 1969; Jacobs, "Constitutional, Statutory, and Judicial History," 4.

39. Title 51, Section 17 of Alabama law was replaced by Title 51, Section 17(1). In 1971, the U.S. District Court for the Northern District of Alabama voided this change as part of a lawsuit on property tax equity. See Jacobs, "Constitutional, Statutory, and Judicial History," 88, and *Weissinger v. Boswell,* 330 F. Supp. 617 (M.D. Ala., 1971); *Birmingham News,* May 27, July 31, 1969; *Montgomery Advertiser,* October 22, 1968, April 20, May 22, July 29, 1969; *Mobile Register,* April 24, May 23, 1969; Brewer address before the opening of the regular session of the 1969 Alabama legislature, no date, ca. May 8, 1969, Brewer Papers, Box 14.

40. *Mobile Register,* April 24, May 23, 1969; *Birmingham News,* May 27, July 31, 1969.

41. *Mobile Register,* May 23, 1969; *Montgomery Advertiser,* July 29, 1969; *Birmingham Post-Herald,* October 29, 1970.

42. The sales tax increase brought in $140 million, the state income tax increase $79.3 million, and the utility tax $48.7 million. *Birmingham News,* January 4, June 21, 25, 1970; *Montgomery Advertiser,* August 7, 9, 22, 1970; *Mobile Register,* February 28, 1971.

43. Brewer address before the annual convention of the Alabama Education Association, March 12, 1970, Birmingham, Alabama, Brewer Speeches, SG 12678, Reel 3; *Birmingham News,* January 4, June 21, 25, 1970; *Montgomery Advertiser,* August 7, 9, 1970; *Mobile Register,* February 28, 1971.

44. *Alabama School Journal* 86 (April 1969): 19.

3. A QUESTION OF JUSTICE: THE 1972 FLORIDA BUSING STRAW VOTE

1. Askew was well read in southern history, especially the work of C. Vann Woodward, whom he quoted when he spoke of the South's burden in his speech at Yale University in 1976; Reubin Askew speech at Yale University, November 16, 1976, Reubin O'D. Askew Papers, S849, Box 6, Florida State Archives (hereafter cited as Askew Papers); Reubin Askew speech before the Symposium on the Contemporary South, January 12, 1972, Tampa, Florida, Askew Papers, S126, Box 20; C. Vann Woodward, *The Burden of Southern History* (Baton Rouge: Louisiana State University Press, 1960).

2. David R. Colburn and Richard K. Scher, *Florida's Gubernatorial Politics in the Twentieth Century* (Tallahassee: University Presses of Florida, 1980), 228–30, 276–81.

3. *Tallahassee Democrat,* August 30, 1970; Kirk campaign press release, February 6, April 5, August 26, September 5, 1970, all in Askew Papers, S126, B7; *Tallahassee Democrat,* August 18, August 23, August 25, 1970; *(Jacksonville) Florida Times-Union,* September 4, 1971.

4. Colburn and Scher, *Florida's Gubernatorial Politics,* 228–30, 276–81; *Famuan,* December 1971; Claude Anderson, "Brainstorming on Busing" in "Facts on Busing," February 28, 1972, in Askew Papers S126, B3.

5. Askew press release, April 20, May 26, 1971, Askew Papers, S126, B7.

6. David R. Colburn and Richard K. Scher, "Race Relations and Florida Gubernatorial Politics since the *Brown* Decision," *Florida Historical Quarterly* 55 (October 1976): 153–69; see also Colburn and Scher, *Florida Gubernatorial Politics,* 222–24; Lamis, *Two-Party South,* 35.

7. Askew interview.

8. Askew commencement speech at the University of Florida, August 28, 1971, Askew Papers, S126, B20; Colburn and Scher, *Florida's Gubernatorial Politics,* 228–30, 276–81.

9. Askew commencement speech at the University of Florida, August 28, 1971, Askew Papers, S126, B20; Colburn and Scher, *Florida's Gubernatorial Politics,* 228–30, 276–81.

10. *(Jacksonville) Florida Times-Union,* September 4, 1971; Edward Brown to Askew, December 28, 1971, Askew Papers, S125, B1; "Statewide Status Report on Schools: 1971," Florida Department of Education, Askew Papers, S126, B9.

11. *Famuan,* December 1971; undated UPI article on Anderson, both in Askew Papers, S126.

12. *St. Petersburg Times,* October 27, 28, 1971.

13. *St. Petersburg Times,* October 28, November 11, 17, 1971.

14. *St. Petersburg Times,* November 1, 3, 16, 20, 1971.

15. Chris Potter to Askew, January 9, 1972, W. Davis to Askew, January 3, 1972, Askew Papers S125, B1. Many of the letters Askew received are located in this container.

16. *Tallahassee Democrat,* January 13, 20, 1972; Askew speech before the Symposium on the Contemporary South, Tampa, Florida, January 12, 1972, Askew Papers, S126, B20.

17. *Tallahassee Democrat,* January 13, 20, 1972; Askew speech before the Symposium on the Contemporary South, Tampa, Florida, January 12, 1972, Askew Papers, S126, B20.

18. The origins of the busing resolution are unclear. Askew believed that the Nixon administration had a direct hand in the issue. He accused Nixon special counsel and South Carolina Republican operative Harry S. Dent of giving Florida legislators the idea. In his memoirs, Dent downplayed his involvement: "Governor Reuben [sic] Askew of Florida accused me of producing the idea of getting the Florida Legislature to put the busing referendum on the primary ballot. I only underscored its importance when the idea was bounced off me by Florida legislators. Anyway, it was a grand idea, and it worked to our benefit—in the GOP side and the Democratic side of the primary." Harry S. Dent, *The Prodigal South Returns to Power* (New York: John Wiley and Sons, 1978), 165, 247; Askew interview; *Tallahassee Democrat,* February 4, 8, 10, 14, 16, March 3, 1972.

19. *Tallahassee Democrat,* February 11, 1972; WTVT Channel 13, Tampa-St. Petersburg, February 10, 1972, transcript in Askew Papers, S126, B7; Askew interview.

20. Askew to Richard Pettigrew, February 14, 1972, Askew Papers, S126, B7; *Tallahassee Democrat,* February 14, 1972; Askew press conference statement, February 15, 1972, Askew Papers, S126, B20; Askew interview.

21. Transcript of Askew press conference, February 15, 1972, Askew Papers, RG103; statement read at press conference, February 15, 1972, Askew Papers, S126, B20; *Tallahassee Democrat,* February 14, 15, 1972.

22. Transcript of Askew press conference, February 15, 1972, Askew Papers, RG103.

23. Askew interview; *Tallahassee Democrat,* February 18, 20, 1972.

24. Colburn and Scher, *Florida Gubernatorial Politics,* 229; *Tallahassee Democrat,* February 21, 1972; *St. Petersburg Times,* February 22, 1972.

25. *Tallahassee Democrat,* March 11, 1972; *St. Petersburg Times,* February 22, 1972; Askew press release, March 7, 1972, Askew Papers, S763, RG100, B5; Rabbi Sheldon Edwards to Askew, March 9, 1972, Askew Papers, S497, B2.

26. *St. Petersburg Times,* February 22, 1972; Rabbi Sheldon Edwards to Askew, March 9, 1972, Askew Papers, S497, B2.

27. *Tallahassee Democrat,* February 21, 23, March 1, 2, 1972; *St. Petersburg Times,* March 1, 1972.

28. *Tallahassee Democrat,* February 26, 29, March 3, 1972; Colburn and Scher, *Florida Gubernatorial Politics,* 229; Askew press conference transcript, March 3, 1972, Askew Papers, RG103, S66, B1; *St. Petersburg Times,* March 5, 1972.

29. *St. Petersburg Times,* March 5, 6, 1972.

30. *Tallahassee Democrat,* March 10, 11, April 16, 1972; Askew press conference transcript, March 10, 1972, Askew Papers, S66, RG103, B1; "Fact Book on Pupil Transportation," from hearings on H.J. Res 620, before Subcommittee No. 5 of U.S. House Committee on Judiciary, March 1, 1972, appendices to testimony of Theodore M. Hesburgh, Chairman, U.S. Commission on Civil Rights, Appendix C, "Public School Desegregation in Hillsborough County, Florida;" "DNC-Special Analysis-Busing," Democratic National Committee, 1974; "Facts About Busing," Jeffrey L. Brezner and Herbert Cambridge, February 28, 1972, Florida School Desegregation Consulting Center, University of Miami, School of Education, all in Askew Papers, S126, B3.

31. *St. Petersburg Times,* March 8, 1972.

32. *Tallahassee Democrat,* March 7, 1972; *St. Petersburg Times,* March 8, 1972.

33. *St. Petersburg Times,* March 8, 1972; *Tallahassee Democrat,* March 7, 11, 1972; Richard Deeb editorial response, WJXT-TV Jacksonville, March 12, 1972, transcript in Bruce Smathers Papers, RG900000, M75-93, Florida State Archives, Tallahassee (hereafter referred to as Smathers Papers).

34. *St. Petersburg Times,* March 13, 1972.

35. Ibid.

36. At a post-primary party celebrating the busing victory, some guests expressed surprise to see blacks there as guests. *Miami Herald,* March 15, 1972; *Tallahassee Democrat,* March 15, 19, 1972; *(Jacksonville) Florida Times-Union,* March 15, 1972; *St. Petersburg Times,* March 15, 1972.

37. *Miami Herald,* March 15, 1972; *Tallahassee Democrat,* March 15, 19, 1972; *(Jacksonville) Florida Times-Union,* March 15, 1972; *St. Petersburg Times,* March 15, 1972; Colburn and Scher, *Florida's Gubernatorial Politics,* 229–30.

38. Hillsborough County (St. Petersburg) voted 78,710 to 23,255 for a ban, Dade County 106,352 to 38,331, Duval County 90,201 to 24,997, Broward 96,927 to 24,719; *Miami Herald,* March 15, 1972; *Tallahassee Democrat,* March 15, 19, 1972; *(Jacksonville) Florida Times-Union,* March 15, 1972; *St. Petersburg Times,* March 15, 1972.

39. Thomas's reversal was quite astonishing given that he had supported most of Askew's bills in the senate, even fighting alongside Askew to see that the straw vote was not passed. Askew campaign internal memo on Thomas voting record, no date,

ca. 1974, Askew Papers, S497, B2; *Miami Herald,* March 15, 1972; *Tallahassee Democrat,* March 22, 1972.

40. Memo to Askew from Gregory Johnson, July 5, 1972, Askew Papers, S497, B3.

41. *Tallahassee Democrat,* February 4, 1973; Claude Anderson memo to Askew, January 5, 1973, Askew Papers, S126, B6.

42. *Pensacola News-Journal,* January 11, 12, 13, 15, 1973; Claude Anderson memo to Askew, January 5, 1973, Askew Papers, S126, B6.

43. *Pensacola News-Journal,* January 12, 13, 14, 15, 16, 1973.

44. *Pensacola News-Journal,* January 12, 17, 19, 23, 24, 25, 26, 27, 1973; *Tallahassee Democrat,* February 4, 1973.

45. *Pensacola News-Journal,* January 12, 17, 19, 23, 24, 25, 26, 27, 1973; *Tallahassee Democrat,* February 4, 1973.

46. Transcript of report by John Hayes, Channel 13 Television, Tampa, January 29, 1973, Askew Papers, S126, B3; *Pensacola News-Journal,* January 26, February 1, 1973; *Tallahassee Democrat,* February 4, 1973.

47. Escambia High principal Sidney Nelson was so emotionally spent and physically drained that he took a leave of absence. Askew to Peaden, February 16, 1973, Askew Papers, S125, B3; *Pensacola News-Journal,* February 1, 3, 1973; *Tallahassee Democrat,* February 4, 5, 10, 1973.

48. Askew interview; "Askew Response to Jerry Thomas Criticisms on 1974 Campaign Issues," 1974, Askew Papers, S126, B20; *Tallahassee Democrat,* September 11, 1974.

49. Article on Askew by Robert Hooker published by the National Urban League, undated, in Askew Papers, S126, B1; speech by Claude Anderson to the American People's Socialist Party, June 3, 1974, Gainesville, Florida, in Askew Papers, S126, B20.

50. Allen Morris, *Florida Handbook, 1997–1998* (Tallahassee: Peninsular Press, 1997), 565; U.S. Bureau of the Census, *Characteristics of the Population, 1970* (Washington, D.C.: Government Printing Office, 1971).

51. Askew speech before the NAACP Freedom Fund Dinner, Orlando, Florida, June 21, 1975, Askew Papers, S849, RG103; Askew speech before the Governor's Conference on Affirmative Action, Florida House of Representatives, January 15, 1975, Askew Papers, S126, B1; Askew interview; Thomas Wolfe quote taken from *You Can't Go Home Again* (New York: Harper and Brothers, 1940).

4. BUILDING A BETTER FLORIDA: THE 1973 FLORIDA EDUCATION REFORMS

1. Floyd Christian memo to education employees, July 1973, Askew Papers, S126, B3; Select Joint Committee on Public Schools of the Florida Legislature, "Im-

proving Education in Florida: A Reassessment," February 1978, Strozier Library, Florida State University, Tallahassee.

2. NEA Estimates of School Statistics, 1967–68, January 4, 1968, Askew Papers, S126 B4; Florida Department of Education Research Brief, no date, ca. 1971, Askew Papers, S126, B9. For other state comparisons see L. L. Ecker-Racz, "More Money for South Carolina Schools," June 1972, NEA State Finance Study, John C. West Papers, Box 52, South Carolina State Archives, Columbia.

3. Askew address to the Florida Education Association (FEA) delegate assembly, Jacksonville, Florida, March 6, 1971, Askew Papers, S126, B11; Askew speech at the University of South Florida, December 6, 1971, Tampa, Florida, Askew Papers, S126, B13.

4. The governor kept his promise and succeeded in repealing sales taxes on household utilities, rental property, and household fuel oil. Askew interview; Askew press conference transcript, November 2, 1971, Askew Papers, RG103, S66, B1; *Miami Herald,* November 2, 3, 1971; *(Jacksonville) Florida Times-Union,* October 24, 1971; *St. Petersburg Times,* November 1, 3, 4, 1971; Askew campaign press release, 1970, Askew campaign press files, RG900000 MSS, M83-8, Florida State Archives, Tallahassee; Jim Apthorp memo to staff, August 10, 1972, Askew Papers, S78, B11; William Maloy, interview by author, December 29, 1998, Pensacola, Florida, tape recording in possession of author (hereafter cited as Maloy interview).

5. The Citizens' Committee on Education was formed by Executive Order No. 71-40, July 27, 1971, Askew Papers, S126, B12; Askew remarks at signing of executive order creating the Citizens' Committee on Education, July 27, 1971, Askew Papers, S763, B1; Ford Foundation to Askew, August 1, 1972, Askew Papers, S763, B4.

6. Askew remarks at signing of executive order creating the Citizens' Committee on Education, July 27, 1971, Askew Papers, S763, B1; Maloy interview.

7. Askew remarks to the Citizens' Committee on Education, no date, ca. spring 1971, Askew Papers, S763, RG100, B4; Florida Citizens' Committee on Education report to Ford Foundation, November 1971, Askew Papers, S126, B4.

8. Bill Maloy memo to Askew, April 25, 1971, Askew Papers, S763, RG100, B1; form letter response to requests for Citizens' Committee on Education membership, July 29, 1971, Askew Papers, S770, RG100, B2; Florida Education Association executive secretary Walford N. Johnson to Askew, August 13, 1971, Askew Papers, S763, RG100, B4.

9. *St. Petersburg Times,* October 27, 1971; Florida Citizens' Committee on Education, "An Interim Report: The Governance of Florida's Educational System" (Tallahassee: Office of the Governor, 1972); *Tallahassee Democrat,* January 16, February 1, 1972; Anne Kelley and Ella L. Taylor, "Florida: The Changing Patterns of Power," in *Interest Group Politics in the South,* ed. Ronald J. Hrebener and Clive S. Thomas

(Tuscaloosa: University of Alabama Press, 1992), 125–51; William Maloy to William Dover, April 29, 1972, Askew Papers, S770, B2; Maloy interview.

10. *St. Petersburg Times,* October 27, 1971; Floyd Christian confidential memo to the Citizens' Committee on Education, undated, ca. spring 1972, Askew Papers, S763, B2; William Maloy to William Dover, April 29, 1972, Askew Papers, S770, B2; *Tallahassee Democrat,* February 3, 1972; Maloy interview.

11. Hugh MacMillan memo to Askew, January 5, 1972, Askew Papers, S126, B15; *St. Petersburg Times,* October 27, 1971; *Tallahassee Democrat,* February 6, 8, 1973.

12. Wilbur Boyd and Mallory Horne press release, February 3, 1972, Askew Papers, S763, RG100, B5; *Tallahassee Democrat,* February 3, 4, 11, 1972.

13. One year later, in February 1973, the Citizens' Committee on Education indeed had proposed a new restructuring plan for education governance. This plan left the education commissioner intact, but proposed a lay board of education appointed by the governor under the existing cabinet board of education. Christian expressed "grave reservations" about even this proposal. He did thank Askew for not trying to eliminate his position this time. The proposal never became law. *Tallahassee Democrat,* February 6, 8, 1973; Floyd Christian to Askew, February 13, 1973, Askew Papers, S497, B2.

14. *Tallahassee Democrat,* February 8, 9, April 18, 19, 1972.

15. *Miami Herald,* June 26, 27, 1972; Marshall Harris (the educational aide) memo to Askew, April 10, 1973, Askew Papers, S497, B2.

16. *Miami Herald,* June 26, 27, 1972; Marshall Harris memo to Askew, April 10, 1973, Askew Papers, S497, B2; Bruce Smathers press release, April 6, 1973, Smathers Papers, RG900000, M75-93, B11.

17. "Successes, Issues, and Goals of the Askew-Democratic Administration-Discussion Draft," summer 1972, unsigned, Askew Papers, S78, B11.

18. Ann Bowman memo to the House Education Committee, spring 1973, Askew Papers, S126, B16; Beverly Frederick to Askew, October 1, 1972, Askew Papers, S126, B5.

19. Notes of conversation with Senator Bob Graham by M. W. Kirst, August 16, 1972; Marshall Harris notes on meeting with Bob Graham, December 15, 1972, both in Askew Papers, S763, B3; Florida Education Association, "Status of the Public School Teacher," January 1972, Askew Papers, S126, B15.

20. "The Monday Report" (weekly newsletter of the Department of Education), October 9, 1972, Askew Papers, S763, RG100, B3; Jim Apthorp memo to staff, August 10, 1972, Askew Papers, S78, B11; Dorothy Davalt to Askew, November 1, 1972, Askew Papers, S126, B11.

21. Stan Crowe memo to the Citizens' Committee on Education, May 5, 1972, Askew Papers, S770, B2; Fred Williamson to Randy White, December 8, 1972; George Barnett memo to George Maloy, December 1972, both in Askew Papers,

S763, RG100, B3; Citizens' Committee on Education minutes, June 12, 13, 1972, Askew Papers, S78, B14.

22. The similarity in name was probably another reason for Askew's reluctance to comment on the meeting. "Proceedings of the Citizens' Conference on Education," Tampa, Florida, February 19–21, 1973; Betty Staton to George Maloy, March 9, 1973, both in Askew Papers, S763, RG100, B4.

23. Fred Schultz to Askew, February 1, 1973, Askew Papers, S497, B2.

24. Florida Governor's Citizens' Committee on Education, *Improving Education in Florida: A Report* (Tallahassee: Citizens' Committee on Education, 1973); "Analysis of Florida's MFP," Citizens' Committee on Education staff report, no date, ca. 1973, Askew Papers, S126, B12; "Financing Elementary and Secondary Education: Moving from a Teacher Unit-Funded System to a Pupil-Funded System," Florida legislative working group report, no date, ca. 1973, Askew Papers S126, B14.

25. "Analysis of Florida's MFP," Citizens' Committee on Education staff report, no date, ca. 1973, Askew Papers, S126, B12.

26. Sessums himself had tried to reform Florida's educational finance system in 1969. That year, he sponsored failed legislation that funded on a per child basis, then subtracted from the state's contribution the equivalent of ten mills in local effort. *(Jacksonville) Florida Times-Union,* September 1, 1971; *Serrano v. Priest,* 487 P2d 1241 (1971) 96 Cal RPTR 601 (1971); Chase Crawford to Terrell Sessums, October 18, 1972, Askew Papers, S763, B4; *Rodriguez v. San Antonio Independent School District* 337 F. Supp. 280 (1971); *Tallahassee Democrat,* March 24, 1973.

27. Florida Governor's Citizens' Committee on Education, *Improving Education in Florida.*

28. Ibid.

29. Ibid.

30. Ibid.

31. Jim Apthorp memo to Hugh MacMillan, March 21, 1973; staff memo to the Citizens' Committee on Education, April 5, 1973, both in Askew Papers, S763, RG100, B4; *Tallahassee Democrat,* March 25, 27, 1973.

32. Askew address before the opening of the 1973 Florida legislature, April 3, 1973, Askew Papers, S126, B14.

33. Staff memo to the Citizens' Committee on Education, April 13 and 20, 1973, Askew Papers, S763, B4; *Tallahassee Democrat,* March 27, 1973.

34. Terrell Sessums to Askew, April 16, 1973, Askew Papers, S78, B4.

35. Ibid.

36. *Tallahassee Democrat,* June 1, 2, 6, 7, 10, 1973; staff memo to the Citizens' Committee on Education, May 4 and June 7, 1973, Askew Papers, S763, B4; Department of Education, "Legislative Report No. 11: Regular Session, 1973," July 1973, Askew Papers, S126, B4.

37. For appropriations figures and an excellent history of educational finance in

Alabama, see Harvey, *History of Educational Finance in Alabama,* 430; see also "Legislative Session Roundup," *Alabama School Journal* 87 (September 1969): 11–13; *Tallahassee Democrat,* June 1, 3, 6, 12, 13, 1973; staff memo to the Citizens' Committee on Education, April 20 and May 4, 1973, both in Askew Papers, S78, RG103, B4; *St. Petersburg Times,* June 10, 1973.

38. *Tallahassee Democrat,* June 1, 3, 6, 1973; staff memo to the Citizens' Committee on Education, April 20 and May 4, 1973, both in Askew Papers, S78, RG103, B4; Associated Industries of Florida, "Summary of Legislation: 1973 Regular and June Special Session," no date, ca. August 1973, Askew Papers, S849, RG103, B4; Senate Education Committee, "Summary of School Finance Bill" (CSHB 734), no date, ca. May 1973, Askew Papers, S126, B14; Lee A. Shiver, "A Historical Review of the Development of Florida's School Finance Plan and the Fiscal Equalization Effects of the Florida Educational Finance Program" (Ph.D. diss., University of Florida, 1982).

39. Abolition of tenure also failed. Staff memo to the Citizens' Committee on Education, June 7, 1973, Askew Papers, S763, B4; "Report of the Second Meeting of the Nevada Educational Seminar," September 19, 1973, Askew Papers, S126, B5; Department of Education, "Legislative Report No. 11: Regular Session," July 1973, Askew Papers, S126, B14.

40. *St. Petersburg Times,* June 7, 10, 1973; *Tallahassee Democrat,* June 7, 8, 9, 1973; Jack Leppert to Mallory Horne, June 14, 1973, Senate Education Committee Bill Files, S18, RG900, B122, Florida State Archives, Tallahassee; Floyd Christian to Bruce Smathers, June 13, 1973, Smathers Papers, RG90000, M75-93, B10.

41. *Tallahassee Democrat,* May 6, June 3, 6, 1973; Bob Graham to Joe Rankshaw, July 10, 1973, Senate Education Committee Bill Files, S18, RG900, B122.

42. Democrats held solid majorities throughout Askew's tenure. In 1970 Democrats held 68.7 percent of house seats and 68.8 percent of senate seats. In 1972 the majority was at its lowest during the Askew years. Democrats held 64.2 pecent of house seats that year, while controlling 62.5 percent in the senate. Anne E. Kelly, *Modern Florida Government* (Temple Terrace, Fla.: MDA Publications, 1981), 194–95; *Tallahassee Democrat,* May 6, 1973; Askew interview; Select Joint Committee on Public Schools of the Florida Legislature, "Improving Education in Florida: A Reassessment," Tallahassee, February 1978, Strozier Library, Florida State University; see also Thomas article on Florida in Hrebener and Thomas, eds., *Interest Group Politics in the South* and William Havard and Loren P. Beth, *The Politics of Mis-Representation: Rural-Urban Conflict in the Florida Legislature* (Baton Rouge: Louisiana State University Press, 1962), 1–40.

43. Select Joint Committee, "Improving Education in Florida"; *St. Petersburg Times,* February 4, 1974; Turner W. Tyson, "A Study of the Impact of the Florida Educational Finance Program Act of 1973 on the State-Local Relationship in Florida" (Ed.D. diss., University of Mississippi, 1977).

44. Select Joint Committee, "Improving Education in Florida"; *St. Petersburg Times,*

February 4, 1974; Tyson, "A Study"; *St Petersburg Times,* February 4, 1974; Steven Mintz, "Analysis of State School Finance Reform Legislation in Florida, 1973" (Washington, D.C.: U.S. Education Resources Information Center, ERIC Document ED 084688, November 1973), 1; R. L. Johns, *The Evolution of Equalization of Educational Opportunity in Florida, 1926 to 1976* (Gainesville, Fla.: Institute for Educational Finance, 1976), 76; see also Shiver, "A Historical Review"; Thomas L. Johns, "School Finance Reform in 1973," *Planning and Changing* 5 (spring 1974): 47.

45. Select Joint Committee, "Improving Education in Florida"; Florida house speaker Terrell Sessums's charges to several house committees, 1974 Regular Session, September 12, 1973; Sessums memo to "all concerned," July 27, 1973, both in Askew Papers, S78, RG100, B11.

5. FORGING A "NEW SOUTH CAROLINA": THE AFTERMATH OF INTEGRATION

1. In this context, pushouts were generally black students who dropped out of school at the school's recommendation or silent urging for lack of remedial class work or attention from the faculty and administration or from being outright ignored in the classroom.

2. Key, *Southern Politics in State and Nation,* 130–34; Edgar, *South Carolina: A History,* 541–42; Edgar, *South Carolina in the Modern Age,* 121.

3. Ernest Hollings address to the South Carolina General Assembly, January 9, 1963, in the Ernest Hollings Papers, Modern Political Collection, South Caroliniana Library, Columbia. See also Maxie Myron Cox, "1963—The Year of Decision: Desegregation in South Carolina" (Ph.D. diss., University of South Carolina, 1996), 2–9.

4. John G. Sproat, "Firm Flexibility: Perspectives on Desegregation in South Carolina," in *New Perspectives on Race and Slavery in America,* ed. Robert H. Abzug and Stephen E. Maizlish (Lexington: University of Kentucky Press, 1986), 164–84; *Mobile Register,* February 3, 1970; West interview.

5. West saw McNair not only as a friend but as a gubernatorial role model. Soon after his own inauguration as governor, West told McNair that he felt more comfortable being governor having had the opportunity to serve under McNair. West to McNair, January 20, 1971, in Governor 1971–1975, General Correspondence 1971, West Papers; Sproat, "Firm Flexibility"; Edgar, *South Carolina in the Modern Age,* 121; Robert McNair, press statement, January 29, 1970, Lt. Governor, Topical Files, Education, John Carl West Papers, Modern Political Collection, South Caroliniana Library, Columbia (hereafter cited as West Private Papers). See also *Theodore Whitmore Stanley et al v. Darlington County School District,* U.S. Court of Appeals for the Fourth Circuit, January 19, 1970, No. 13,904-13,905; and *Alexander v. Holmes County,* 396 U.S. 19, October 26, 1969; Maxie Cox in "1963—The Year of Decision" does a

first-rate job of recounting the history of Clemson's desegregation and the general political mood of the state in that year as it faced an end of dual school systems.

6. West interview; Jack Bass and Jack Nelson, *The Orangeburg Massacre* (Macon: Mercer University Press, 1984), 32–33, 94–95. The Bass and Nelson work on Orangeburg is superior, the standard account of the incident and of the state's racial situation as illustrated by the massacre.

7. West later recalled that as the black students sat in the senate gallery, one woman became extremely disruptive, and he ordered her removed from the chamber. As the sergeant at arms carried her out, West recalled that he heard her yelling repeatedly, "I'll make Huntley-Brinkley tonight!" West interview; Bass and Nelson, *Orangeburg Massacre,* 95–97; West to South Carolina State College Student Government Association Vice President, March 15, 1968; Lt. Governor, Topical Files, Education, South Carolina State College, West Private Papers.

8. Robert Scott to West, March 18, 1968; Harry Avinger to West, March 25, 1968; Brenda Arledge to West, March 22, 1968; "Bo Bo Bo" to West, March 22, 1968. All in Lt. Governor, Topical File, S.C. State, West Private Papers. See also "Petition to the Senate of the State of South Carolina," March 12, 1968; John West to Alexander Nichols, March 12, 1968. Both in Lt. Governor, Topical Files, Education, South Carolina State College, West Private Papers; and interview with Lt. Governor John West, July 18, 1969, Lt. Governor, Public Papers, Miscellaneous, West Private Papers.

9. Jack Bass, "John C. West of South Carolina: His Emphasis on Health, Hunger, Race Relations Reflects Changed Tone of State's Politics," *South Today,* July–August 1972, 9–10; West interview.

10. Sproat, "Firm Flexibility;" John Hammond Moore, *Columbia and Richland County: A South Carolina Community, 1740–1990* (Columbia: University of South Carolina Press, 1993), 414–31.

11. West interview; Sproat, "Firm Flexibility"; Cox, "1963—The Year of Decision," 2.

12. West Inaugural Address, January 19, 1970, *South Carolina House Journal,* 99th Assembly, First Session, January 19, 1970, 154–61; *Columbia (S.C.) State,* January 20, 1970; West to Gus Stratacos, May 28, 1971, John C. West Papers, Box 58 (11284), South Carolina Department of Archives and History, Columbia, South Carolina (hereafter cited as West Papers).

13. The "Dr. No" label comes from Dan Carter's book, *The Politics of Rage: George Wallace, the Origins of the New Conservatism, and the Transformation of American Politics* (New York: Simon and Schuster, 1995), 329; see also Dent, *Prodigal South; New York Post,* January 29, 1970; *New York Times,* January 20, 1970.

14. *New York Post,* January 20, 1970; *New York Times,* January 20, 1970.

15. It came as no surprise that in the election, Watson won Darlington County easily. West's county manager, A. Lee Chandler, had hoped that West might split the

county. A. Lee Chandler to West, November 11, 1970, Lt. Governor, General Correspondence, November 1970, West Private Papers; "Your Schools: Newsletter of the South Carolina Community Relations Program," April 1970, in Lt. Governor, Topical files, Campaign 1970, Persons, Watson, Record, West Private Papers.

16. News of the incident reached as far as Manchester, England. *Manchester Guardian,* March 4, 6, 1970; *New York Times,* March 5, 6, 8, 10, 11, 1970; *Columbia Record,* March 3, 1970; *National Observer,* March 9, 1970; West interview; Cole Blease Graham, *South Carolina Politics and Government* (Lincoln: University of Nebraska Press, 1994), 92.

17. *New York Times,* March 5, 6, 8, 10, 11, 1970; *Columbia Record,* March 3, 1970. During his campaign, West briefly sunk to Watson's level of court baiting. He even wrote Jeryl Best, giving his assurance that he was sympathetic with his concerns. Said West: "The disruption of the educational process of your children by the tyranny of the federal courts is the most senseless judicial act that I have ever seen in my nearly twenty-five years as a practicing attorney. I stand ready at all times to assist any citizen or citizens' groups in an attempt to continue to provide quality education for children and to resist by every legal means the disruption caused by such acts as the recent orders of the federal courts which have precipitated the crisis in Darlington County." West to Jeryl Best, February 20, 1970, John C. West Collection, Camden Archives, Camden, South Carolina.

18. Later in 1971, Judge Weatherford came under fire for allowing the jailed rioters to go home on weekends. He later reduced their sentences to probation. The state attorney general appealed this decision to the state supreme court, which ruled in the state's favor that Weatherford had overstepped his bounds. See *Columbia (S.C.) State,* November 13, December 7, 1971, January 9, 1972; for details on the conviction see *Columbia (S.C.) State,* March 3, 4, 1971; *New York Times,* March 11, 1971.

19. *New York Times,* March 23, 1971, May 27, 1973; H2283, a bill prohibiting discrimination in the schools, Papers of the House Committee on Education and Public Works, February 10, 1971, Box 79 (S165131), South Carolina State Archives, Columbia; *Florence Morning News,* no date, ca. 1971, in the John C. West clipping file at the South Caroliniana Library, Columbia.

20. *New York Times,* January 20, 1971; *Columbia (S.C.) State,* March 14, 1971; *Charleston News and Courier,* September 15, 1971, August 2, 1972.

21. Mizell was a lightning rod for controversy in Columbia. As early as his college years at the University of South Carolina, Mizell had been called a "double-dipped integrationist" by the *Columbia State.* See M. Hayes Mizell, "The Impact of the Civil Rights Movement on a White Activist" (paper presented at the annual meeting of the Southern Historical Association, Ft. Worth, Texas, November 4, 1999), in possession of author; *New York Times,* May 11, 1971; *Charleston News and Courier,* June 10, 1971; John West to James D. Hodgson, March 12, 1971, West Papers, Box 58 (11284).

22. "Public Mobilization for Educational Reform: A Proposal Synopsis," Papers of the South Carolina Council on Human Relations, South Caroliniana Library, Columbia; *Columbia (S.C.) State,* December 17, 1971.

23. The *Columbia State* wondered when South Carolina's "sin" of segregation would be absolved and held out hope that *Swann* would finally enable the South to "be free of its ancient sins." *Columbia (S.C.) State,* June 24, 1971; *Swann v. Charlotte-Mecklenburg Board of Education,* 402 U.S. 1, 1971; quoted in Davison M. Douglas, *Reading, Writing, and Race: The Desegregation of the Charlotte Schools* (Chapel Hill: University of North Carolina Press, 1995), 190; *Columbia (S.C.) State,* April 21, 1971.

24. West's campaign generally stayed away from race and integration save for this brief outburst. A memo West issued to his campaign staff revealed his growing disgust with the racial tone of the campaign. In nothing short of a personal manifesto, West reached several conclusions about himself and the campaign: "I cannot project the image of a die hard segregationist who will 'require federal marshals and court orders.' I cannot in the space of three months hope to gain the political charisma of a Fritz Hollings. I cannot change a personality and an image of sixteen years accumulated, even if it means that failure to attain the goal which we all seek." West to Crawford Cook, July 17, 1970; West to B. B. Bryson, February 9, 1970; both in 1970 Campaign, General, February 1970, West Private Papers; and West to Jeryl Best, February 20, 1970, Lt. Governor Topical Files, Desegregation, West Private Papers; *Columbia (S.C.) State,* January 27, 1970; see also John C. West clipping file in the Workman Papers; Bass, "John C. West"; West campaign news release, October 16, 1970, West Papers, Box 113 (RCB 20147); *Columbia (S.C.) State,* October 29, November 1, 11, 1970.

25. Mississippi showed the most dramatic increase in private school growth; 62,676 pupils attended the state's three hundred private schools, an *increase* of 43,278 pupils since 1964. See analysis of Southern Regional Council report on private schools in *Columbia (S.C.) State,* July 12, 1971; John West to G. Bumgardner, March 27, 1970, West Papers, Box 14; *Columbia (S.C.) State,* July 14, 1970, June 10, 1971, July 12, 1971, September 13, 1971, April 7, 1972, February 11, 1973; *Charleston News and Courier,* August 6, 1971, September 2, 3, 1971.

26. "More Money for South Carolina Schools: A State Finance Study," June 1972, West Papers, Box 52.

27. The same type of "tipping" occurred in Alabama. See Heron, "Growth of Private Schools." West interview; *Columbia (S.C.) State,* July 1, 12, 24, 1971.

28. U.S. civil rights director J. Stanley Pottinger told the district that barring any future U.S. Supreme Court ruling, Columbia was finished with desegregation. *Columbia (S.C.) State,* August 4, 1971.

29. *Columbia (S.C.) State,* July 1, August 2, 1971.

30. *Columbia (S.C.) State,* July 1, 23, August 2, 3, 4, 15, 1971.

31. Ibid.

32. *Columbia (S.C.) State,* July 23, August 8, 1971; Edgar, *South Carolina in the Modern Age,* 127; Edgar, *South Carolina: A History,* 545.

33. Richard Gergel, "School Desegregation: A Student View," *New South* 26 (winter 1971): 34–38; M. Hayes Mizell, "The Myth of Quality Education," *New South* 26 (winter 1971): 26–33.

34. John West, "Quality Education: The Best Education for All Students," *South Carolina Education Journal* (winter 1971): 6; West speech before the Columbia, South Carolina, Rotary Club, quoted in the *South Carolina Education News* (January 1967): 9–10.

35. Minutes from organizational meeting for Project Helping Hand, held in West's office, April 8, 1971; "Concept Paper for Project Helping Hand," prepared by South Carolina State College, April 22, 1971, both in West Papers, Box 58 (11284); *New York Times,* April 25, 1971.

36. Project Summary for Project Helping Hand, no date, ca. June 1973; Jack David memo to West, April 8, 1971, both in West Papers, Box 58 (11284).

37. West to Preston Torrence, September 21, 1971; West to Elliot Richardson, September 21, 1971; Richardson to West, December 7, 1971; all in West Papers, Box 58 (11284); *Columbia (S.C.) State,* November 10, 1971; *New York Times,* April 25, 1971.

38. *Los Angeles Times,* August 23, 1971; *Columbia (S.C.) State,* August 12, 13, 1971.

39. West to Olivia Williamson, August 30, 1971; West to Lois Yancey, September 13, 1971; West to Raymond W. Green, September 16, 1971, all in West Papers, Box 58; *Columbia (S.C.) State,* August 12, 13, 1971.

40. Campaign news release, July 13, 1970, West Papers, Box 113; campaign news release, October 21, 1970; weekly campaign newsletter to local headquarters, July 24, 1970, both in West Papers, Box 114; West education advisor Jack David to Ronald Hurtenbaum, no date, ca. 1972, West Papers, Box 58 (11284).

41. *Columbia (S.C.) State,* October 12, 1971.

42. Madge Robinson to West, October 21, 1971; West to Robinson, November 11, 1971, both in West Papers, Box 58.

43. *Columbia (S.C.) State,* September 16, 1971; *Charleston News and Courier,* September 16, 29, 1971; "Proposed Policy Position for the National Governor's Conference, 1971," Jimmy Carter and Winfield Dunn, no date; "Position Paper on Busing," Jimmy Carter and Winfield Dunn, no date, ca. 1971; Wallace Resolution on Busing, September 13, 1971, National Governor's Conference, all in Box 58, West papers.

44. *Columbia (S.C.) State,* November 7, 8, 11, 14, 1971; James O. Young to West, September 8, 1971; West to Fred Atkinson, February 28, 1972; Jack David to Jinx Roberts, February 25, 1972; all in West Papers, Box 58.

45. Many letters to West asked or even commanded him to follow Wallace's lead. One in particular told West to "get with Wallace now!" Another told West to support

Wallace and "be a man not a robot." James Young to West, August 15, 1971; Brantley Jordan to West, August 15, 1971; Thomas Alessi to West, August 15, 1971; Doug Collins to West, August 18, 1971; Larry Mitchell to West, August 15, 1971; West to Larry Mitchell, September 2, 1971; all in West Papers, Box 58.

46. *Columbia (S.C.) State,* August 17, 19, 1971; West to Raymond Green, September 16, 1971; West to Lois Yancey, September 13, 1971, both in West Papers, Box 58.

47. *Columbia (S.C.) State,* March 9, 1972.

48. *Columbia (S.C.) State,* March 9, 10, 11, 1972, August 28, September 1, 1974; *Charleston Evening Post,* March 16, 1972; "West Statement on School Disruptions," March 9, 1972, West Papers, Box 46; *Charleston News and Courier,* June 10, 1972, August 31, 1972.

49. *Columbia (S.C.) State,* June 6, 1971; *Charleston News and Courier,* February 9, 1973; Sproat, "Firm Flexibility."

50. Sproat, "Firm Flexibility"; *Charleston News and Courier,* August 28, 1971; West Inaugural Address, 154–61.

51. *Charleston News and Courier,* January 20, 1973.

52. Gov. John C. West Annual Address to the South Carolina General Assembly, January 9, 1974, *South Carolina House Journal,* 100th Assembly, January 9, 1974, 40–57; *Columbia (S.C.) State,* December 29, 1974.

53. *Columbia (S.C.) State,* August 18, 23, 1974; *Kershaw County Record,* July 3, 1974.

54. Gov. John C. West Farewell Address to the South Carolina General Assembly, January 14, 1975, *South Carolina House Journal,* 101st Assembly, First Session, January 14, 1975, 38–43.

6. SUNBELT TO THE RESCUE: EDUCATION REFORM IN SOUTH CAROLINA

1. West, "Quality Education"; *Charleston News and Courier,* January 3, 1971; for information on the Sunbelt South see Bartley, *New South,* 431–33, and Bruce J. Schulman, *From Cotton Belt to Sunbelt: Federal Policy, Economic Development, and the Transformation of the South, 1938–1980* (New York: Oxford University Press, 1991); West interview.

2. *Charleston News and Courier,* January 1, 1971; John West speech before the Columbia, South Carolina, Rotary Club, quoted in the *South Carolina Education News* (January 1967): 9–10; Richland County Legislative Delegation, "Public Education: A Statement of Findings and Policy," May 23, 1972, Papers of the League of Women Voters–South Carolina, South Caroliniana Library, Columbia, South Carolina, Box 4 (hereafter cited as LWV-SC Papers).

3. The 1971 average per pupil expenditures in South Carolina were $654, in Georgia $680, North Carolina $657, Alabama $523, Florida $819, and the U.S. av-

erage $868. South Carolina paid its teachers in 1971 an average of $7,300, North Carolina $7,948, Georgia $8,010, Alabama $7,525, Florida $9,230, Virginia $8,892. L. L. Ecker-Racz, "More Money for South Carolina Schools," West Papers, Box 52.

4. Practically all the statutes that governed property assessment and valuation were enacted in the 1880s. Heyward Belser, "A Hard Nut or Statewide Equalization and Reassessment of Real Property?" (speech before the Kosmos Club, Columbia, South Carolina, November 10, 1967), Workman Papers, Box 24.

5. Ecker-Racz, "More Money"; Belser, "A Hard Nut." The South Carolina Constitution (1895), Sec. 29, Art. III, provided that "all taxes on property, real and personal, shall be laid upon the actual value of the property taxed."

6. Belser provided this example in his speech. The Richland County assessment rate was 8.3 percent, whereas the millage rate in Columbia was .20 percent. The result of assessing property at one-tenth its value, then taxing a tenth of that amount was an effective rate of 1 percent. Belser, "A Hard Nut."

7. Ibid.; Ecker-Racz, "More Money."

8. West position paper sent to Carlos Gibbons, October 5, 1970, West Papers, Box 114 (RCB 20148); *Columbia (S.C.) State,* November 18, 1970; West news release, January 12, 1970, West Papers, Box 113 (RCB 20147); West interview.

9. The information about the tax honeymoons was deleted from the final draft of West's correspondence to Gibbons. See both draft and final copy of the West position paper sent to Gibbons, October 5, 1970, West Papers, Box 114 (RCB 20148); Ecker-Racz, "More Money."

10. Average daily membership was only 86.2 percent of the school-aged population in 1969, revealing the severity of the dropout situation. This figure had increased from 80.8 percent in 1968. "SCEA Legislative Program, 1970–1971," West Papers, Box 52.

11. "SCEA Legislative Program, 1970–1971," West Papers, Box 52; Richland County legislative delegation, "Public Education," *Columbia (S.C.) State,* January 7, 1971.

12. Gibbons memo to South Carolina Education Association local and state leaders, August 18, 1970; Gibbons memo to South Carolina Education Association county presidents, November 11, 1970, both in West Papers, Box 52.

13. *Columbia (S.C.) State,* January 12, 14, 15, 1971; *Columbia Record,* January 15, 1971.

14. *Columbia (S.C.) State,* January 12, 14, 15, 1971; *Columbia Record,* January 15, 1971. The flow of letters to West's office was so great that several form letters were produced to respond. Later, the governor's staff started sending more personal letters lest teachers start to compare the letters they received from the governor. See West Papers, Box 52.

15. West address to the General Assembly, January 27, 1971, *Journal of the South Carolina House of Representatives,* 99th Assembly, First Session, 275–85.

16. In 1969, the average South Carolina teacher's salary was $6,883, and the

southeast average was $7,108. In 1971 the state average was $7,355, while the south-eastern average reached $8,113; Edith Jensen, "Public School Teacher's Salaries in South Carolina," March 1971, LWV-SC Papers, Box 14. State Education Department figures support the League of Woman Voters' numbers. See Cyril Busbee to R. A. Durham, September 19, 1972, West Papers, Box 46; *Sumter Daily Item,* January 28, 1971; *Columbia (S.C.) State,* February 4, 9, 14, 15, 1971.

17. *Columbia (S.C.) State,* February 4, 9, 14, 15, 1971.

18. *Columbia (S.C.) State,* February 11, 16, 1971; West interview.

19. *Columbia (S.C.) State,* February 6, 11, 16, 1971.

20. *Columbia (S.C.) State,* February 5, 11, 12, 19, 1971.

21. Jensen, "Public School Teachers' Salaries"; *Columbia (S.C.) State,* February 10, 19, 1971, March 2, 1971.

22. *Columbia (S.C.) State,* March 5, 10, 12, 18, 1971.

23. *Columbia (S.C.) State,* March 21, 1971.

24. *Columbia (S.C.) State,* March 26, 27, 28, 1971.

25. *Columbia (S.C.) State,* March 26, 27, 1971.

26. Ibid.

27. Gibbons to West, April 13, 1971, West Papers, Box 52.

28. Richard E. Tukey to West, March 11, 1971, West Papers, Box 52; *Columbia (S.C.) State,* March 27, 28, 1971; April 8, 1971.

29. *Columbia (S.C.) State,* April 8, 21, 1971.

30. West told Superintendent Busbee that although he donated his portion of the pay raise to kindergarten expansion, he authorized Busbee to use it "where it would do the most good." He also inscribed the bottom of the letter: "Cyril: Hope this helps kindergartens 'cause it sho' hurts old JCW." West to Cyril Busbee, July 26, 1971, Governor, 1971–1975 General Correspondence, and Busbee to West, June 22, 1972, General Correspondence, January–June 1972, West Private Papers; West interview; *Columbia (S.C.) State,* May 5, 6, 8, 11, 1971.

31. West to Claude Kitchens, May 13, 1971, West Papers, Box 52; *Columbia (S.C.) State,* April 18, 20, 1971.

32. *Columbia (S.C.) State,* May 5, 8, June 14, July 3, August 2, 1971.

33. Gibbons to West, June 23, 1971, West Papers, Box 52; *Columbia (S.C.) State,* June 17, 20, July 3, 1971.

34. *Charleston News and Courier,* August 9, 13, 1971; West interview.

35. West to Kitchens, May 13, 1971, West Papers, Box 52; *Columbia (S.C.) State,* August 4, 13, 1971; *Charleston News and Courier,* August 13, 1971; *Columbia (S.C.) State,* March 5, 1972.

36. Leonard Silk, *Nixonomics: How the Dismal Science of Free Enterprise Became the Black Art of Controls* (New York: Praeger Publishers, 1972), 63–80; *Columbia (S.C.) State,* August 19, 21, September 1, 1971; *Charleston News and Courier,* August 19, September 1, 1971.

37. South Carolina Republican chairman C. Kenneth Powell criticized West for not supporting Nixon's economic policy. He accused the governor of avoiding issues that might hurt him politically. West was "somewhat weak when it comes to political courage," he said. *Charleston News and Courier,* August 28, September 1, 4, 18, 24, 1971; *Columbia (S.C.) State,* September 18, 30, 1971.

38. In September 1971, the first full month of the freeze, South Carolina took in $46.3 million in tax revenues. In the same month in 1970, the state garnered only $37.7 million. *Charleston News and Courier,* October 6, 1971; *Columbia (S.C.) State,* October 7, 1971.

39. *Columbia (S.C.) State,* September 11, October 6, 13, 15, 1971; *Charleston News and Courier,* August 26, October 5, 8, 1971.

40. *Columbia (S.C.) State,* October 20, 1971; *Charleston News and Courier,* October 21, 1971.

41. *Columbia (S.C.) State,* October 20, 24, 1971.

42. *Columbia (S.C.) State,* October 21, 1971; *Charleston News and Courier,* October 24, 1971.

43. *Columbia (S.C.) State,* October 21, 1971.

44. *Charleston News and Courier,* October 26, 1971; *Columbia (S.C.) State,* October 26, 30, 1971; Sara Powers to West, November 8, 1971, West to Powers, November 12, 1971, both in West Papers, Box 52.

45. *Columbia (S.C.) State,* November 4, 1971.

46. Neil Reeves to West, November 12, 1971, West Papers, Box 52.

47. *Greenville News,* August 27, 1971; *Columbia Record,* April 21, 1971; *Columbia (S.C.) State,* November 6, 1971; A. T. Clarkson memo to West, December 22, 1971, West Papers, Box 45.

48. South Carolina taxed cigarettes at six cents per pack. Only North Carolina at 2 cents, Virginia at 2.5 cents, Kentucky at 3 cents, Washington, D.C., and Oregon at 4 cents, and Colorado at 5 cents were lower. A. T. Clarkson memo to West, December 22, 1971; Greg Johnson memo to Jim Apthorp, December 30, 1971 (this memo is between two aides to Florida Governor Reubin Askew. Why they researched South Carolina's tax structure is unclear. Most likely it was done for comparison to Florida's tax system); Carlos Gibbons to Silas Pearman, January 3, 1972, all in West Papers, Box 45.

49. *Columbia (S.C.) State,* January 2, 4, 9, 1972.

50. Gibbons to West, January 6, 1972, West Papers, Box 52; *Columbia (S.C.) State,* January 2, 5, 6, 7, 1972.

51. John C. West address to the General Assembly, January 12, 1972, *Journal of the South Carolina House of Representatives,* 99th Assembly, 2d Session, 60–75; *Columbia (S.C.) State,* January 13, 14, 1972.

52. Quoted in *Columbia (S.C.) State,* January 21, 1971.

53. *Columbia (S.C.) State,* January 11, 21, 1972. Many citizens wrote West taking

opposite sides of the issue. One teacher asked him what good raises would do if he planned to tax the money right back from teachers. See "Agnes, A Friend" to West, February 1, 1972; Harold Ridgeley to West, December 30, 1971; West to Ridgeley, January 5, 1972; R. L. Utsey to West, December 30, 1971; West to Utsey, January 5, 1972, all in West Papers, Box 155.

54. Tax revenues in the six months between July and December 1972 reached $264 million. For the same period in 1971, they amounted to $233 million. *Columbia (S.C.) State,* January 7, 12, March 4, 9, 22, 1972; Bass, "John C. West of South Carolina."

55. West also sought federal grants. He hired a lobbyist in Washington, D.C., to garner almost $28 million in federal money, 75 percent of which came between 1972 and 1973. *Charlotte Observer,* undated article, ca. 1973, West Clippings, Governor 1973, March–August, West Private Papers; Douglas Carlisle, "The Administration of John Carl West, Governor of South Carolina, 1971–1975," unpublished manuscript, 1975, Modern Political Collection, South Caroliniana Library, Columbia; League of Women Voters–South Carolina, "The South Carolina Voter," October 1970, in Workman Papers, Box 6; *Greenville News,* July 25, 1972.

56. South Carolina's cheap labor force and non-unionized labor force were attractive to Michelin. James C. Cobb, *The Selling of the South: The Southern Crusade for Industrial Development, 1936–1990,* 2d ed. (Urbana: University of Illinois Press, 1993), 190; "Schedule for Trip to Europe for an International Textile Machine Show," n.d., ca. June 1971, Public Papers, Governor Schedule, January–October 1971, West Private Papers; West to William Workman, May 5, 1972, Governor, General Correspondence, January to June 1972, West Private Papers; German Consul Roland H. A. Gottlieb to West, November 5, 1971, Governor General Correspondence, 1971, West Private Papers; Carlisle, "The Administration of John Carl West," Bass, "John C. West of South Carolina"; *Columbia (S.C.) State,* October 19, 1971, February 14, 1973; West news release, February 13, 1973, Governor, Speeches, 1973, West Private Papers; *Wall Street Journal,* n.d., ca. October 1973, Clipping File 1973, Governor, September–December 1973, West Private Papers; West press release, June 28, 1971, Press Releases, June–July 1971, West Private Papers.

57. *Columbia (S.C.) State,* October 19, 1971, September 6, 1972, February 14, 1973; *Wall Street Journal,* n.d., ca. October 1973, Clipping File 1973, Governor, September–December 1973, West Private Papers.

58. Per capita income in South Carolina in 1972 was $3,400, still only 80 percent of the national average. West address before the National Clinic on Technical Education, Columbia, South Carolina, March 29, 1974, West Papers, Box 56; Harold Crawford to House Education and Public Works Committee, April 22, 1972; Representative Harold Brezeale to Charles E. Palmer, March 6, 1972; Brezeale to Judge Winston W. Vaught, April 1, 1972, all in Papers of the Committee to Study the Educational System of South Carolina, 1963–1975, RG-153, S-153001, South Carolina

State Archives, Columbia; Annual Report of the Advisory Council on Vocational and Technical Education, 1972, West Papers, Box 116; Cobb, *Selling of the South,* 166; *Wall Street Journal,* n.d., ca. October 1973, Clipping File 1973, Governor, September–December 1973, West Private Papers.

59. By August 1974, South Carolina had sixteen Technical Education Centers in Aiken, Beaufort, Cheraw, Denmark, Florence, Greenville, Conway, Columbia, Orangeburg, Piedmont, Spartanburg, Sumter, Pendleton, Charleston, Kingstree, and York. See West Papers, Box 116; Carlisle, "Administration of John Carl West"; West interview; see also West campaign press release, September 19, 1966, Campaign Press Releases 1966, Lt. Governor files, West Private Papers.

60. West interview; *Columbia (S.C.) State,* February 9, 10, 24, 1972; National Education Association, "Inconsistent School Governance: Personnel Practices in Disarray, South Carolina Special Study," October 1972, West Papers, Box 58.

61. Edith Manfredi to West, March 21, 1972, West Papers, Box 58; *Columbia (S.C.) State,* November 18, 1971, February 10, 1972.

62. See *Green v. County School Board,* 391 U.S. 430, 438 (1968). National Education Association, "Inconsistent School Governance"; Cyril Busbee to West, April 10, 1974, West Papers, Box 58.

63. The Educational Testing Service did not favor the four-year National Teacher Exam phase-out. Busbee argued that to implement a salary schedule all at once would create fiscal chaos. The Educational Testing Service agreed to allow the phase-out as long as the state showed good faith. Agnes Wilson (president of the South Carolina Education Association) to Busbee, December 8, 1972; "Report to the State Board of Education by the Committee to Study Teacher Education and Certification Requirements," June 8, 1973; Winton H. Manning (vice president of the Educational Testing Service) to Cyril Busbee, June 18, 1973, and March 5, 1974; "ETS Policy on Reporting NTE Scores to the South Carolina Department of Education," June 18, 1973; James R. Deneen (director of teacher programs and services, Educational Testing Service) to Busbee, June 22, 1973; "State Board of Education Position Paper Regarding the Use of the NTE for Salary Purposes for Experienced Teachers," April 10, 1974; Cyril Busbee to West, April 10, 1974, all in West Papers, Box 58; West interview.

64. Sixteen of the state's economic indicators jumped, including a decline in initial unemployment claims; unemployment dropped below 3.6 percent in early 1973, and the work week grew to 41.6 hours. *SCEA Legislative Newsletter,* January 2, 1973, West Papers, Box 52; Dorothy Massie to Robert E. "Jack" David, October 12, 1972, West Papers, Box 59; *Greenville News,* July 25, 1972; *Charleston News and Courier,* January 7, 8, 10, February 7, 10, 1973; West interview.

65. John C. West address before the South Carolina General Assembly, January 16, 1973, *Journal of the South Carolina House of Representatives,* 100th Assembly, 1st Session, January 16, 1973, 104–22.

66. *Columbia (S.C.) State,* January 21, 1973; "Resume of Legislation Passed by the General Assembly: January to June, 1973," West Papers, Box 155; *Charleston News and Courier,* February 3, 6, 7, 10, 1973.

67. "Report from Governor John C. West," September 28, 1973, in the John C. West Clipping File, South Caroliniana Library, Columbia; *Columbia (S.C.) State,* September 1, 1974; *Columbia Record,* September 28, 1973; West interview.

68. "Report from Governor John C. West," September 28, 1973, in the John C. West Clipping File, South Caroliniana Library, Columbia; West interview; *Columbia (S.C.) State,* September 1, 1974.

CONCLUSION

1. Sabato, "New South Governors," 194–213.

2. *St. Petersburg Times,* October 31, 1971.

3. *1970 Census of Population* (Washington D.C.: U.S. Department of Commerce, 1973); David R. Colburn, "Florida Politics in the Twentieth Century," in *The New History of Florida,* ed. Michael Gannon (Gainesville: University Press of Florida, 1996), 344–72.

4. National Education Association, *Rankings of the States, 1972* (Washington, D.C.: National Education Association, 1972).

5. Bass and De Vries, *Transformation of Southern Politics,* 57–86.

6. Walter B. Edgar, "Reform and Reformers in South Carolina: A Historical Perspective," in *Proceedings of the South Carolina Historical Association 1992,* ed. Peter W. Becker (Columbia: South Carolina Historical Association, 1992), 35–39; Walter Edgar, unpublished history of South Carolina, 919–21, in possession of author; see also Edgar, *South Carolina in the Modern Age.*

7. Edgar, *South Carolina in the Modern Age,* 130–32; Michael Gannon, *Florida: A Short History* (Gainesville: University Press of Florida), 136–39.

8. Sabato, "New South Governors."

9. "The South Today: Carter Country and Beyond," *Time,* September 27, 1976.

10. Ibid.

11. Ibid.

Bibliography

PRIMARY SOURCES

Manuscript Collections

Alabama Department of Archives and History, Montgomery, Alabama (ADAH)

Alabama Governor Legal Advisor, Hugh Maddox Papers
Alabama State Sovereignty Commission Papers
Albert P. Brewer Papers
Governor Albert P. Brewer Administrative Papers
Governor Albert Brewer Speeches

Auburn University Archives, Auburn, Alabama

Harry M. Philpott Papers

Auburn University Special Collections, Auburn University, Auburn, Alabama

Report of the Alabama Education Commission, 1959

Ralph Brown Draughon Library, Auburn University, Auburn, Alabama

Alabama House Journal, Special Session 1969
Alabama Senate Journal, Special Session 1970
Preliminary Report of the Alabama Education Commission, 1919
Report of the Alabama Education Study Commission, 1969
Summary of Laws and Resolutions Enacted during the Special Session of the Alabama
    Legislature, February 23, 1970

Florida State Archives, Tallahassee, Florida

Bruce Smathers Papers
Florida Senate Education Committee Bill Files
Governor Reubin O'D. Askew Papers
Reubin O'D. Askew Campaign Files

Robert Manning Strozier Library, Florida State University, Tallahassee, Florida

Improving Education in Florida: A Report, 1973

South Carolina State Archives, Columbia, South Carolina

Committee to Study the Educational System of South Carolina, 1963–1975 Papers
Governor John C. West Papers
South Carolina House Committee on Education and Public Works Papers

South Carolina State Library, Columbia, South Carolina

South Carolina House Journal, 99th Assembly, 1970–1972
South Carolina House Journal, 100th Assembly, 1973–1974
South Carolina House Journal, 101st Assembly, 1975–1976

Camden Archives, Camden, South Carolina

John C. West Collection

Modern Political Collections, South Carolina Library, Columbia, South Carolina

Governor Ernest Hollings Papers
John C. West Clipping File
John C. West Private Papers
William D. Workman, Jr. Papers

South Caroliniana Library, Columbia, South Carolina

John C. West Clipping File
South Carolina Council on Human Relations Papers
South Carolina League of Women Voters Papers

Thomas Cooper Library, University of South Carolina, Columbia, South Carolina

South Carolina Education Journal

Author's Interviews

Albert P. Brewer, October 15, 1997
John C. West, August 20, 1997
Reubin O'D. Askew, September 2, 1997
William Maloy, December 29, 1998

Newspapers and Magazines

Alabama Journal, 1963, 1968–1969
Alabama School Journal, 1968–1969

Anniston Star, 1969

Auburn Bulletin, 1968

Baldwin Times, 1969

Birmingham News, 1968–1970

Birmingham Post-Herald, 1968–1970

Charleston Evening Post, 1971

Charleston News and Courier, 1971–1973

Columbia Record, 1970–1971

Columbia (S.C.) State, 1970–1975

Current Biography, 1973

Decatur Daily, 1969

Florence Morning News, 1971–1972

Florida A & M University Famuan, 1971

Geneva Reaper, 1968

Greenville News, 1971–1972

Huntsville Times, 1969

(Jacksonville) Florida Times-Union, 1970–1974

Kershaw County Record, 1974

Los Angeles Times, 1971

Lowndes Signal, 1968

Manchester Guardian, 1970

Miami Herald, 1972

Mobile Register, 1968–1969

Montgomery Advertiser, 1968–1970

Montgomery Independent, 1969

Nashville Tennessean, 1969–1970

National Observer, 1970

New York Post, 1970

New York Times, 1970–1973

Opelika Daily News, 1969

Pensacola News-Journal, 1972–1973

Phenix City Citizen-Herald, 1968

Sand Mountain Reporter, 1969

South Carolina Education Journal, 1971

South Carolina Education News, 1971

South Today, 1970–1972

St. Petersburg Times, 1970–1974

Sumter Daily Item, 1971

Tallahassee Democrat, 1970–1975

Time, 1976

Wall Street Journal, 1973

Court Cases

Birdie Mae Davis, et al and U.S. v. Board of School Commissioners, Mobile County, Civil Action No. 3003-3063, U.S. District Court for the Southern District of Alabama

Brown v. Board, 347 US 483 (1954)

Davis v. Board, 333 F2d 53, 356 (1970–71)

Green v. New Kent County, Virginia, School Board, 391 US 430, 438 (1968)

Harris v. Crenshaw County, Alabama, Board of Education, Civil Action No. 2455-N, U.S. District Court for the Middle District of Alabama

Lee v. Macon, Civil Action No. 604-E, U.S. District Court for the Middle District of Alabama

Louisville and Nashville Railroad Company v. State of Alabama, Montgomery County Circuit Court, Nos. 36393, 36642, and 36936 (April 4, 1967)

Rodriguez v. San Antonio Independent School Board, 337 F Supp. 280 (1971)

Serrano v. Priest, 487 P2d 1241 (1971) 96 Cal RPTR 601 (1971)

Shuttlesworth v. Birmingham Board of Education, 162 F Supp. 372 (1957)

State of Alabama v. Robert Finch, Motion of leave to file complaint, Supreme Court of the United States, October Term, 1969

Swann v. Charlotte-Mecklenburg Board of Education, 402 US 1 (1971)

Trial Brief of the United States, Lee v. Macon, 267 F Supp. 464, 469

Weissenger v. Boswell, 330 F Supp. 617 (M.D. Alabama, 1971)

SECONDARY SOURCES

Bailyn, Bernard. *Education in the Forming of American Society.* New York: Basic Books, 1977.

Bartley, Numan. *The New South, 1945–1980.* Baton Rouge: Louisiana State University Press, 1995.

Bartley, Numan, and Hugh D. Graham. *Southern Elections: County and Precinct Data, 1950–1972.* Baton Rouge: Louisiana State University Press, 1978.

———. *Southern Politics and the Second Reconstruction.* Baltimore: Johns Hopkins University Press, 1975.

Bass, Jack. *Taming the Storm: The Life and Times of Judge Frank M. Johnson, Jr. and the South's Fight over Civil Rights.* New York: Doubleday, 1993.

———. *Unlikely Heroes: The Dramatic Story of the Southern Judges Who Translated the Supreme Court's Brown Decision into a Revolution for Equality.* New York: Touchstone, 1981.

Bass, Jack, and Walter De Vries. *The Transformation of Southern Politics: Social Change and Political Consequence since 1945.* New York: Basic Books, 1976.

Bass, Jack, and Jack Nelson. *The Orangeburg Massacre.* Mercer, Ga.: Mercer University Press, 1984.

Black, Earl. *Southern Governors and Civil Rights: Racial Segregation as a Campaign Issue in the Second Reconstruction.* Cambridge: Harvard University Press, 1976.

Black, Earl, and Merle Black. *Politics and Society in the South.* Cambridge: Harvard University Press, 1987.

Boles, John B. *The South through Time: A History of an American Region.* Englewood Cliffs, N.J.: Prentice Hall, 1995.

Brezner, Jeffrey C., and Herbert Cambridge. *Facts about Busing.* Miami: Florida School Desegregation Consulting Center, University of Miami, 1972.

Brown, Stuart. *Financing Education.* University, Ala.: Auburn University Office of Public Service and Research, 1980.

Cain, Henry C. "Redistribution Effects of Funding Florida's Elementary and Secondary Educational System." Ph.D diss., Florida State University, 1978.

Carlisle, Douglas. "The Administration of John Carl West, Governor of South Carolina, 1971–1975," unpublished manuscript, 1975, Modern Political Collection, South Caroliniana Library, Columbia, South Carolina.

Carter, Dan T. *The Politics of Rage: George Wallace, the Origins of the New Conservatism, and the Transformation of American Politics.* New York: Simon and Schuster, 1995.

Cash, W. J. *The Mind of the South.* New York: Vintage Books, 1941.

Cobb, James C. *The Selling of the South: The Southern Crusade for Industrial Development, 1926–1990.* Urbana: University of Illinois Press, 1993.

Colburn, David R. "Florida's Governors Confront the Brown Decision: A Case Study of the Constitutional Politics of School Desegregation." In *An Uncertain Tradition: Constitutionalism and the History of the South,* edited by Kermit L. Hall and James W. Ely Jr., 326–55. Athens: University of Georgia Press, 1989.

———. "Florida Politics in the Twentieth Century." In *The New History of Florida,* edited by Michael Gannon, 344–72. Gainesville: University Presses of Florida, 1996.

Colburn, David R., and Richard K. Scher. *Florida's Gubernatorial Politics in the Twentieth Century.* Tallahassee: University Presses of Florida, 1980.

Cooper, Charles R. "Four Key Issues in the 1969–1970 School Integration Crisis." *Bulletin of the National Association of Secondary School Principals* 54 (November 1970): 40–57.

Cox, Maxie Myron. "1963—The Year of Decision: Desegregation in South Carolina." Ph.D. diss., University of South Carolina, 1996.

Cremin, Lawrence A. *American Education: The Metropolitan Experience, 1876–1980.* New York: Harper and Row, 1988.

Dauer, Manning J., ed. *Florida's Politics and Government,* 2d ed. Gainesville: University Presses of Florida, 1984.

Dent, Harry S. *The Prodigal South Returns to Power.* New York: John Wiley and Sons, 1978.

Douglas, Davison. *Reading, Writing, and Race: The Desegregation of the Charlotte Schools.* Chapel Hill: University of North Carolina Press, 1995.

Edgar, Walter B. "Reform and Reformers in South Carolina: A Historical Perspective." In *Proceedings of the South Carolina Historical Association,* edited by Peter W. Becker, 35–39. Columbia: South Carolina Historical Association, 1992.

———. *South Carolina: A History.* Columbia: University of South Carolina Press, 1998

———. *South Carolina in the Modern Age.* Columbia: University of South Carolina Press, 1992.

Ergstrom, Richard L. "Black Politics and the Voting Rights Act, 1965–1982." In *Contemporary Southern Politics,* ed. James F. Lea, 83–106. Baton Rouge: Louisiana State University Press, 1988.

Fite, Gilbert C. *Cotton Fields No More: Southern Agriculture, 1865–1980.* Lexington: University Press of Kentucky, 1984.

Florida Legislature. House. *Florida Educational Accountability: A 1975–76 Staff Report to the Committee on Education, Florida House.* Tallahassee: N.p., 1976.

Fulton, Mary, and David Long. *School Finance Litigation: A Historical Summary.* Denver: Education Commission of the States, 1993.

Gannon, Michael. *Florida: A Short History.* Gainesville: University Presses of Florida, 1993.

———, ed. *The New History of Florida.* Gainesville: University Presses of Florida, 1996.

Gergel, Richard. "School Desegregation: A Student View." *New South* 26 (winter 1971): 34–38.

Goldfield, David. *Black, White, and Southern: Race Relations and Southern Culture, 1940 to the Present.* Baton Rouge: Louisiana State University Press, 1990.

Gooderow, Ronald K., and Arthur O. White, eds. *Education and the Rise of the New South.* Boston: G. K. Hall and Company, 1981.

Graham, Cole Blease, Jr., and William V. Moore. *South Carolina Politics and Government.* Lincoln: University of Nebraska Press, 1994.

Grantham, Dewey W. *The South in Modern America: A Region at Odds.* New York: Harper Perennial, 1994.

Gray, Fred D. *Bus Ride to Justice, Changing the System by the System: The Life and Works of Fred D. Gray.* Montgomery: Black Belt Press, 1995.

Harris, James Tyra. "Alabama Reaction to the Brown Decision, 1954–56: A Case Study in Early Massive Resistance." D.A. diss., Middle Tennessee State University, 1978.

Harvey, Ira W. *A History of Educational Finance in Alabama: 1819–1986.* University, Ala.: Truman Pierce Institute for the Advancement of Teacher Education, Auburn University, 1989.

Hathorn, Billy B. "The Changing Politics of Race: Congressman Albert William Watson and the South Carolina Republican Party, 1965–1970." *South Carolina Historical Magazine* 89 (October 1988): 227–41.

Havard, William C., ed. *The Changing Politics of the South.* Baton Rouge: Louisiana State University Press, 1972.

Havard, William, and Loren P. Beth. *The Politics of Mis-Representation: Rural-Urban Conflict in the Florida Legislature.* Baton Rouge: Louisiana State University Press, 1962.

Heron, William John. "The Growth of Private Schools and Their Impact on the Public Schools of Alabama (1955–1977)." Ed.D. diss., University of Alabama, 1977.

Holland, Davis Rutledge. "A History of the Desegregation Movement in the South Carolina Public Schools during the Period 1954–1976." Ph.D. diss., Florida State University, 1978.

Ingram, Bob. *That's the Way I Saw It.* Montgomery: B and E Press, 1986.

Jacobs, Grover Tolbert. "Constitutional, Statutory, and Judicial History of Property Tax as a Source of Support for Public Education in Alabama, 1819–1976." Ed.D. diss., Auburn University, 1976.

Jacoway, Elizabeth, and David R. Colburn. *Southern Businessmen and Desegregation.* Baton Rouge: Louisiana State University Press, 1982.

Johns, Roe L. *The Evolution of the Equalization of Educational Opportunity in Florida, 1926 to 1976.* Tallahassee: University of Florida Institute for Educational Finance, 1976.

Johns, Thomas L. "School Finance Reform in 1973." *Planning and Changing* 5 (spring 1974): 47.

Jones, Lewis P. *Books and Articles on South Carolina History.* Columbia: University of South Carolina Press, 1991.

Kallina, Edmund F. *Claude Kirk and the Politics of Confrontation.* Gainesville: University Presses of Florida, 1993.

Kelly, Anne E. *Modern Florida Government.* Temple Terrace, Fla.: MDA Publications, 1981.

Kelly, Anne E., and Ella L. Taylor. "Florida: The Changing Patterns of Power." In *Interest Group Politics in the Southern States,* edited by Ronald J. Hrebener and Clive S. Thomas, 125–51. Tuscaloosa: University of Alabama Press, 1992.

Key, V. O., Jr. *Southern Politics in State and Nation.* Knoxville: University of Tennessee Press, 1984.

Kovacik, Charles F., and John J. Winberg. *South Carolina: A Geography.* Boulder, Colo.: Westview Press, 1987.

———. *South Carolina: The Making of a Landscape.* Columbia: University of South Carolina Press, 1989.

Lamis, Alexander. *The Two-Party South.* 2d ed. New York: Oxford University Press, 1990.

Lander, Ernest M., and Robert K. Ackerman. *Perspectives in South Carolina History: The First Three Hundred Years.* Columbia: University of South Carolina Press, 1973.

Lawson, Stephen F. *Black Ballots: Voting Rights in the South, 1944–1969.* New York: Columbia University Press, 1976.

Lea, James F., ed. *Contemporary Southern Politics.* Baton Rouge: Louisiana State University Press, 1988.

Levine, Leonard, and Kitty Griffith. "The Busing Myth: Segregation Academies Bus More Children and Further." *South Today* (May 1970): 7.

Lofton, Paul, Jr. "Calm and Exemplary: Desegregation in Columbia, South Carolina." In *Southern Businessmen and Desegregation,* edited by Elizabeth Jacoway and David R. Colburn, 70–81. Baton Rouge: Louisiana State University Press, 1982.

McNeill, Paul Wesley. *School Desegregation in South Carolina, 1963–1970.* Ed.D. diss., University of Kentucky, 1979.

Mahan, Howard F., and Joseph W. Newman, eds. *The Future of Public Education in Mobile.* Mobile: South Alabama Review, 1982.

Mahan, Thomas W. "Busing Students for Equal Opportunity." *Journal of Negro Education* (summer 1968): 293.

Mizzell, M. Hayes. "The Myth of Quality Education." *New South* 26 (winter 1971): 26–33.

Moore, John Hammond. *Columbia and Richland County: A South Carolina Community, 1740–1990.* Columbia: University of South Carolina Press, 1993.

———. *South Carolina Newspapers.* Columbia: University of South Carolina Press, 1988.

Morris, Allen. *The Florida Handbook, 1997–1998.* Tallahassee: Peninsular Press, 1997.

National Education Association. *Rankings of the States, 1971.* Washington, D.C.: National Education Association, 1971.

———. *Rankings of the States, 1972.* Washington D.C.: National Education Association, 1972.

———. *Rankings of the States, 1973.* Washington D.C.: National Education Association, 1973.

———. *Rankings of the States, 1974.* Washington D.C.: National Education Association, 1974.

Naylor, Thomas, and James Clotfelder. *Strategies for Change in the South.* Chapel Hill: University of North Carolina Press, 1975.

Newman, Joseph W., and Betty Brandon. "Integration in the Mobile Public Schools." In *The Future of Public Education In Mobile,* edited by Joseph W. Newman and Howard F. Mahan, 45–54. Mobile: South Alabama Review, 1982.

Norrell, Robert J. *Reaping the Whirlwind: The Civil Rights Movement in Tuskegee.* New York: Knopf, 1985.

O'Brien, Michael. *The Idea of the American South, 1920–1941.* Baltimore: Johns Hopkins University Press, 1979.

Permaloff, Anne, and Carl Grafton. *Political Power in Alabama: The More Things Change . . .* Athens: University of Georgia Press, 1995.

Raines, Howell, and Robert Hooker. "Reubin Who?" *Floridian,* February 12, 1978, 7–10.

Ravitch, Diane. *The Troubled Crusade: American Education, 1945–1980.* New York: Basic Books, 1983.

Rogers, George C., Jr., and C. James Taylor. *A South Carolina Chronology, 1497–1992,* 2d ed. Columbia: University of South Carolina Press, 1994.

Rogers, William Warren, Robert David Ward, Leah Rawls Atkins, and Wayne Flynt. *Alabama: The History of a Deep South State.* Tuscaloosa: University of Alabama Press, 1994.

Sabato, Larry. *Goodbye to Goodtime Charlie: The American Governorship Transformed,* 2d ed. Washington, D.C.: CQ Press, 1983.

———. "New South Governors and the Governorship." In *Contemporary Southern Politics,* edited by James F. Lea, 194–213. Baton Rouge: Louisiana State University Press, 1988.

Scher, Richard K. *Politics in the New South: Republicanism, Race, and Leadership in the Twentieth Century.* New York: Paragon House, 1992.

Schulman, Bruce J. *From Cotton Belt to Sunbelt: Federal Policy, Economic Development, and the Transformation of the South, 1938–1980.* New York: Oxford University Press, 1991.

Shiver, Lee A. "A Historical Review of the Development of Florida's School Finance Plan and the Fiscal Equalization Effects of the Florida Education Finance Program." Ph.D diss., University of Florida, 1982.

Sick, Leonard. *Nixonomics: How the Dismal Science of Free Enterprise Became the Black Art of Controls.* New York: Praeger, 1972.

Simun, Patricia Bates. "Exploring the Myths of School Integration." *Integrated Education* (December 1967): 59–65.

Southern Regional Council. *The South and Her Children: School Desegregation, 1970–71.* Atlanta: Southern Regional Council, 1971.

Sproat, John G. "'Firm Flexibility': Perspectives on Desegregation in South Carolina." In *New Perspectives on Race and Slavery in America: Essays in Honor of Kenneth M. Stampp,* edited by Robert H. Abzug and Stephen E. Maislish, 164–84. Lexington: University Press of Kentucky, 1986.

Stern, Mark. "Florida's Elections." In *Florida's Politics and Government,* edited by Manning J. Dauer, 73–91. Gainesville: University Presses of Florida, 1980.

Stovall, James Glen, Patrick R. Cotter, and Samuel H. Fisher III. *Alabama Political Almanac.* 2d ed. Tuscaloosa: University of Alabama Press, 1997.

Thomas, James D., and William Stewart. *Alabama Government and Politics.* Lincoln: University of Nebraska Press, 1988.

Tindall, George Brown. "Business Progressivism: Southern Politics in the Twenties." *South Atlantic Quarterly* 42 (winter 1963): 92–106.

———. *The Emergence of the New South, 1913–1945.* Baton Rouge: Louisiana State University Press, 1967.

Tyson, Turner W. "A Study of the Florida Educational Finance Program Act of 1973 on the State-Local Relationship in Florida." Ed.D. diss., University of Mississippi, 1977.

United States Commission on Civil Rights. *Inequality in School Financing: The Role of Law.* Washington D.C.: U.S. Commission on Civil Rights, 1972.

Wolfe, Thomas. *You Can't Go Home Again.* New York: Harper and Brothers, 1940.

Woodward, C. Vann. *The Burden of Southern History.* Baton Rouge: Louisiana State University Press, 1960.

Wright, Gavin. *Old South, New South: Revolutions in the Southern Economy since the Civil War.* New York: Basic Books, 1986.

Yarbrough, Tinsley E. *Judge Frank Johnson and Human Rights in Alabama.* Tuscaloosa: University of Alabama Press, 1981.

Index

About the Author

GORDON E. HARVEY is Assistant Professor of History at the University of Louisiana at Monroe. He has published articles on liberalism in New Deal Alabama and Woodrow Wilson's foreign policy, as well as a biographical essay on Governor Albert Brewer in *Alabama Governors: A Political History of the State*.